Police Powers

Brian Moorcroft

Howie Page

Cecelia Reilly

Toronto, Canada

2015

Emond Montgomery Publications Limited
60 Shaftesbury Avenue
Toronto ON M4T 1A3
http://www.emond.ca/highered

Printed in Canada.
Reprinted June 2017.

We acknowledge the financial support of the Government of Canada through the Canada Book Fund for our publishing activities.

Emond Montgomery Publications has no responsibility for the persistence or accuracy of URLs for external or third-party Internet websites referred to in this publication, and does not guarantee that any content on such websites is, or will remain, accurate or appropriate.

Acquisitions editor: Lindsay Sutherland
Managing editor, development: Kelly Dickson
Director, editorial and production: Jim Lyons
Developmental editor: Su Mei Ku
Copy editor: Jamie Bush
Production editor and coordinator: Laura Bast
Proofreader: David Handelsman
Permissions editor: Monika Schurmann
Indexer: Paula Pike
Cover and text designer and typesetter: Tara Wells
Cover image: Geoffrey Holmes

Library and Archives Canada Cataloguing in Publication

Moorcroft, Brian, author
    Police powers / Brian Moorcroft, Howie Page, Cecelia Reilly.

Includes index.
ISBN 978-1-55239-616-2 (pbk.)

    1. Police power—Ontario.   2. Police regulations—Ontario.   3. Police—Ontario.
4. Ontario. Police Services Act.   I. Page, Howie, author   II. Reilly, Cecelia, author
III. Title.

KEO887.M66 2015   344.71305'2   C2014-906447-0
KF5399.M66 2015

Dedicated to Lynda, Michael, Christopher, and Angela, my motivation and support.

—*Brian Moorcroft*

For my wife, Gail, and my two sons, Shawn and Mark. I thank each of them for their patience and support through the many hours it took to bring this project to completion. Without their help, it would not have been possible.

—*Howie Page*

For my husband, John, and my daughter, Morgan. I also dedicate my work to my late mother, Eunice. Without her encouragement, and without the patience and unrelenting support of John and Morgan, this work would not have been possible.

—*Cecelia Reilly*

Contents

3

Arrest Powers   47

4

Location of Arrest and Feeney Laws   79

8

9

10

Preface

Canadian police officers are entrusted with extraordinary powers to fulfill their duties. These powers include the authority to arrest, to detain, to use force, and to enter private dwellings. As a police officer, you will be expected to know and understand the law well enough to use these powers in a reasonable and lawful manner. And you will be required to justify your use of these powers when you are questioned by the courts, by your supervisors, or one of several civilian oversight bodies. Police powers are far from absolute or unquestionable; their use is regularly reviewed by the courts and by civilian oversight bodies whose role and purpose will be covered in this text

The purpose of this book is to provide you with a complete understanding of police powers and their sources. The latter include relevant federal and provincial legislation, as well as case law. By covering current case law and providing excerpts from statutes related to police powers, this book will enable you to exercise police powers in a legally justifiable manner. Each chapter includes review questions that will test your understanding of its contents. The "It's Your Move" scenarios included throughout the book will teach you how to determine the best course of action in real-life policing situations.

Chapter 1: Sources of Police Powers

As a law enforcement officer, it is important that you understand the sources of your authority. This chapter explores the Canadian laws that constitute these sources. It focuses on constitutional sources as well as other legislative and judicial sources.

Chapter 2: Ontario Police Services Act

The Ontario *Police Services Act* defines the roles and responsibilities of individual police officers and of police organizations serving the citizens of Ontario, and establishes internal and external processes for ensuring effective and efficient police services. This chapter explores the principles of the *Police Services Act* and its regulations from various points of view—that of a police officer, that of police service management, and that of the citizens of Ontario.

Chapter 3: Arrest Powers

In order to ensure that the *Canadian Charter of Rights and Freedoms* is upheld, Canadian police officers' extraordinary arrest and detention powers come with very specific limitations. The chapter identifies the steps a police officer must follow in order to make a lawful and justifiable arrest. Just as importantly, it indicates when an arrest should not be made. It explores the concepts of voluntary accompaniment and investigative detention. As a police officer, you must understand citizens' powers of arrest and how these powers differ from police powers in this area. This chapter highlights these differences and explains the police officer's role once a citizen has made an arrest.

Chapter 4: Location of Arrest and Feeney Laws

This chapter discusses the locations where an arrest can be made and the conditions under which arrests may occur. The Supreme Court of Canada case of *R v. Feeney* (1997) is discussed extensively from the perspective of a police officer who intends to make an arrest within a dwelling-house. The chapter sets out the legal requirements that police officers must meet before entering a dwelling-house to make an arrest.

Chapter 5: Use of Force and Officer Safety

Canadian legislators have recognized that police officers must sometimes use force to perform their duties. This chapter explains the concepts of reasonable and unreasonable levels of force. Under federal and provincial legislation, police officers have rights and duties regarding the use of force, and this chapter explains what these rights and duties are. It uses the Use-of-Force Continuum model to show possible police responses in relation to different levels of threat. It also considers a controversial issue of today—whether police should use force in dealing with persons with mental health issues.

Chapter 6: Releasing and Charging a Suspect

A police officer's responsibilities concerning the suspect do not end with the decision to arrest. The suspect must be properly charged with an appropriate offence(s) and compelled to attend court to answer to the charge(s). This chapter explores the concepts of interim and judicial interim release, as well as the role of the *Canadian Charter of Rights and Freedom* in the release process. It includes examples of the documents that are used to compel an accused to attend court and to charge an accused, and it describes the circumstances under which each is used, and by whom.

Chapter 7: Police Discretion

Canadian police officers are given discretion over how and when they use their powers. This chapter identifies the factors that influence police discretion and presents many of the challenges and benefits of exercising police discretion.

Chapter 8: Warrantless Search and Seizure

Police officers' powers to search may be divided into two categories: (1) search with prejudicial authorization (that is, with a warrant), and (2) search without such authorization. This chapter explores the second of these categories, and it considers, in the process, the relationship between search authorities and the *Canadian Charter of Rights and Freedoms*. Various search circumstances are examined: search incident to arrest and to investigative detention; search of motor vehicles; and searches of schools. The chapter also explains certain legal concepts, including consent, exigent circumstances, and the plain-view doctrine.

Chapter 9: Search with a Warrant

This chapter covers the first of the two categories of searches—search with a warrant. It explains, among other things, the purpose and the general requirements of the search warrant, and it includes a detailed explanation of how to obtain one. The chapter explains and covers the disclosure requirements a warrant application must meet (that is, the Three Fs), as well as the process of executing a search warrant.

Chapter 10: Accountability of Police

Powers over life and death, over freedom and imprisonment—these are among the extra-ordinary powers given to police. This chapter considers the many processes and procedures that are in place to ensure that police exercise these powers responsibly, in a way that earns the public's confidence. In the context of accountability, this chapter explains the role of an officer's notes, of the *Canadian Charter of Rights and Freedoms*, and of the police chain of command, and it discusses the effect of external oversight bodies—the civil courts, new technology, and social media—on police accountability.

Acknowledgments

The creation of this text would not have been possible without the extraordinary support of the Emond Montgomery Publications team, and of our families, friends, and colleagues. We would particularly like to thank Lindsay Sutherland, Su Mei Ku, and Kelly Dickson— our EMP editorial team—and Dr. Frank Trovato of Centennial College.

We are thankful for the valuable thoughts and suggestions provided by the review team of Judy Manherz, Algonquin College; Mike Winacott, Georgian College; Lisa Myers, Lambton College; and Ann Corbold, Seneca College of Applied Arts and Technology.

Brian Moorcroft

Howie Page

Cecelia Reilly

About the Authors

Brian Moorcroft, MA Ed (Central Michigan University), BAA Justice (University of Guelph Humber), is a faculty member of Centennial College. He is currently the Police Foundations Program coordinator, and he teaches the Criminal Code and Police Powers course in that program. He is a retired staff sergeant of the Toronto Police Service.

Howie Page has been a member of the Toronto Police Service for 33 years. He was an inspector with 52 Division before becoming the unit commander of the Toronto Drug Squad in March 2014. From 1999 to 2010, Howie was a part-time instructor in multiple subjects at the Toronto Police College, and for the past four years he has been a part-time professor in the Police Foundations course at Humber College. Howie holds a BAA in Justice Studies from the University of Guelph.

Cecelia Reilly has taught Justice Studies at Loyalist College for 23 years and has been the coordinator of the Police Foundations course at this institution for eight years. She is currently Eastern Region Rep on OCAT Provincial Coordinator Committee. Prior to teaching, Cecelia was employed with Peterborough Lakefield Police Service as a constable—one of the first two women hired by the service. Cecelia holds a Law and Security diploma, a diploma in Adult Education, and a BA in Psychology from Queen's University.

Sources of Police Powers

1

LEARNING OUTCOMES

After completing this chapter, you should be able to:

- Identify the constitutional sources of police powers.
- Identify the legislative and judicial sources of law.
- Describe the limits to legislative and police powers.

```
ON SCENE
```

It's 4:00 p.m. on January 1. Officers are conducting a roadside check when a 46-year-old woman pulls into the check stop and rolls down her window. The officer approaches the vehicle and advises the driver that he is conducting a traffic stop under the RIDE program. "Have you had anything to drink today?" he asks her.

The woman, who has never been stopped by police in her life, becomes agitated and indignant. "What are you people doing setting up a roadblock at this time of day? Don't you have better things to do? There are criminals out there committing real crimes."

The officer assures the woman that the roadblock is just a way of keeping citizens safe. But she continues her tirade. "You know, I work hard and pay my taxes. What gives you the right to pull me over without any cause at all? I've done nothing wrong!"

The officer, continuing to speak calmly to the driver, notices a partly empty bottle of liquor on the floor of the car. He asks the woman to step out of the car and advises her that he is going to conduct a search of the vehicle.

She says, "This is ridiculous! Are we living in a police state? This is Canada! First you stop me without cause, and now you're going to go through my belongings? What gives you that right?" Then she exclaims angrily, "I don't know what authority you think you are operating under, but I'll have you explain that to my lawyer." Fortunately, the officer is fully aware of the authority he has and the source from which this power is derived.

What do you think? Is the officer acting lawfully? Where does his authority come from?

Introduction

As a police officer, you will be entrusted with exceptional powers, powers that exceed those of other individuals in our society. You will regularly find yourself in situations like the one in the scenario above, where you will disregard ordinary rules about trespassing upon another person's physical self, home, and possessions. You will have the power to arrest and detain individuals, search and seize private property, and, in exceptional situations, use appropriate force. Where do these powers come from? Who decides that you will have these rights? On what authority are your powers based? As a law enforcement officer, you need to understand where your authority comes from.

A short answer to these questions is the following: "It is the laws of Canada that give you the authority to do your job as a police officer." As a society, we have decided upon a set of laws that reflect our values, and we punish actions and activities that we believe violate them. Included in this set of laws are measures to ensure that police officers have the power to enforce our laws. Of course, a fuller answer to the question concerning the source of police powers must answer the question of where laws come from: Who creates them? On what authority do those law-making bodies act?

In this chapter, you will be introduced to the different sources of police powers. You will explore how laws are created, by whom, and on what authority law-making bodies operate. You will also see how the ultimate source of legal authority in Canada has evolved over time.

Constitutional Sources of Police Power

Canada is a **federation**—in other words, a group of independent states (that is, provinces and territories) that are united under a central, or federal, government. Each province and territory operates independently with regard to internal affairs, but any issue or service that affects all of the provinces and territories is handled by the federal government.

The relationship between the provinces/territories and the federal government was laid out in Canada's first Constitution, created in 1867. This was the *Act of Confederation*, which united the separate colonies of Quebec, Ontario, Nova Scotia, and New Brunswick to form the new country of Canada. This Act was originally called the **British North America Act (BNA Act)**, but in 1982 its name was changed to the *Constitution Act, 1867*. That is how we will refer to it in this text.

A **constitution** is the fundamental law of a nation or state. It provides the principles by which a country is governed. It has been described (Cheffins & Tucker, 1975, p. 4) as a "badge of nationhood" and "a mirror reflecting the national soul." Unlike other laws, those included in a constitution are considered to be a part of the social and national fabric. All other laws and decisions are measured against the principles of the constitution. Making changes, or **amendments**, to any part of a constitution is a long, involved process.

Law-Making Powers Under the Constitution

Canada's Constitution and its system of government were modelled on the British system. The *Constitution Act, 1867* begins with the following statement:

> WHEREAS the Provinces of Canada, Nova Scotia and New Brunswick have expressed their Desire to be federally united into One Dominion under the Crown of the United Kingdom of Great Britain and Ireland, with a Constitution similar in Principle to that of the United Kingdom.

Under the British system, Parliament was considered an extension of the monarch (king or queen). As such, Parliament had supreme authority to enact laws: to **legislate**. This idea is called **parliamentary supremacy**. Today, the monarch's role in Canada's government is purely symbolic, but we still see the everyday authority of the monarch in our courtrooms. The official name of every criminal prosecution begins with "R," which refers to *Rex* or *Regina*—the king or queen.

Police officers enforce the laws of the country, which are developed through Parliament. By extension, they represent the Crown, or government. Under s. 1 of O. Reg. 268/10, police officers swear an oath of office in which they "will uphold the Constitution of Canada." The officer in the opening scenario is doing just that.

Power Splitting Between the Federal and Provincial Governments

One of the main objectives of the *Constitution Act, 1867* was to describe the **division of powers** between the provinces and the federal government. It laid out which level of government would have legislative authority over which areas of social concern. While there is a clear division of responsibilities between the federal and provincial/territorial governments, there is often overlap in how these responsibilities are carried out. The sharing of responsibility for criminal justice is a good example of this. According to the *Constitution Act, 1867*, criminal law is under the **jurisdiction** of both federal and provincial governments.

---

federation
a group of independent states, provinces, or territories that have agreed to unite under a central or federal government

British North America Act
Canada's original constitution, which united the separate colonies of Quebec, Ontario, Nova Scotia, and New Brunswick to form Canada

constitution
the fundamental law of a nation or state, written or unwritten, that establishes the character and conception of the nation's government

amendments
changes made to enacted legislation to modify and improve it

legislate
to make or enact laws

parliamentary supremacy
a doctrine that places final law-making power in the hands of the legislature

division of powers
refers to the specific powers granted to the federal and provincial levels of government, respectively, by ss. 91 and 92 of the *Constitution Act, 1867*

jurisdiction
a body's sphere of authority to do a particular act—for example, the authority of a court to hear and determine a judicial proceeding

The Constitution says that both levels of government would have parliaments of their own to watch over and administer their areas of responsibility, and to make laws within their jurisdictions. The responsibilities of each level of government were defined and limited in ss. 91 and 92 of the Act.

Section 91: What the Federal Government Does

Section 91 of the *Constitution Act, 1867* says,

> It shall be lawful for the Queen, by and with the Advice and Consent of the Senate and House of Commons, *to make Laws* [emphasis added] for the Peace, Order, and good Government of Canada, in relation to all Matters not coming within the Classes of Subjects by this Act assigned exclusively to the Legislatures of the Provinces.

Further, according to s. 91(27), the Parliament of Canada has exclusive legislative authority over "Criminal Law, except the Constitution of Courts of Criminal Jurisdiction, but including the Procedure in Criminal Matters."

This means that the federal government, through the debates and discussions of the Senate and House of Commons, has the exclusive power to create criminal laws for all of Canada. That is why there is a single criminal code that is enforceable across the country. All persons who work in criminal justice use the same set of laws. The powers given to police officers and civilians are the same across the country, from British Columbia to Newfoundland and Labrador. The *Criminal Code* outlines the scope of law enforcement power with respect to arrest and detention and with respect to police procedures in search, seizure, and surveillance related to criminal law. This section of the Constitution also granted the federal government the power to create judicial procedures, establish levels and types of courts, and appoint judges. The federal government was also given the power to create a federal police force, and the result was the Royal Canadian Mounted Police (RCMP), which has a broad, nationwide law enforcement mandate.

Another important aspect of s. 91 was that federal powers were limited; the federal Parliament did not have the right to pass laws in areas where the provinces had already been given that authority. Neither the federal nor provincial governments were permitted to step on each other's legislative toes.

Section 92: What the Provincial Governments Do

Section 92 of the *Constitution Act, 1867* outlined the legislative powers of the provinces. Subsections 14 and 15 are of particular interest:

> 92. In each Province the Legislature may exclusively make Laws in relation to Matters coming within the Classes of Subjects next hereinafter enumerated; that is to say, …
>
>> 14. The Administration of Justice in the Province, including the Constitution, Maintenance, and Organization of Provincial Courts, both of Civil and of Criminal Jurisdiction, and including Procedure in Civil Matters in those Courts.
>> 15. The Imposition of Punishment by Fine, Penalty, or Imprisonment for enforcing any Law of the Province made in relation to any Matter coming within any of the Classes of Subjects enumerated in this Section.

These subsections granted the provincial governments power over the enforcement of criminal law: laying charges and prosecuting offenders. It also gave the provinces the authority to make their own laws governing such things as driving rules, liquor possession and consumption, and trespassing on private property. Provinces, which create and oversee municipalities, also had the power to establish and maintain municipal police forces through the municipal councils. This means that police forces created by the provinces enforced the *Criminal Code* and dealt with all provincial and municipal offences. Section 92(14) also established that criminal trials took place in provincial courts, even though the rules of evidence and criminal procedure were initially created federally.

It is worth noting that the legislative powers of the territories are different from those of the provinces, and that, since their creation, the territories have been controlled by the federal government. To this day, the territories have a different relationship with the federal government than the provinces do; they have fewer powers over lands and resources, and less say in constitutional matters. There are also some differences with regard to policing and the court systems. The powers that the territories have and the relationship that they have with the federal government are evolving over time.

Administration of Policing

One of the consequences of sharing responsibility for policing across federal, provincial, and municipal jurisdictions is that policing in Canada is highly complex.

As you have already seen, the federal government established a federal police force, the RCMP, which has jurisdiction over all federal laws throughout all Canadian provinces and territories (for example, the *Criminal Code*, the *Controlled Drugs and Substances Act*, the *Canada Transportation Act*). Each province also has the power to establish its own provincial police force, even though only three provinces have done so. Quebec, Ontario, and Newfoundland and Labrador have created the following:

- the Sûreté du Québec (SQ)
- the Ontario Provincial Police (OPP)
- the Royal Newfoundland Constabulary (RNC)

The rest of the provinces and territories contract the services of the RCMP to enforce the *Criminal Code*, provincial statutes, and, in many cases, municipal bylaws. In the case of the RNC, policing is conducted side by side with the RCMP, with each of the two services responsible for certain areas within the province.

The agreements made between the provinces/territories and federal government do not necessarily cover municipalities. Each municipality has the right to establish its own police force under provincial law. For example, Moncton, New Brunswick has its own police service, while the RCMP polices much of the rest of the province. In most large municipalities, policing is provided by either a municipal force, the provincial force, or a regional force. Where the provinces have opted for a provincial force and numerous municipal police forces, the RCMP still maintains a presence in all regions to enforce the federal mandate, such as the *Controlled Drugs and Substances Act*. RCMP officers frequently work directly with local law enforcement in enforcing this mandate.

While the different jurisdictions and levels of police create complexity and administrative challenges, they also provide some room for checks and balances. For example, one police force, such as the Ontario Provincial Police (OPP), can investigate a complaint about another police service, such as a municipal police force. This provides an appearance of objectivity and fairness in the review process.

1. Provincial governments have the power to establish provincial and municipal police services, lay charges, and prosecute offenders. Where does this power come from?
2. Explain what is meant by the doctrine of parliamentary supremacy.
3. Describe the powers that reside in ss. 91 and 92.

Legislative and Judicial Sources of Power

We will now explore three other sources of police powers:

1. statutes,
2. regulations and bylaws, and
3. common law and case law.

Statutes

The laws that we have been discussing to this point, including those in the Constitution and the *Criminal Code*, are called **statutes**. A statute is a law that has been

- written down, or **codified**;
- enacted by a legislative body (the Parliament of Canada or a provincial or territorial legislature); and
- given **royal assent**, which means that it has received the approval of the monarch through his or her representative (the **governor general** at the federal level, the **lieutenant governor in council** at the provincial level, or the commissioner at the territorial level).

Federal, provincial, and territorial governments each enact hundreds of statutes. These statutes are posted on the Internet and updated continually. Every day, police officers (like the one in the opening scenario) enforce these laws, so they need to know which level of government is the authority for the statute(s) they are enforcing (see Table 1.1 for examples). Officers also need to stay current with changes in legislation, whether the change is in the form of an amendment to the law, or a case that provides a significant interpretation of a law that affects day-to-day policing. Figure 1.1 sets out the basics of statutes.

statutes
codified legal provisions developed and adopted through the parliamentary and legal process

codified
written down

royal assent
approval of the British monarch through his or her representative

governor general
the monarch's representative in the federal legislature

lieutenant governor in council
the monarch's representative in the provincial legislature; official name for the provincial Cabinet

TABLE 1.1   Examples of Statutes

Statute	Passed by	Enforceable	Examples
Federal	Canadian Parliament	across Canada	Income tax International trade Aviation Criminal records Tariff laws Fisheries
Provincial/territorial	the provincial/territorial legislatures	in the province or territory in which the statute was enacted	Residential tenancy laws Labour laws Conservation laws Highway traffic laws

FIGURE 1.1   What Is a Statute?

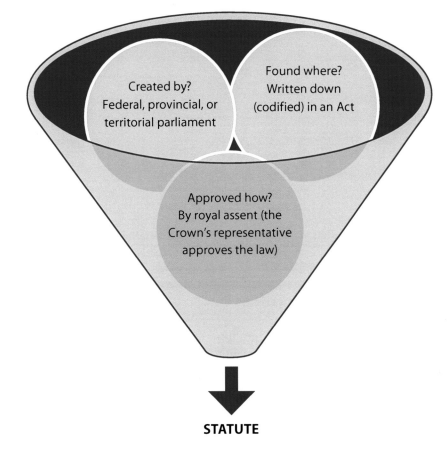

Creating Statutes

To understand how statute law or legislation is made, we will look at a simplified model of the **legislative process** in the provincial and federal governments. Municipal bylaws often go through a similar process, also described below, but without the requirement of receiving royal assent.

All federal, provincial, and territorial laws are made by members of the federal Parliament or of provincial or territorial legislatures. These government officials act as representatives of the people.

Every statute begins its life as a **bill**. A bill is introduced by being read out in the House (legislature). Called the first reading, this is the first of three readings that the bill must pass through. At each reading, a majority of the members in the House must vote to send the bill to the next stage. Usually, between the second and third reading, the bill is sent to various committees for closer consideration. The committee reports back to the House, making any recommendations for improvement. The legislative assembly considers the recommendations of the committee, making any changes it feels necessary. The bill then goes through a third reading. If the legislature votes in favour of the bill at third reading, the bill is said to have passed. It is then sent to be signed by the monarch's representative, and the bill becomes an act. This final stage is called royal assent. (See Figure 1.2.)

The process for passing a federal statute is the same as the process for the provinces and territories up to the point where the bill passes third reading. The difference is that, at the federal level, a bill must pass through two legislative houses: the House of Commons and the Senate. So, once the bill passes third reading in the first house, it is then sent to the

legislative process
process by which the elected representatives of government make laws

bill
a proposed new or amended law in the provincial/territorial or federal legislative process

FIGURE 1.2 Legislative Process

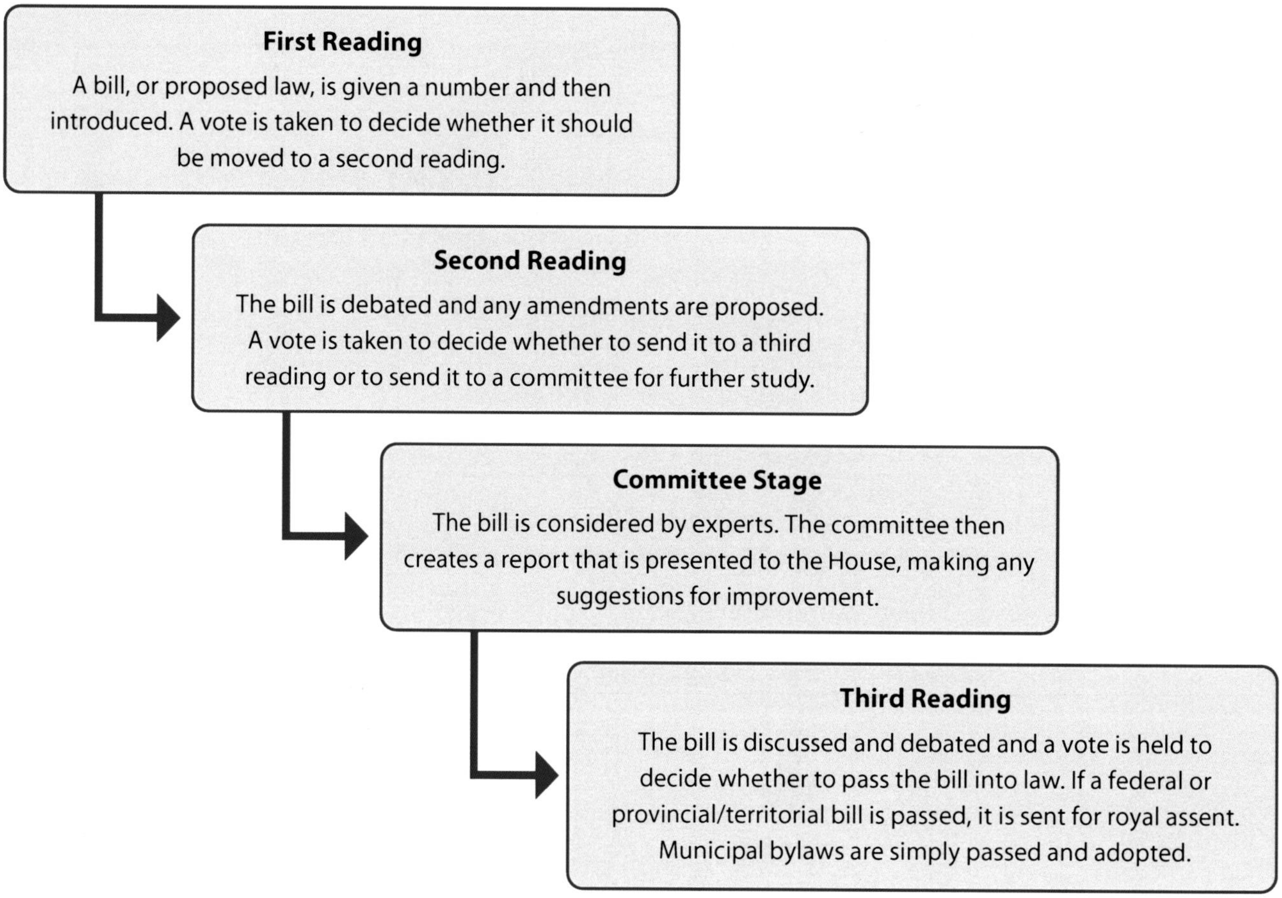

First Reading

A bill, or proposed law, is given a number and then introduced. A vote is taken to decide whether it should be moved to a second reading.

Second Reading

The bill is debated and any amendments are proposed. A vote is taken to decide whether to send it to a third reading or to send it to a committee for further study.

Committee Stage

The bill is considered by experts. The committee then creates a report that is presented to the House, making any suggestions for improvement.

Third Reading

The bill is discussed and debated and a vote is held to decide whether to pass the bill into law. If a federal or provincial/territorial bill is passed, it is sent for royal assent. Municipal bylaws are simply passed and adopted.

second house to go through the process again. It is not until both houses have passed the bill that it is sent to the governor general for royal assent. It is possible, however, that the second house may send the bill back to the first house with recommended changes. Once the bill has received royal assent, it still needs to come into force. It may be proclaimed into force on the date it passes, on a date specified in the law, or on a date determined by the governor general.

Once a law is enacted, it is necessary to keep it current and workable in the face of societal changes. This is done through an amending process. All police officers have to keep up to date not only with new laws, but also with amendments to the law and the regulations. The officer in the introductory scenario had to be aware of current highway traffic and liquor laws and regulations, and he needed to be able to articulate his grounds for stopping, detaining, and searching a member of the public. We will be able to see some of these amendments in action as we study legislation and regulations throughout this text.

Regulations and Bylaws

Regulations and **bylaws** are usually an extension to a statute. When a legislature passes a law, it often includes a section at the end of the statute that describes the power that a subordinate body has to modify the statute. This is usually done through passing regulations, which provide further details about a particular subject in a statute. Because the power to create regulations and bylaws is delegated to a subordinate body, these types of legislation are called **delegated legislation**.

regulations
a type of subordinate legislation that carries out the intent of the statute under which it is made; generally concerned with the detail and technical aspects of the law

bylaws
regulations and rules adopted by local or municipal governments

delegated legislation
legislation such as regulations and bylaws created by subordinate governmental bodies such as branches and agencies rather than the legislature

Here are two examples of regulations that have been created to clarify particular statutes:

- Section 106 of Ontario's *Highway Traffic Act* (HTA) outlines offences regarding the proper use of seatbelts: when, where, and how they are to be worn. Regulation 613 of this Act ("Seat Belt Assemblies") provides further information, describing the design and location of a restraint system.
- Section 214.1 of the HTA provides that the council of a municipality may designate a part of a provincial highway under its jurisdiction as a community safety zone. Ontario Regulation 510, passed in 1999 (O. Reg. 510/99), provides details about the locations of these community safety zones in some Ontario municipalities. Regulations and statutes function hand in hand.

Similarly, the provincial/territorial legislature gives local councils the responsibility of making bylaws for their communities. Bylaws regulate the day-to-day affairs of businesses and residents within a municipality. For example, a bylaw might restrict the hours that construction equipment can be operated, or it might legislate the minimum temperatures in rental housing. Various law enforcement agents, including police, bylaw enforcement officers, and special constables, are responsible for enforcing these bylaws. No law is too insignificant for the attention of law enforcement.

The process for creating regulations and bylaws can be similar to creating statutes; it may involve several readings and a committee stage, even though regulations and bylaws do not require royal assent. However, regulations and bylaws are often passed much more rapidly than statutes are. The creation of a statute is a very formal, careful, and rigorous process, and the time for implementation can be lengthy, sometimes as long as a year. Regulations and bylaws, by contrast, can be proposed, passed, and implemented very rapidly, often within weeks or even less. Sometimes these pieces of legislation can be proposed, passed, and adopted in a single meeting.

IT'S YOUR MOVE, OFFICER!

Scenario 1.1

As a new officer, you receive a call to respond to a noise complaint. The noise is caused by the banging of doors in a warehouse at the edge of a residential district. After listening to the complainant's side of things, you go to the warehouse to speak with the property manager, whose name is Deb. She objects to your presence, claiming that "there ain't no laws against warehouse doors banging." She says, "Prove it to me. Until then, I ain't quietin' down for nobody."

1. Where would you find a law against excessive noise?
2. Locate an example of this offence, using the Internet, and if possible describe the powers a police officer might have to minimize the disturbance to the area residents.

Common Law and Case Law

All of Canada, except for Quebec, follows the British tradition of **common law**, which is also referred to as *case law*. This tradition decides criminal and civil cases based on previous court decisions and long-standing principles. It is founded on the concept of *stare decisis*, which is Latin for "to stand by things decided." (This concept is also referred to as the **doctrine of precedent** or **rule of precedent**.) It is based on the belief that it is unfair to deliver different rulings or impose different punishments for crimes that have similar circumstances.

common law
the body of judge-made law not found in statute

stare decisis
a common law doctrine stating that the decision of a higher court in a particular jurisdiction acts as a binding authority on a lower court in the same jurisdiction

doctrine of precedent or rule of precedent
a doctrine that requires a judge, in resolving a particular case, to follow the decision in a previous case where the facts in the two cases are similar

The implication of this is that statute law is shaped by case law decisions. The courts, through the judges, must interpret both the intention and language of statutes. In doing so, they shape how that statute is applied in future cases. For this reason, common law is sometimes referred to as "judge-made law." The implication for police officers is that they must be aware of court decisions, so that they are able to make better decisions about whether a crime has been committed.

Police officers must be aware of changes in case law. An example of an everyday police practice that is authorized not by any legislation but by case law is the police officer's right to search a person upon his or her arrest. Based on safety considerations, the right to search is a "common law power" given to police officers; it is accepted and practised without being in statute. The Supreme Court of Canada confirmed this common law authority in *R v. Golden* (2001, para. 84), when it said that search incident to arrest is "an established exception to the general rule that warrantless searches are *prima facie* unreasonable." That statement has not been written into legislation, but, because it is judge-made law, it is as powerful as legislation. Common law provides the authority; case law affirms it.

IT'S YOUR MOVE, OFFICER!

Scenario 1.2

It's Friday night and you and your partner, both relatively new recruits, have just been dispatched to a 911 call. The caller stated that he was in his house and that he heard his next-door neighbour, a 73-year-old male, calling for help. The caller said that his neighbour, George Macklin, sounded as if he was in the basement. Mr. Macklin could be heard by the complainant yelling, "She's locked me in again!"

When you arrive at the home, you notice an elderly woman sitting on the front porch, drinking tea and working on a crossword puzzle. You greet her with, "Good evening, ma'am, I'm Officer Kalid and this is my partner, Officer McNulty. May we ask you some questions?"

Mrs. Macklin eyes you suspiciously and asks what brings you to her house. You reply that you have received a 911 call concerning the well-being of her husband and suggest that he may be in the basement.

Mrs. Macklin laughs, stating that her husband died three years ago. She tells you that you have been the victim of "that crazy old creep next door." You are unsure now of your facts.

1. Do you have a right to enter the home?

2. What is the basis in case law for your decision?

3. If you decide to enter the house, how would you explain your decision in court?

CHECK YOUR UNDERSTANDING

1. What is a statute and how is it different from a regulation and a bylaw?

2. What is a bill and what are the steps required for it to pass into law?

3. Describe the concept of *stare decisis* and its relationship to the development of law.

Limiting Legislative and Police Powers

As discussed above, the *Constitution Act, 1867* gave Parliament supremacy over law-making, so Parliament was one of the main sources of police powers (the other being common law). The problem with parliamentary supremacy was that even though Parliament was responsible for protecting individual rights, it could enact any law, however restrictive, as long as it was within its jurisdiction. There was no concept of an unconstitutional law, since Parliament had supreme law-making powers, and it was the source of the Constitution.

The Canadian Bill of Rights

In 1960, Prime Minister John Diefenbaker proposed the *Canadian Bill of Rights*. Diefenbaker had seen discrimination against different religious and cultural groups, and he believed that the rights of individuals needed to be protected under federal laws. On the night before he introduced the *Bill of Rights* to Parliament, Diefenbaker (1960) said,

> What will a Canadian Bill of Rights do? It will declare that the following rights and freedoms are in existence and that no Act of the Parliament of Canada in the past or in the future (subject to the security demands of war) shall be permitted to interfere with them:
> - The right of the individual to life, liberty, security of person and enjoyment of property and the right not to be deprived thereof except by due process of law;
> - The right of the individual to protection of the law without discrimination by reason of race, national origin, colour, religion or sex;
> - Freedom of religion;
> - Freedom of speech;
> - Freedom of the press.

In this speech, Diefenbaker expressed a hope that no act of Parliament would interfere with these rights, but he also acknowledged that the effectiveness of the statute was limited because it was not part of the Constitution. His hope, he said, was that the Bill would at least make Parliament more "freedom-conscious." Unfortunately, Diefenbaker was correct about the limited effectiveness of the statute. Because these rights were not **entrenched** in the Constitution, the *Bill of Rights* had little effect on legal decisions and procedures.

entrenched
firmly established

Policing Under the Constitution Act, 1982

Twenty years after John Diefenbaker introduced the *Canadian Bill of Rights*, Prime Minister Pierre Elliott Trudeau took up the cause of protecting the rights of Canadians.

At the beginning of the 1980s, Trudeau's government was involved in amending the Constitution so that Canada's Parliament would control Canadian legislation and thus eliminate the traditional role of the British Parliament in Canadian affairs. This process is called the **patriation** of the Constitution. Trudeau took this opportunity to introduce other amendments into the Constitution, including the addition of the **Canadian Charter of Rights and Freedoms**. This part of the Constitution enshrines the individual rights of Canadians. The Charter is of particular interest to law enforcement because it defines the limits of police powers. Another amendment to the *Constitution Act, 1982* was the recognition and affirmation of Aboriginal rights. This amendment has had significant implications for legislation and policing in respect to traditional Aboriginal lands and traditional First Nations activities, such as fishing, hunting, and logging.

patriation
the process of changing the Canadian Constitution so that control of legislation was moved from the British Parliament to the Canadian Parliament

Canadian Charter of Rights and Freedoms
a constitutional document that sets out the rights and freedoms of all people in Canada

Source: Robert Cooper/National Archives of Canada fonds/e008300499.

Prime Minister Pierre Trudeau and Queen Elizabeth are shown at the signing of Canada's *Constitution Act, 1982.*

The Charter expresses and entrenches basic civil liberties, which are highly valued in a free and democratic country. These rights and freedoms include

- equality under the law,
- protection of the individual from the intrusion of the state, and
- the freedoms of religion, the press, speech, assembly, and association

These changes redefined and limited the powers of police and legislators. The implication of these constitutional changes was deepened by s. 52(1), which says the following: "The Constitution of Canada is the supreme law of Canada, and any law that is inconsistent with the provisions of the Constitution is, to the extent of the inconsistency, of no force or effect." This phrase marks a shift away from the idea of a parliamentary supremacy to a concept of **constitutional supremacy**.

constitutional supremacy
a doctrine that places final decision-making power in legal matters in the hands of the judiciary

Constitutional Challenges to Laws

With the introduction of the Charter, there arose a uniquely Canadian tension between the concept of constitutional supremacy and the concept of parliamentary supremacy. Acts of Parliament were now weighed against constitutional guarantees, and the phrase "of no force or effect" has been heard again and again as laws are challenged and found to be unconstitutional. Examples of this in Canada's *Criminal Code* include laws pertaining to abortion, minimum sentencing, and prostitution. These laws, created by Parliament, have been challenged, found wanting, and struck down as unconstitutional. (In the case of abortion, the law has been left in the *Criminal Code*, but it is not enforceable.) This process has often forced the amendment of legislation or the creation of new legislation.

The Charter provides protections to all Canadians and, in the case of criminal prosecutions, to the public (victims, witnesses) and to the accused. This attention to the rights of the accused has been one of the Charter's more controversial byproducts. For example, the Supreme Court of Canada (SCC) reviewed rape shield provisions in the context of the 1991 case *R v. Seaboyer*. Rape shield provisions prohibited defence lawyers from asking rape victims about their sexual history. The SCC decided that these limitations violated the defendant's Charter rights. The court stated that the provisions infringed the principles of **fundamental justice** by depriving the accused of the right to full answer and defence. In this way, the Constitution was used to set express limits against "rape shield provisions." In consequence, a new set of principles had to be enacted to protect the rights of the accused.

fundamental justice
rights that belong to us all and originate either in the express terms of the Constitution or, by implication, in common law

Another example of this tension between the rights of the accused and the rights of the public comes from the Ontario Court of Appeal. In the case of *R v. Nur* (2013), the court was called upon to consider the fairness of s. 95(1) of the *Criminal Code*, which said that the possession of a prohibited or restricted firearm, either loaded or with accessible ammunition, would result in a mandatory minimum sentence of three years' imprisonment. This penalty was levelled regardless of the purpose or use of the firearm.

Five justices in the Court of Appeal looked at sentences that had been handed down in similar cases prior to the introduction of the mandatory minimum sentence. They compared the earlier sentences with the three-year mandatory sentence and found the gap between the two to be disproportional. As a result, the court determined that the mandatory three-year sentence was a "cruel and unusual punishment," which is prohibited by s. 12 of the Charter. The law was struck down as unconstitutional—of no force or effect.

Charter Rights Have Limits

The introduction of the *Canadian Charter of Rights and Freedoms* was not without some controversy. Many people were concerned that the Charter and the move to constitutional supremacy reduced the ability of Canadian governments to legislate effectively and, in some cases, limited the powers of police to police effectively. Police were not used to having their activities judged according to a law that provided rights to all and that could result in the dismissal of cases.

Partly in response to these concerns, the government introduced into the Constitution the concept of "reasonable limits" to individual rights and freedoms. What this means is that legislatures are able to place limits on Charter rights as long as these limits can be shown to be "justified to protect a free and democratic society." It is this part of the Constitution that enables laws against hate speech and child pornography.

CANADIAN CHARTER OF RIGHTS AND FREEDOMS: LEGAL RIGHTS

LIFE, LIBERTY AND SECURITY OF PERSON

7. Everyone has the right to life, liberty and security of the person and the right not to be deprived thereof except in accordance with the principles of fundamental justice.

SEARCH OR SEIZURE

8. Everyone has the right to be secure against unreasonable search or seizure.

DETENTION OR IMPRISONMENT

9. Everyone has the right not to be arbitrarily detained or imprisoned.

ARREST OR DETENTION

10. Everyone has the right on arrest or detention
(a) to be informed promptly of the reasons therefor;

(b) to retain and instruct counsel without delay and to be informed of that right; and

(c) to have the validity of the detention determined by way of *habeas corpus* and to be released if the detention is not lawful.

PROCEEDINGS IN CRIMINAL AND PENAL MATTERS

11. Any person charged with an offence has the right

(a) to be informed without unreasonable delay of the specific offence;

(b) to be tried within a reasonable time;

(c) not to be compelled to be a witness in proceedings against that person in respect of the offence;

(d) to be presumed innocent until proven guilty according to law in a fair and public hearing by an independent and impartial tribunal;

(e) not to be denied reasonable bail without just cause;

(f) except in the case of an offence under military law tried before a military tribunal, to the benefit of trial by jury where the maximum punishment for the offence is imprisonment for five years or a more severe punishment;

(g) not to be found guilty on account of any act or omission unless, at the time of the act or omission, it constituted an offence under Canadian or international law or was criminal according to the general principles of law recognized by the community of nations;

(h) if finally acquitted of the offence, not to be tried for it again and, if finally found guilty and punished for the offence, not to be tried or punished for it again; and

(i) if found guilty of the offence and if the punishment for the offence has been varied between the time of commission and the time of sentencing, to the benefit of the lesser punishment.

TREATMENT OR PUNISHMENT

12. Everyone has the right not to be subjected to any cruel and unusual treatment or punishment.

SELF-CRIMINATION

13. A witness who testifies in any proceedings has the right not to have any incriminating evidence so given used to incriminate that witness in any other proceedings, except in a prosecution for perjury or for the giving of contradictory evidence.

INTERPRETER

14. A party or witness in any proceedings who does not understand or speak the language in which the proceedings are conducted or who is deaf has the right to the assistance of an interpreter.

One of the main roles of the criminal courts in Canada is to interpret the Charter. A defendant may choose to complain, for example, that a Charter right was violated by the police in their pursuit of the investigation. Rosenberg (2009) has noted that much case law has developed in answer to constitutional questions concerning ss. 7 through 10 of the Charter. After a case has exhausted the lower courts, it is these questions that most often form the basis of an appeal to the Supreme Court. The court, for its part, refers to these Charter provisions when having to make decisions that limit or confirm law enforcement practices. The court's interpretations have generated a large body of case law that has become an important part of police training.

In this chapter's introductory scenario, the officer would have received training regarding his appropriate power to stop a vehicle. This police power to stop a vehicle in order to check for the driver's sobriety is found in case law, and it has been confirmed that this practice, along with the detention of the citizen in order to enforce the *Criminal Code*, is reasonable. Therefore, a police officer is not violating the Charter when he or she stops a vehicle to check the driver's sobriety or detains the driver in the process. In police training, reading and understanding case law decisions that affirm or deny police powers is a routine academic exercise. These cases are a source of police power: they provide the police with an indirect, external set of guidelines regarding their own power in relation to the rights of an ordinary citizen, and they help the police avoid exercising their power in a way that interferes with the rights of an ordinary citizen.

CHECK YOUR UNDERSTANDING

1. Describe the doctrine of constitutional supremacy and its relationship to the development of law.
2. Describe the role of the Charter in limiting police powers.
3. What is the role of case law as a source of law enforcement power?

CHAPTER SUMMARY

Reread the introductory scenario. What do you think now? As you have learned, police derive their powers from several sources within the Canadian system. One source is statutes, regulations, and bylaws, created by different levels of government. Another is common law and case law. One of the functions of our court system is to determine that laws are appropriately used by police and that the *Charter of Rights and Freedoms* protects Canadian society from misuse of power by police. The woman who was stopped by the officer in the opening vignette is as well protected as any Canadian citizen by this intricate system of checks and balances on police power. In order to be an effective police officer, you need to study and understand the appropriate use of police powers. This book will help you do this.

KEY TERMS

amendments, 3
bill, 7
British North America Act, 3
bylaws, 8
Canadian Charter of Rights and Freedoms, 11
codified, 6
common law, 9
constitution, 3
constitutional supremacy, 12
delegated legislation, 8
division of powers, 3
doctrine of precedent or rule of precedent, 9
entrenched, 11

federation, 3
fundamental justice, 13
governor general, 6
jurisdiction, 3
legislate, 3
legislative process, 7
lieutenant governor in council, 6
parliamentary supremacy, 3
patriation, 11
regulations, 8
royal assent, 6
stare decisis, 9
statutes, 6

REFERENCES

Canadian Charter of Rights and Freedoms. (1982). Part I of the *Constitution Act, 1982,* RSC 1985, app. II, no. 44.

Cheffins, R., & Tucker, R. (1975). *The constitutional process in Canada* (2nd ed.). Toronto: McGraw-Hill.

Constitution Act, 1867. (1867). (UK), 30 & 31 Vict., c. 3.

Constitution Act, 1982. (1982). RSC 1985, app. II, no. 44.

Criminal Code. (1985). RSC 1985, c. C-46, as amended.

Diefenbaker, J. (1960, June 30). Address on the nation's business. Library and Archives Canada. https://www.collectionscanada.gc.ca/primeministers/h4-4052-e.html.

Golden, R v. (2001). [2001] 3 SCR 679, 2001 SCC 83.

Highway Traffic Act, O. Reg. 510/99. (1999). Community safety zones.

Highway Traffic Act, RRO 1990, Reg. 613. (1990). Seat belt assemblies.

Nur, R v. (2013). 2013 ONCA 677.

Police Services Act, O. Reg. 268/10. (2010). General.

Rosenberg, M. (2009). Twenty-five years later: The impact of the *Canadian Charter of Rights and Freedoms* on the criminal law. *Supreme Court Law Review, 45* (2nd Series). Markham, ON: LexisNexis Canada. http://www.ontariocourts.ca/coa/en/ps/publications/twenty-five_years_later.htm.

Seaboyer, R v.; Gayme, R v. (1991). [1991] 2 SCR 577.

FURTHER READING

Federal Justice Laws: http://laws.justice.gc.ca/eng/

Federal Parliament of Canada: http://www.parl.gc.ca

Ontario e-Laws: http://www.e-laws.gov.on.ca

Ontario Legislative Assembly, Bills & Lawmaking: http://www.ontla.on.ca/lao/en/bills/

Shiner, R.A. (1994). Citizens' rights and police powers. In R.C. MacLeod & D. Schneiderman (Eds.), *Police powers in Canada: The evolution and practice of authority*. Toronto: University of Toronto Press.

REVIEW QUESTIONS

Multiple Choice

1. In the interests of protecting society, police have the power to
   a. arrest and detain
   b. search and seize
   c. use force
   d. all of the above

2. The principle of *stare decisis* refers to
   a. the principle according to which the courts use precedent cases to decide new, similar cases
   b. the principle according to which the courts use dissimilar cases to decide new cases
   c. the police practice of applying the same law to everyone
   d. the police practice of applying the same investigative processes to everyone

3. Which of the following provinces have provincial police forces?
   a. Saskatchewan, Quebec, and Alberta
   b. Ontario, Prince Edward Island, and Manitoba
   c. Nova Scotia, New Brunswick, and Ontario
   d. Ontario, Newfoundland and Labrador, and Quebec
   e. all provinces

4. A provision of a statute may be "struck down" by a judge if he or she finds it to be
   a. unethical
   b. unconstitutional
   c. an abuse of power
   d. in violation of the *Criminal Code*

5. Criminal trials take place in
   a. provincial courts
   b. special criminal courts
   c. federal criminal courts
   d. all of the above

True or False

_____ **1.** The Constitution provides that specific responsibilities for different types of laws belong to either the provincial or the federal government.

_____ **2.** The duty to enforce the criminal justice system is the sole responsibility of the federal government.

_____ **3.** Section 91(27) of the *Constitution Act, 1867* governs the provincial government in its power to enact criminal law and procedure.

_____ **4.** The *Canadian Charter of Rights and Freedoms* was enacted in 1987.

_____ **5.** *Stare decisis* is a doctrine that requires judges to follow precedents.

_____ **6.** The Canadian Constitution is the supreme law of the land, as stated in s. 52(1) of the *Constitution Act, 1982.*

_____ **7.** A regulation must go through three readings in the legislature.

_____ **8.** The federal and provincial governments rarely have any disputes over the jurisdiction of each level of government.

_____ **9.** The provinces are permitted to establish their own police forces or may contract with the RCMP to provide police services on their behalf.

_____ **10.** The *Criminal Code* applies to all provinces and territories in Canada.

Short Answer

1. a. How do judicial decisions affect the activities of the police?

   b. When will a judge strike down a law?

   c. Give an example of a law that would be unconstitutional.

2. What is the main function of Canada's Constitution with respect to the division of powers?

3. a. How does the enactment of a statute differ from the making of a regulation?

   b. Is a regulation law?

4. Take a look at the legal rights from the Charter on pages 13 and 14. Consider how the concept of reasonable limits redefines how these rights may be applied. How might the wording of some of these rights affect how you perform your job as a police officer?

It's Your Move, Officer!

A. It is your first day in court to testify at a trial. On the witness stand, under oath, you are asked by the Crown attorney to explain how the accused came to your attention. You explain that you had reasonable grounds to arrest him; he had committed an indictable offence—theft over $5,000. You then explain your next steps: you searched the accused after handcuffing him. When you are questioned by the defence attorney, she asks why you went to the trouble of searching her client, since the search did not turn up any incriminating evidence. She claims your search was unreasonable.

1. How would you respond to the defence attorney?

2. Did you have a lawful power of search? From where did this power come?

3. What were you searching for?

B. It is Saturday night at 3:00 a.m. You are part of a RIDE team, stopping vehicles to check for impaired drivers. A vehicle approaches you, and you ask the driver if he has consumed any alcoholic beverages. He replies "no," but you can clearly smell alcohol on his breath. The car also smells strongly of liquor, and there is an empty liquor bottle on the floor of the front passenger seat.

You ask the driver to step out of the car, then you turn him over to the officer who is conducting the roadside screening tests. He fails the test and is arrested by the officer conducting the test. The officer demands, pursuant to s. 254(3)(a)(i) of the *Criminal Code*, a breath sample. Because the location of your RIDE program is very isolated, you decide to wait with the arresting officer for a tow truck to tow the driver's car. Freezing rain begins, and you learn that the tow truck will be delayed by 30 minutes. You know that the law in s. 254(3) regarding impaired driving requires that an officer demand a breath sample "as soon as practicable." Section 258(1)(c) requires that the first breath sample be taken not later than two hours after the offence.

1. What would you do?

2. Would you continue to wait for the tow truck? Explain.

3. Do you think that waiting would mean the breath test results might not be admitted? Explain.

Ontario Police Services Act

2

LEARNING OUTCOMES

After completing this chapter, you should be able to:

- Explain the history of policing in Canada and why the Ontario *Police Services Act* (PSA) was formed.

- Identify the basic principles upon which the PSA was founded.

- Explain how police services are delivered in Ontario.

- Describe how members of police services are hired and what their duties are.

- Describe the roles, responsibilities, and duties of various civilian oversight bodies, and explain why these oversight bodies are important.

- Summarize what constitutes police misconduct.

- Describe how complaints against police officers and services are handled.

ON SCENE

In the course of their duties, police officers regularly search government and police databases. They might conduct these checks from office-based computers or from mobile computers in police cars. Much of the information contained in these databases is not readily available to the public.

Over several years, a municipal police officer holding a supervisory position conducted a number of Canadian Police Information Centre (CPIC) and Ministry of Transportation (MOT) computer checks for personal reasons, not work-related ones. The police officer was searching for information, including criminal records and driver's-licence records, to use against individuals with whom he was having an ongoing dispute.

Becoming aware of the officer's actions, the police service conducted an investigation. The investigation showed the officer had carried out over 200 non-employment checks from the computer in his police car, using his own personal password.

When confronted with the allegations, the officer made a full confession. However, he clearly stated that he did not use any of the information against the subjects of the checks.

What is your reaction to this officer's conduct? Should police officers be held to a higher standard of conduct than the average community member? What should these standards be and what should the consequences of failing to meet the standards be? How do you think the public would view this case?

Introduction

> The public must be confident that police officers will strive to set the example for those in the community. Anything short of this will be seen as a contradiction and serve no other purpose but to undermine the efforts of all police officers and the explicit goals of the service. ... efficient operation of a police service depends upon the existence of mutual respect and trust between members of the police service and the community itself.
>
> Terence Kelly, Hearing Officer, September 26, 2012
> (quoted in Ottawa Police Service, 2012)

It is important that the standards of police conduct, as well as the consequences of failing to meet these standards, be clear and available to all. These standards should apply to all police, from the lowest constable to the chief of police, as well as to police services boards and to politicians tasked with creating and funding police services for their community.

The average member of the public would be angered if a police officer used his or her position for personal gain, especially if that officer was in a supervisory position.

In the opening scenario, the actions of the police officer, who was an experienced member of the force, did not meet the standard of conduct expected of police. As a police officer, you are granted a great deal of power by law. It is crucial that this power not be misused and that the public's trust in police not be compromised. It is essential that you understand how to conduct yourself, both on duty and off duty. You must also understand your roles and responsibilities, as well as the roles and responsibilities of all governing bodies within the Ontario policing system.

In this chapter, you will explore the *Police Services Act* (PSA) and its related regulations. The PSA is legislation that provides detailed information about a number of areas of policing.

It describes the duties, responsibilities, and various activities of a police service—of its members and of its oversight bodies. The PSA also outlines the services that police must provide in order to be "adequate and effective." The goal of the PSA and its regulations is to guarantee competent and uniform police services to all citizens of Ontario.

History of the Police Services Act

To understand why the PSA exists, you need to understand the state of policing before the Act was created. It is difficult for us to imagine a time when policing did not exist; it is such a fundamental part of our society. Yet the modern concept of a police force is relatively new. The creation of the PSA was an important moment in the evolution of policing.

Early Law Enforcement in Canada

Historically, Canadian law enforcement was closely tied to the British system of law enforcement. Prior to the mid-1700s, Canada, like Britain, deployed a system of citizen night watches and constables who patrolled parishes, towns, and villages. It was the responsibility of male householders to take turns patrolling the streets at night. Citizens were also expected to serve as part-time constables. These unpaid duties were often dangerous. The watchmen and constables, armed only with a staff, would encounter criminals who were more apt to be carrying a sword or some other weapon.

The ineffectiveness of this system of policing was recognized in Britain in the early 1800s, as crime proliferated in the cities and caused anxiety in the growing middle class. In 1829, the British government, under Prime Minister Robert Peel, passed the *Metropolitan Police Act*. This Act created a force of 3,000 uniformed men who carried batons and patrolled London on foot and horseback. It is for this reason that Robert Peel is considered by many to be the father of modern policing. (The English term for a police officer—*bobby*—comes from his name.) The new concept of paid constables was also adopted in Canada, and in 1834 York (which later became Toronto) got its first full-time, paid constable.

Policing After Confederation

Following Confederation in 1867, there were further developments in Canadian policing. At the federal level, the Dominion Police Force (DPF) was created in 1868 to police Ottawa and eastern Canada. The North-West Mounted Police (NWMP) was created in 1873 to police the west; it enforced liquor-trafficking laws and created relationships with First Nations peoples. The DPF and NWMP were later merged in 1920 to form the Royal Canadian Mounted Police (RCMP).

As for policing in Ontario, there were two acts that were particularly influential to law enforcement:

1. The *Municipal Institutions of Upper Canada Act* (1858) shaped how policing was carried out in municipalities. This legislation was in force even before Canada became a country. Enacted in 1858, the Act made a Board of Commissioners of Police the governing authority for municipal police forces. The Act stated that a municipal police force would comprise a chief constable and "as many constables, other officers and assistants, as the Council from time to time deems necessary."

2. The *Constables Act*, passed in 1877, created a force of part-time provincial constables. These constables were generally underpaid and under-trained. However, they led the way for the creation of the Ontario Provincial Police (OPP) in 1909.

POLICING TIMELINE

pre-1750s:	A system of citizen night watches and constables helps keep law and order.
1829:	Robert Peel's government passes the *Metropolitan Police Act* in Britain.
1834:	York (present-day Toronto) adopts the concept of full-time paid constables.
1858:	The *Municipal Institutions of Upper Canada Act* is enacted.
1868:	The Dominion Police Force (DPF) is created to police Ottawa and eastern Canada.
1873:	The North-West Mounted Police (NWMP) is created to police western Canada.
1877:	The *Constables Act* is passed.
1909:	The Ontario Provincial Police (OPP) is formed.
1920:	The DPF and the NWMP merge to form the Royal Canadian Mounted Police (RCMP).
1946:	The *Ontario Police Act* (OPA) is passed.
1990:	The *Police Services Act* (PSA) is passed.

These Acts continued to evolve and take shape over the years, but they had two main flaws when it came to policing:

1. They did not clearly outline the duties of a constable in relation to other municipal personnel. A constable might find himself responsible for everything from road repair to a weights-and-measures inspection. In 1850, for example, Peterborough's first chief constable, William Cummings, found that he was responsible for everything from inspecting wood and shingles, to weighing bread, to ensuring that customers got what they paid for, to caring for the town's fire engine (Hotson, 2011). Early constables worked long hours for little pay.

2. The *Municipal Institutions of Upper Canada Act* clearly put the power over policing and over the local constables in the hands of politicians. The Act stated that the number of constables to be kept on staff was at the discretion of the board; a constable could be removed at the whim of board members. This made policing highly susceptible to political interference. A constable had no means of negotiating his position or appealing a decision to remove him.

It was these two flaws that led to the first *Ontario Police Act* (OPA), created in 1946. It replaced the *Constables Act* and the *Municipal Institutions of Upper Canada Act*, providing a far more robust and detailed vision for policing in Ontario than these Acts had.

Modern Policing in Canada

The OPA, enacted in 1946, addressed some of the gaps in the earlier policing legislation. For one thing, it established **collective bargaining rights** for police officers. Although police officers were, and still are, prohibited from joining a union, the OPA allowed them to be represented by a police association. This development made the job of a police constable more secure, and it reduced the potential for political interference.

The OPA accomplished the following:

- It defined the responsibilities of police in municipalities and the responsibilities of the OPP.
- It established that a board was required, responsible for policing and for the maintenance of law and order.
- It prescribed the duties of the chief of police and of police officers.

collective bargaining rights
the rights of employees, such as safety, wage, and working hours, negotiated through a process called collective bargaining; the PSA allows police officers to be members of an association for the purpose of negotiating these rights with their employer

The OPA was in force until 1990, when it was replaced by the *Police Services Act*. This new Act made some important changes. In particular, it introduced a public complaints system, a concept that was not part of the OPA. It also gave rise to other regulations, such as O. Reg. 268/10, which included a code of conduct for police chiefs and police officers. In this chapter, we will look at these regulations as well as at the PSA.

CHECK YOUR UNDERSTANDING

1. Identify at least three statutes that have governed policing in Ontario since Confederation.

2. List the major accomplishments of the *Ontario Police Act* of 1946.

3. When was a public complaints system first included in legislation concerned with police governance?

Basic Principles of the Police Services Act (PSA)

OVERVIEW OF THE PSA

Section 1: Declaration of principles
Section 2: Definitions

Part I	Responsibility for police services
	• Solicitor general: duties, responsibilities
	• Municipalities: operation, responsibilities, composition agreements
	• Ontario Provincial Police (OPP): composition, responsibilities
Part II	Ontario Civilian Commission on Police Services
Part II.1	Independent Police Review Director
Part III	Municipal police services boards
Part IV	Police officers and other police staff
	• Chief of police: duties
	• Police officers: powers and duties, oaths, political activity
	• Other members of police forces
	• Special constables
	• First Nations constables
Part V	Complaints and disciplinary proceedings
	• Review and investigation of complaints
	• Withdrawal of public complaints
	• Internal complaints
	• Offences
	• Misconduct
	• Hearings
	• Suspension
Part VI	[Repealed]
Part VII	Special investigations
Part VIII	Labour relations
Part VIII.1	Transfer of assets between pension plans
Part IX	Regulations and miscellaneous
Part X	Court security

The PSA begins with a declaration of principles—six basic principles on which the Act is founded and which guide how it may be interpreted. These six principles constitute a philosophy of how to police in a democracy. This philosophy emphasizes that, though policing is complex and dangerous, it must avoid being oppressive while fulfilling its mandate of enforcing the law. This philosophy is sophisticated, modern, and consensual, and it is based on the participation and support of the population being policed.

The six basic principles of the PSA are as follows.

1. *The need to ensure the safety and security of all persons and property in Ontario.* This principle recognizes that the primary responsibility of police officers is to protect life and property and to prevent and investigate crimes. Police are empowered, and required by law and the Constitution, to enforce laws and to protect all citizens from harm. Police work hard, in partnership with the community, to ensure an ordered society where every person may enjoy his or her rights and freedoms in a peaceful environment. Police services are available at all times and for every citizen.

2. *The importance of safeguarding the fundamental rights guaranteed by the Charter and the Human Rights Code.* The right of an individual to certain basic freedoms is the hallmark of a civilized society. This PSA principle recognizes the importance of the *Canadian Charter of Rights and Freedoms* (1982) and the *Human Rights Code* (1990) and police officers' responsibility to protect and respect these rights. These rights apply equally to all members of the community. Police often find themselves having to balance the rights of one group with those of another. For example, police might be called to close roads to enable a group to march in protest and exercise its right to **freedom of expression**. At the same time, these officers have a duty to protect the security of citizens and their property, which might be damaged by such protests.

3. *The need for cooperation between providers of police services and the communities they serve.* Police organizations recognize that police services cannot fulfill their duties without the assistance and support of the communities they serve. With **community-based policing**, the community is in the position of a client or partner in the effort to manage local crime and enhance community safety. The presence of civilians on police boards, on the Ontario Civilian Police Commission (formerly the Ontario Civilian Commission on Police Services), and in volunteer positions in the service itself reflects a desire to broaden community involvement in policing.

4. *The importance of respecting victims of crime and understanding their needs.* The Ontario *Victims' Bill of Rights* (1995) was passed in 1996. This Act set guidelines on how officials of the justice system should treat victims of crime. This principle in the PSA recognizes that police have an important role in protecting victims' rights to be treated with compassion and fairness. To uphold these rights, many police services have set up specialized units to assist victims of sexual assault, domestic violence, trauma, and other injuries, physical or mental. Police officers who have witnessed or been involved in traumatic situations may themselves become vulnerable and in need of specialized services.

5. *The need for sensitivity to the pluralistic, multiracial, and multicultural character of Ontario society.* Immigration has played an important role in the development of Ontario for hundreds of years. The fifth PSA principle reflects the belief that all community members, regardless of ethnic or cultural background, have a role within the greater community of Ontario. Police services and their officers must recognize the need to respect our differences when providing services.

6. *The need to ensure that police forces are representative of the communities they serve.* This principle is enshrined in s. 1(6) of the PSA. Since the time of Sir Robert Peel,

freedom of expression
a right guaranteed under s. 2(b) of the Charter that ensures everyone the right to manifest thoughts, opinions, and beliefs, including all expressions of the heart and mind regardless of how unpopular or distasteful they may be

community-based policing
police policy and philosophy that includes the people of the local community in the operations and activities of a police service

having a police service that represents the community it serves has been an elusive goal, but not an impossible one. Ontario police services are continually recruiting members from all cultural and ethnic groups within the community in order to create a representative police service. Women, minorities, First Nations, and other traditionally underrepresented groups bring new ideas and world views into the service. A police service that is representative of the community it serves will tend to share its community's values and beliefs, and it will have a better understanding of diverse situations.

These principles guide policing practices in Ontario. However, the PSA does not in every case lay out how these principles are to be implemented. This work is done through regulations, made by the lieutenant governor in council, and through policy statements and directives issued by the **solicitor general of Ontario**. These regulations and directives supplement the Act and flesh out its framework. For example, the Act is very direct about the need to strengthen the links between police and the surrounding community, but it does not indicate how this goal is to be achieved. Instead, regulations such as O. Reg. 3/99 set out recommendations for enhancing community policing.

CHECK YOUR UNDERSTANDING

1. List the basic principles of the PSA.
2. What is the purpose of the basic principles of the PSA?
3. Where can directions regarding how to implement the principles be found?

Delivering Police Services

Police services are delivered at municipal, provincial, and federal levels. In this section, we will focus on municipal and provincial levels.

Municipal Police Services

The PSA provides that each municipality must provide "adequate and effective police services" according to its needs. The police services must, at a minimum, include the five **core police services**, set out in s. 4 of the Act and shown in Figure 2.1.

In 2001, O. Reg. 3/99 came into force. Entitled "Adequacy and Effectiveness of Police Services," this regulation to the PSA spells out what constitutes an adequate and effective police service. It identifies what specific services each of the five core services must comprise.

Municipal police services are to be under the control and direction of a police services board. The board establishes what priorities, objectives, and policies are needed to meet the requirements of adequate and effective police services in that municipality. The structure and function of the board are clearly defined in the PSA. Board members are drawn from the community and have no particular expertise in policing. They represent the views and concerns of their municipality. The number of board members is determined by the municipality's population, as shown in Table 2.1.

solicitor general of Ontario
the elected official and Cabinet member of the political party in power in Ontario; charged with duties pertaining to law enforcement and correctional services in Ontario; this position is held by the minister of community safety and correctional services

core police services
a collection of services required to be performed by every police service in Ontario; failure to provide these services may lead to a dismantling of a police service and the installation of another police service

FIGURE 2.1   Core Police Services

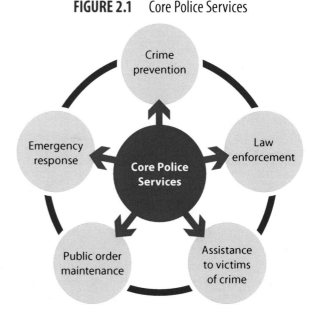

TABLE 2.1   Composition of Police Services Boards

Small communities	Medium-sized cities, regional districts, or metropolitan districts	Large communities
Population under 25,000	Population exceeds 25,000	Population exceeds 300,000
Three board members* • head of council or delegate; • council appointee, neither a city councillor nor a city employee; and • member appointed by lieutenant governor in council.	Five board members† • head of council or delegate; • member of council appointed by resolution of council; and • three members appointed by lieutenant governor in council.	Seven board members • head of council or delegate; • two members of council appointed by resolution of council; • one member appointed by council, neither a city councillor nor a city employee; and • three members appointed by lieutenant governor in council.

* May increase size of board to five members by resolution of council.

† May increase size of board to seven members by resolution of council.

Municipalities have a number of options available when it comes to providing police services. The council can

- appoint its own board to create a police service, or form a partnership with one or more other councils to form a joint board;
- enter into an agreement with one or more councils to **amalgamate** their police forces if there are existing forces in place; or
- enter into an agreement with another council or the OPP to provide police services in the community.

amalgamate
combine two or more existing organizations to form one; in policing, two or more municipal police forces may be combined to form one police force serving multiple municipalities

If a municipality does not provide adequate and effective police service, then the OPP will take over the municipality's policing role. The municipality then has to pay the OPP for performing this role.

Ontario Provincial Police

Unlike municipal police services, the OPP is not directed by a police services board. The commissioner, or head, of the OPP, under the direction of the solicitor general, has general control and administration of the OPP, as provided by s. 17(2) of the PSA.

The PSA stipulates very specific roles for the OPP, which are somewhat different from those of a municipal police service. Section 19(1) of the PSA describes the responsibilities of the OPP as follows:

1. Providing police services in respect of the parts of Ontario that do not have municipal police forces other than municipal law enforcement officers.
2. Providing police services in respect of all navigable bodies and courses of water in Ontario, except those that lie within municipalities designated by the Solicitor General. [*Note*: The duties of the solicitor general are performed by the minister of community safety and correctional services.]
3. Maintaining a traffic patrol on the King's Highway, except the parts designated by the Solicitor General.

4. Maintaining a traffic patrol on the connecting links within the meaning of section 21 of the *Public Transportation and Highway Improvement Act* that are designated by the Solicitor General.
5. Maintaining investigative services to assist municipal police forces on the Solicitor General's direction or at the Crown Attorney's request.

First Nations Policing

The federal government, provincial or territorial governments, and First Nations or Inuit communities have a tripartite, or three-way, policing agreement for delivering policing services. There are two types of policing models under the agreement:

1. a self-administering agreement, whereby First Nations or Inuit communities manage their own police services according to provincial policing legislation. In Ontario, that legislation is the PSA.

2. a community tripartite agreement, whereby dedicated officers from an existing police service provide policing services to a First Nations community.

Section 54 of the PSA allows the OPP commissioner to appoint First Nations constables to perform specific duties. If these duties relate to a reserve, the appointment requires the approval of the reserve's police-governing authority or band council. The definition of a police officer found in s. 2 of the PSA does not include First Nations constables. However, these constables do possess the powers of police officers when they are engaged in specified duties. Section 54(3) provides as follows: "The appointment of a First Nations Constable confers on him or her the powers of a police officer for the purpose of carrying out his or her specified duties." Most agreements between the Ontario government and First Nations peoples state that the specific duties of First Nations constables are the same as those of police officers as defined in the PSA.

CHECK YOUR UNDERSTANDING

1. List five core police services that all municipalities are required to provide.
2. Explain the difference between the policing responsibilities of the OPP and those of municipal police services.
3. Who polices First Nations or Inuit communities?

Members of Police Services and Their Duties

Police services boards are the employers of municipal police services. As such, a board hires police officers, police civilian employees, and various other positions. The board also negotiates collective bargaining agreements with police associations.

Hiring Requirements

The position of police constable is a very desirable one, and the selection process in most police services is highly competitive. Section 43(1) of the PSA provides that no person shall be hired as a police officer unless he or she:

(a) is a Canadian citizen or a permanent resident of Canada;
(b) is at least eighteen years of age;

(c) is physically and mentally able to perform the duties of the position, having regard to his or her own safety and the safety of members of the public;

(d) is of good moral character and habits; and

(e) has successfully completed at least four years of secondary school education or its equivalent.

While the PSA sets out minimum criteria, the Ontario Association of Chiefs of Police (OACP), in partnership with the Ministry of Community Safety and Correctional Services, has developed a common selection process that is used by most Ontario police services. The Constable Selection System (OACP, n.d.) provides that this process involves tests and interviews conducted by an independent testing service and by the police service to ensure that the best candidates are selected.

A chief of police, with the approval of the board, may hire a police cadet to undergo training to become a police constable. It is common for a candidate for a police constable to be first hired as a police cadet. Once the cadet has successfully completed the required training, he or she is then appointed as a police constable. Police cadets are considered members of the police force but are not police officers as defined in s. 2 of the PSA.

Oaths of Office and Probationary Period

Under s. 45(1) of the PSA, before starting his or her job, each police officer who has been hired must take an oath, or affirmation, of office and an oath of secrecy to ensure that he or she will perform his or her duties faithfully and confidentially when required. Each police officer must also serve a probationary period of either one year from the date of his or her appointment or one year from the completion of his or her initial period of training at the Ontario Police College. A probationary police officer's employment may be terminated at any time during the probationary period if the board provides reasonable support for doing so. However, s. 44(3) of the PSA provides that the officer has the opportunity to respond orally or in writing in the event of such termination.

Duties of Law Enforcement Officers

Before the enactment of the OPA in 1946, police officers were regularly assigned duties that had little or nothing to do with policing as we now define it. Today, the PSA defines in very specific terms the duties of the chief of police and of police officers. The duties and responsibilities are the same throughout the province, ensuring consistent policing regardless of location. Part IV of the PSA and the Act's regulations define the duties of the chief of police and other police officers.

Duties of the Chief of Police

> A chief of police is the senior law enforcement officer in the community. This is a significant responsibility. A chief of police is expected to effectively manage his or her service and provide the necessary leadership, example, and direction.
>
> Ontario Civilian Commission on Police Services (2007a)

The chief of police is responsible for the day-to-day operation of the police service, and is expected by his or her employer—the police services board—to carry out its objectives, priorities, and policies. It is the role of the chief to make this happen on a day-to-day basis. It is also the chief's responsibility to ensure that the members of the police service perform their duties as set out in the PSA and its regulations.

The duties of a chief of police, as outlined in s. 41(1) of the PSA, are as follows:

(a) in the case of a municipal police force, administering the police force and overseeing its operation in accordance with the objectives, priorities and policies established by the board under subsection 31(1);

(b) ensuring that members of the police force carry out their duties in accordance with this Act and the regulations and in a manner that reflects the needs of the community, and that discipline is maintained in the police force;

(c) ensuring that the police force provides community-oriented police services;

(d) administering the complaints system in accordance with Part V.

Duties of Police Officer

A police officer has the authority to act as an officer throughout Ontario. Although the duties of police officers are found in s. 42 of the PSA, they have additional duties and responsibilities not listed in that section. For example, s. 8 of O. Reg. 267/10, a regulation created under the Act, provides that a police officer designated as a witness officer in a Special Investigations Unit (SIU) matter must meet with investigators when requested and answer all questions.

As set out in s. 42(1), the duties of a police officer include

(a) preserving the peace;

(b) preventing crimes and other offences and providing assistance and encouragement to other persons in their prevention;

(c) assisting victims of crime;

(d) apprehending criminals and other offenders and others who may lawfully be taken into custody;

(e) laying charges and participating in prosecutions;

(f) executing warrants that are to be executed by police officers and performing related duties;

(g) performing the lawful duties that the chief of police assigns;

(h) in the case of a municipal police force and in the case of an agreement under section 10 (agreement for provision of police services by OPP), enforcing municipal by-laws;

(i) completing the prescribed training.

Duties of Auxiliary Officers

With the solicitor general's approval, a board may appoint auxiliary members of the local police service. In the OPP, the commissioner has the authority to make these appointments. Auxiliary officers are members of the police force, but are not considered to be police officers as defined in s. 2. Auxiliary members have the authority of police officers if they are accompanied or supervised by a police officer and are so authorized by the chief of police. Section 52 of the PSA provides that the chief may authorize auxiliary members to perform police duties only in special circumstances, when there are not enough police officers to handle the situations. For example, auxiliary members may help with crowd control during special events.

Duties of Special Constables

Section 53 of the PSA permits a board or the OPP commissioner to appoint special constables, with the solicitor general's permission. Special constables are given the powers of a police officer with respect to the purpose of the appointment. These constables are not to be used to perform the usual duties of a police officer.

Special constables provide policing services in various parts of the community. For example, they police many university campuses throughout Ontario. They also police the courts, attending to prisoner care and transport.

CHECK YOUR UNDERSTANDING

1. List the minimum requirements that a police constable must meet.

2. Is a police cadet considered a police officer as defined in the PSA? Explain.

3. Explain the duties of the chief of police.

Ensuring the Accountability of Police Services

accountable
required to explain actions
or decisions to someone

oversight
the management of
police activity, both
internally and externally

It is important that police services are delivered to the community efficiently, equitably, and with transparency, and that police are held **accountable** for their actions. The PSA ensures that there are various levels of civilian **oversight** of the police services in the province. These civilians include elected representatives at both the provincial and municipal levels, and they include appointed members of the community. Let's take a look at some of the key positions and agencies that ensure the accountability of police services and police officers. (See Figure 2.2.)

Ministry of Community Safety and Correctional Services

The Ministry of Community Safety and Correctional Services oversees policing services throughout the province and has considerable influence over the policies, procedures, and general operations of the provincial and municipal police services. Led by a minister (also known as the solicitor general), the Ministry has an extensive list of duties, defined in s. 3 of the PSA.

One of the most important duties of the Ministry is to monitor all municipal police services as well as the provincial police to ensure they are delivering adequate and effective services. The Ministry provides a support network for the policing community by developing and promoting programs to enhance professional police practices and standards and training, and it serves as a consultant to the various boards and community committees within the policing community.

The Ontario Civilian Police Commission (OCPC)

Working under the Ministry of Community Safety and Correctional Services, the Ontario Civilian Police Commission (OCPC) performs an independent quasi-judicial function. In other words, the commission has authority to investigate police conduct and mete out appropriate penalties to ensure that police services comply with prescribed standards of service. It is through the commission that police services boards and police services are accountable to the public (OCPC, 2014).

For example, what happens when a board, a police chief, or a municipal police service fails to comply with the prescribed standards of police services? Sections 22-26 of the PSA set out the powers and duties of the commission to address such failure. These powers and duties include conducting hearings, investigations, and inquiries on the advice of the solicitor general. Where appropriate, as its mission statement affirms, the commission may

FIGURE 2.2   Police Services Organizational Chart

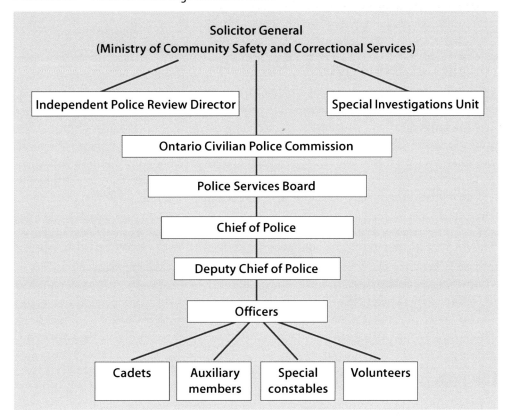

impose sanctions, such as suspending or removing a police chief or one or more members of a board, disbanding a police service, or appointing an administrator for a specified period.

The commission is also responsible for internal police matters. It may—at the solicitor general's request, at a municipal council's request, or by way of its own motion—investigate and report on the conduct or performance of police chiefs, board members, auxiliary members of a service, special constables, and bylaw enforcement officers. Under s. 26 of the PSA, the commission is also responsible for conducting inquiries into crime and law enforcement matters at the direction of the solicitor general.

Office of the Independent Police Review Director (OIPRD)

The Office of the Independent Police Review Director (OIPRD) operates under the Ministry of the Attorney General, which oversees Ontario's justice system. The OIPRD was created by the *Independent Police Review Act* (2007) and began operating in 2009.

The OIPRD was created to "provide an objective, impartial office to receive, manage, and oversee the investigation of public complaints against Ontario's police" (McNeilly & Simmonds, 2013). To ensure objectivity and impartiality, the OIPRD is composed of civilians. Employees cannot be police officers, but they can include former police officers. However, the director of the OIPRD, who is appointed by the lieutenant governor in council on the advice of the attorney general, cannot be a police officer or former police officer.

Sections 26.4-26.9 of the PSA outline the OIPRD's powers to carry out investigations into complaints. One of these powers is the authority to appoint investigators. These investigators have the power to obtain an order from a justice of the peace or provincial justice to enter and search police premises for anything related to an investigation. All employees of the police are obliged to assist with these investigations.

Although the OIPRD is accountable to the attorney general, day-to-day decisions are the responsibility of the director. The decisions of the OIPRD are independent, and separate from the government, police, and the community.

The Special Investigations Unit (SIU)

At one time, police services conducted their own criminal investigations into their own members. In other words, it was police investigating police. The conclusions of this process were not always trusted by members of the community. To ensure confidence in such investigations, the government of Ontario passed legislation in 1990 creating the Special Investigations Unit (SIU). The SIU is a civilian law enforcement body that conducts criminal investigations into interactions between the police and civilians that have resulted in serious injury, death, or an allegation of sexual assault. This unit is independent of the police and works under the direction of the Ministry of the Attorney General. The director of the SIU reports the results of each investigation to the attorney general (SIU, 2011).

Part VII of the PSA sets out the responsibilities of the SIU and its staff. The objective of each SIU investigation is to determine, through a rigorous independent investigation, whether there is evidence of criminal wrongdoing by a police officer(s). The director of the SIU has the duty to determine if there exist reasonable grounds for believing the officer(s) has committed a criminal offence. When the director forms such reasonable grounds, he or she will lay an appropriate criminal charge(s), which is prosecuted by the **Crown attorney**.

Crown attorney
a lawyer responsible for prosecuting criminal offences in the province of Ontario

The Police Services Board

As noted above, a police services board is responsible for providing adequate and effective police services as defined in s. 31 of the PSA and in the Act's related regulations. Police services boards are the employers of municipal police services and they appoint police officers, special constables, and police civilian employees. They conduct labour talks and negotiate collective agreements with police associations. The police services board is also responsible for establishing priorities, objectives, and policies, and—in order to ensure accountability—for monitoring the performance of both the chief of police and the police service.

The Chief of Police

misconduct
improper behaviour; behaviour that contravenes certain standards or laws; an Ontario police officer is guilty of misconduct if he or she commits an offence described in s. 80 of the PSA or O. Reg. 268/10

unsatisfactory work performance
work performance that does not meet the standards established by the policies of chiefs of police

The chief of police reports directly to the police services board. Under s. 41(2) of the PSA, he or she is required to obey the lawful orders and directions of the board. It is the chief's responsibility to ensure the discipline of the members of his or her service. Section 76 of the PSA provides that if there is a complaint about the conduct or work performance of a police officer in his or her police force, the police chief is responsible for having the complaint investigated and the results reported to him or her in writing. If the chief concludes, after reviewing the report, that the officer's conduct constitutes either **misconduct** (as defined in s. 80 of the PSA) or **unsatisfactory work performance**, he or she will hold a hearing.

CHECK YOUR UNDERSTANDING

1. Who leads the Ministry of Community Safety and Correctional Services, and what is the role of this person?
2. Describe a key function of the OCPC and OIPRD.
3. Under what circumstance will the SIU conduct an investigation?

Conduct of Police Officers On Duty and Off Duty

Police officers are given extraordinary powers to carry out their duties. The community expects them to use these powers solely for the purposes for which they were intended. Police officers are also expected to perform their duties in a fair and responsible manner. Therefore, police officers are held to a higher standard of conduct than average citizens are.

Code of Conduct

The PSA and the regulations created under it define the standards of police conduct and the consequences of failing to follow these standards. The code of conduct for police officers is found in O. Reg. 268/10, a regulation created under the PSA. Simply put, the code of conduct defines what unacceptable behaviour is for a police officer. (The actual text of the code is reproduced in the box below.) The following is a list of the behaviours that are considered misconduct, under the code of conduct:

- *Discreditable conduct.* This covers a wide range of conduct, including the manner in which a police officer treats members of the public or other members of the police force. Swearing at members of the public or the police force, withholding a complaint or making a false complaint against a member of the police force, or being found guilty of a criminal offence—these are examples of discreditable conduct. Such actions could cause embarrassment to the police force or negatively affect the public's confidence in the police force.

- *Insubordination.* An officer commits insubordination by not following the orders of a superior. This may include outright refusal to follow a lawful order or failing to carry out an order.

- *Neglect of duty.* This covers the general duties of a police officer as defined in the PSA and the regulations. An officer who fails to cooperate with investigators of the SIU, who does not follow orders, who allows a prisoner to escape, who does not complete required reports, who misses duty without excuse, or who dresses improperly is guilty of neglect of duty.

- *Deceit.* An officer who provides a false or misleading statement or destroys a record has committed deceit. For example, an officer might enter into his or her memo book an entry stating that he or she was patrolling an area of the community when in fact he or she was dining at a restaurant.

- *Breach of confidence.* When an officer provides secret information to a person not entitled to this information, such as a reporter or a wanted person, he or she is in breach of confidence.

- *Corrupt practice.* Examples of corrupt practice by officers include taking bribes, placing themselves in a position where they are indebted to a licensee (such as a bar owner) when they or another member of the force are required to provide a negative report on a licensee, or using their position to their private advantage, such as receiving goods at a discounted price.

- *Unlawful or unnecessary exercise of authority.* It is important that officers only arrest individuals when lawfully entitled to do so and use force only when necessary.

- *Damage to clothing or equipment.* An example of this would be when an officer who is operating a police vehicle causes a collision owing to lack of attention.

- *Consuming drugs or alcohol in a manner prejudicial to duty*. Police officers are not strictly prohibited from consuming alcohol when on duty. Whether and how much an officer can drink while on duty often depends on the work he or she is doing. For example, a uniform officer generally is prohibited from drinking on duty. An undercover officer, on the other hand, would be permitted to drink some alcohol in order to fit in with the people he or she is investigating. No officers, regardless of their assignment, are permitted to drink to the point where their ability to perform policing duties is affected. Officers can consume alcohol or legally prescribed drugs while off duty provided they are fit for duty when required. It is safe to say that police officers are never permitted to consume illegal drugs.

SCHEDULE

Code of Conduct

2(1) Any chief of police or other police officer commits misconduct if he or she engages in,

(a) Discreditable Conduct, in that he or she,

(i) fails to treat or protect persons equally without discrimination with respect to police services because of race, ancestry, place of origin, colour, ethnic origin, citizenship, creed, sex, sexual orientation, age, marital status, family status or disability,

(ii) uses profane, abusive or insulting language that relates to a person's race, ancestry, place of origin, colour, ethnic origin, citizenship, creed, sex, sexual orientation, age, marital status, family status or disability,

(iii) is guilty of oppressive or tyrannical conduct towards an inferior in rank,

(iv) uses profane, abusive or insulting language to any other member of a police force,

(v) uses profane, abusive or insulting language or is otherwise uncivil to a member of the public,

(vi) wilfully or negligently makes any false complaint or statement against any member of a police force,

(vii) assaults any other member of a police force,

(viii) withholds or suppresses a complaint or report against a member of a police force or about the policies of or services provided by the police force of which the officer is a member,

(ix) is guilty of a criminal offence that is an indictable offence or an offence punishable upon summary conviction,

(x) contravenes any provision of the Act or the regulations, or

(xi) acts in a disorderly manner or in a manner prejudicial to discipline or likely to bring discredit upon the reputation of the police force of which the officer is a member;

(b) Insubordination, in that he or she,

(i) is insubordinate by word, act or demeanour, or

(ii) without lawful excuse, disobeys, omits or neglects to carry out any lawful order;

(c) Neglect of Duty, in that he or she,

(i) without lawful excuse, neglects or omits promptly and diligently to perform a duty as,

(A) a member of the police force of which the officer is a member, if the officer is a member of an Ontario police force as defined in the *Interprovincial Policing Act, 2009*, or

(B) a police officer appointed under the *Interprovincial Policing Act, 2009*,

(ii) fails to comply with any provision of Ontario Regulation 267/10 (Conduct and Duties of Police Officers Respecting Investigations by the Special Investigations Unit) made under the Act,

(iii) fails to work in accordance with orders, or leaves an area, detachment, detail or other place of duty, without due permission or sufficient cause,

(iv) by carelessness or neglect permits a prisoner to escape,

(v) fails, when knowing where an offender is to be found, to report him or her or to make due exertions for bringing the offender to justice,

(vi) fails to report a matter that it is his or her duty to report,

(vii) fails to report anything that he or she knows concerning a criminal or other charge, or fails to disclose any evidence that he or she, or any person within his or her knowledge, can give for or against any prisoner or defendant,

(viii) omits to make any necessary entry in a record,

(ix) feigns or exaggerates sickness or injury to evade duty,

(x) is absent without leave from or late for any duty, without reasonable excuse, or

(xi) is improperly dressed, dirty or untidy in person, clothing or equipment while on duty;

(d) Deceit, in that he or she,

(i) knowingly makes or signs a false statement in a record,

(ii) wilfully or negligently makes a false, misleading or inaccurate statement pertaining to official duties, or

(iii) without lawful excuse, destroys or mutilates a record or alters or erases an entry in a record;

(e) Breach of Confidence, in that he or she,

(i) divulges any matter which it is his or her duty to keep secret,

(ii) gives notice, directly or indirectly, to any person against whom any warrant or summons has been or is about to be issued, except in the lawful execution of the warrant or service of the summons,

(iii) without proper authority, communicates to the media or to any unauthorized person any matter connected with,

(A) the police force of which the officer is a member, if the officer is a member of an Ontario police force as defined in the *Interprovincial Policing Act, 2009*, or

(B) the police force with which the officer is working on a joint forces operation or investigation, if the officer is appointed as a police officer under the *Interprovincial Policing Act, 2009*, or

(iv) without proper authority, shows to any person not a member of the police force described in sub-subclause (iii)(A) or (B), as the case may be, or to any unauthorized member of that police force any record that is the property of that police force;

(f) Corrupt Practice, in that he or she,

(i) offers or takes a bribe,

(ii) fails to account for or to make a prompt, true return of money or property received in an official capacity,

(iii) directly or indirectly solicits or receives a gratuity or present without the consent of,

(A) the chief of police, if the officer is a member of an Ontario police force as defined in the *Interprovincial Policing Act, 2009*, or

(B) the person who appointed the police officer under Part II or III of the *Interprovincial Policing Act, 2009*,

(iv) places himself or herself under a pecuniary or other obligation to a licensee if a member of the following police force may have to report or give evidence concerning the granting or refusing of a licence to the licensee:

   (A) the police force of which the officer is a member, if the officer is a member of an Ontario police force as defined in the *Interprovincial Policing Act, 2009*, or

   (B) the police force with which the officer is working on a joint forces operation or investigation, if the officer is appointed as a police officer under the *Interprovincial Policing Act, 2009*, or

(v) improperly uses his or her character and position as a member of a police force for private advantage;

(g) Unlawful or Unnecessary Exercise of Authority, in that he or she,

(i) without good and sufficient cause makes an unlawful or unnecessary arrest, or

(ii) uses any unnecessary force against a prisoner or other person contacted in the execution of duty;

(h) Damage to Clothing or Equipment, in that he or she,

(i) wilfully or carelessly causes loss or damage to any article of clothing or equipment, or to any record or other property of,

   (A) the police force of which the officer is a member, if the officer is a member of an Ontario police force as defined in the *Interprovincial Policing Act, 2009*, or

   (B) the police force with which the officer is working on a joint forces operation or investigation, if the officer is appointed as a police officer under the *Interprovincial Policing Act, 2009*, or

(ii) fails to report loss or damage, however caused, as soon as practicable; or

(i) Consuming Drugs or Alcohol in a Manner Prejudicial to Duty, in that he or she,

(i) is unfit for duty, while on duty, through consumption of drugs or alcohol,

(ii) is unfit for duty when he or she reports for duty, through consumption of drugs or alcohol,

(iii) except with the consent of a superior officer or in the discharge of duty, consumes or receives alcohol from any other person while on duty, or

(iv) except in the discharge of duty, demands, persuades or attempts to persuade another person to give or purchase or obtain for a member of a police force any alcohol or illegal drugs while on duty.

IT'S YOUR MOVE, OFFICER!

Scenario 2.1

Constable K was on uniform patrol when he stopped a car that had its rear licence plate hanging loose. The motorist, named AF, did not have registration and insurance documents with him, but provided his name, address, and driver's licence number. Upon checking the motorist's information on his mobile data terminal, Constable K discovered that the plate was registered to the motorist's wife and belonged on another vehicle. Further inquiries revealed that there was another person by the name of AF, and that this other person was a suspended driver.

Constable K served the motorist with five summonses for violations of the *Highway Traffic Act* and the *Compulsory Automobile Insurance Act*. A court date of January 5, 2001 was set on the summonses. Constable K also prepared, and insisted that he served the motorist with, a further six summonses based on the second AF's driving history. The court date identified on the further summonses was January 9, 2001. The motorist insisted that he was never served with these additional summonses.

The motorist appeared in court on January 5, 2001, but Constable K did not appear; nor did he appear on the trial date. The five charges faced by the motorist were later withdrawn. On January 9, 2001, when Constable K went to court for the additional six summonses, the motorist failed to appear. A trial date was set, and Constable K appeared on this date while the motorist did not. The motorist was convicted in absentia and was fined $15,000 and sentenced to 15 days' imprisonment for driving under suspension. A warrant was issued for the arrest of the motorist.

Two years later, the motorist (the first AF) was stopped by another patrol officer and arrested for the outstanding warrant. He spent five days in jail before he could convince the authorities he was not the second AF.

The motorist later brought a lawsuit against the police service, which was settled out of court (OCCPS, 2007b).

1. If you were an officer investigating this matter for the chief, how would you view this case? Assuming that all the facts are true, did Constable K violate any of the codes of conduct? Explain.

2. What do you believe would be an appropriate penalty for Constable K?

Off-Duty Conduct

Police officers have many responsibilities while on duty, but they also have certain off-duty rules that they have to follow.

Restrictions on Off-Duty Activities

Police officers are restricted in what activities they can participate in during their off-duty time. Section 49 of the PSA prohibits police officers from engaging in off-duty activities that

- will negatively interfere with or influence their performance as police officers;
- place them in a position of conflict of interest;
- would constitute full-time employment for another person; or
- gives them an advantage derived from their status as police officers.

Police officers must disclose to the chief or board when they have taken part or plan to take part in an activity that may violate these restrictions. Under s. 49(3)(4) of the PSA, the chief or board will decide whether the officer is permitted to take part in the activity, and the police officer must comply with the decision.

IT'S YOUR MOVE, OFFICER!

Scenario 2.2

Constable B is off duty and attends a local restaurant and bar. Upon arrival, Constable B sees that there is a long line of patrons waiting to enter. The constable, known to management and employees at the establishment, jumps the line and is witnessed doing so by the other patrons (OCCPS, 2001).

If you were the officer who received this complaint, how would you view Constable B's action? Did the constable violate an off-duty code of conduct? Why or why not?

Political Activity

Ontario Regulation 268/10 regulates the political activity of police officers. Police officers may in general participate in all aspects of the political process. For example, they may vote, be a member of a political party, and contribute money to a political party. There are some restrictions on off-duty officers. When a police officer is off duty, any political views he or she expresses cannot relate directly to his or her responsibilities as a police officer or be represented as those of a police service.

When police officers are on duty, greater restrictions apply; they must stay politically neutral, neither supporting nor opposing a candidate or political party or a position taken by a candidate or political party.

Generally speaking, a police officer who wishes to run for federal, provincial, or municipal office must take an unpaid leave of absence. If elected, the police officer must resign from the police service immediately. Sections 11–18 of O. Reg. 268/10 provide for an exception to this rule: If an officer is elected into a municipal council that does not receive police services from the municipality in which the officer is employed, then the officer does not need to resign.

CHECK YOUR UNDERSTANDING

1. Identify two kinds of misconduct an on-duty police officer might engage in.
2. Under what circumstances can a police officer remain as a police officer once elected to a public office?
3. Who decides if a police officer may engage in an off-duty secondary activity?

Complaints Against Police Officers and Police Services

As you have learned, one of the main differences between the original *Ontario Police Act* (1946) and the PSA is that the latter established a province-wide complaints system under the authority of the Police Complaints Commissioner.

External Complaints

Citizens' complaints (external complaints) fall into two categories: (1) complaints regarding the conduct of a police officer; and (2) complaints about a police service's policy or service standard. As discussed earlier in this chapter, the Office of the Independent Police Review Director (OIPRD) is responsible for administering the public complaints system as well as for processing and investigating public complaints.

Part V of the PSA deals with the public complaints system and resulting disciplinary proceedings. Not all complaints made by community members are investigated. Under ss. 60(4)-(6) of the PSA, the director of the OIPRD may determine not to deal with a complaint for a number of reasons, including the following:

- the complaint is frivolous or without sufficient grounds;
- the complaint would be better dealt with under another Act;
- dealing with the complaint would not be in the public interest;
- the complaint is about a policy or service that has no direct effect on the complainant;

- the complainant is neither the person at whom the conduct was directed, nor the person who saw or heard the conduct, nor a person who, because he or she was in a relationship with the person affected by the conduct, suffered loss, damage, distress, danger, or inconvenience as a result of the conduct.

The director of the OIPRD has a number of options when dealing with complaints about the conduct of a police officer. The director can

- refer the complaint to the chief of police of the force to which the complaint relates,
- refer the complaint to the chief of police of another force, or
- retain the complaint.

Complaints against the policies of the OPP are handled somewhat differently than are those against the policies of a municipal police service. An individual may make a complaint against the OPP policies, which apply throughout the OPP, or against local OPP detachment policies. Many OPP detachments provide municipal police services to municipalities throughout Ontario. These detachments may have local policies that only apply to that individual detachment.

Table 2.2 summarizes some of the complaints that might be made against police officers and police services, and it lists the individuals responsible for dealing with them.

TABLE 2.2   Who Deals with What Types of Complaints?

Complaints about ...	→	Referred to ...
Policies of and services provided by a municipal police force	→	Police chief
OPP policies and services	→	Commissioner
Local OPP policies	→	Detachment commander
Police chief	→	Police services board
Commissioner	→	Solicitor general

Internal Complaints

The chief of police initiates internal complaints. Internal complaints are the discipline system within the police service. These complaints can involve behaviours as minor as being late for work to something as serious as a criminal offence. As with external complaints, unacceptable behaviour in a police officer is defined by the code of conduct. Internal complaints are handled in a similar way to external complaints: an investigation is conducted and a written report is sent to the chief of police.

Under ss. 76(8)-(10) of the PSA, internal complaints will result in one of three conclusions:

1. If, at the end of the investigation, the chief concludes that the complaint is unsubstantiated, no further action will be taken.

2. If the chief concludes there are reasonable grounds to believe that the officer's conduct constitutes misconduct or unsatisfactory work performance, the chief will hold a hearing.

3. If the chief believes that the misconduct or unsatisfactory work performance was not serious, the chief may propose an informal resolution without a hearing. The police officer involved must agree to the resolution proposed by the chief.

If a hearing takes place and the police officer is found to have committed misconduct or unsatisfactory work performance on clear and convincing evidence, the chief, under s. 85(1) of the PSA, has a number of different penalties that could be imposed:

> (a) dismiss the police officer from the police force;
> (b) direct that the police officer be dismissed in seven days unless he or she resigns before that time;
> (c) demote the police officer, specifying the manner and period of the demotion;
> (d) suspend the police officer without pay for a period not exceeding 30 days or 240 hours, as the case may be;
> (e) direct that the police officer forfeit not more than three days or 24 hours pay, as the case may be;
> (f) direct that the police officer forfeit not more than 20 days or 160 hours off, as the case may be; or
> (g) impose on the police officer any combination of penalties described in clauses (c), (d), (e) and (f).

If an informal resolution is attempted but not achieved, the chief may impose penalty (d), (e), or (f). Section 76(12) of the PSA provides that, if the police officer refuses to accept the penalty, the chief will hold a hearing.

Suspensions

One of the more controversial subjects of late is the viability of suspending, with pay, police officers accused of serious offences or misconduct. Section 89 of the PSA gives the chief of police the authority to make this decision for any police officer who is suspected of or charged with an offence under a federal, provincial, or territorial law, or is suspected of misconduct. This suspension can be revoked or imposed repeatedly as the chief considers appropriate. However, under s. 89(6) of the PSA, the chief can only impose a suspension *without pay* when an officer is convicted of an offence and sentenced to prison, and he or she may impose this sentence even if the officer's conviction is under appeal.

How this controversy will play out is yet to be seen. As you have seen with the OIPRD, civilian involvement in the accountability of police services has gone from almost none in the years before the PSA to multiple levels of civilian oversight and control under the current legislation. In response to complaints from community members, from the media, and from other members of the police services, the Ontario Association of Chiefs of Police (OACP) has started to demand that the provincial government amend the PSA to allow police officers to be suspended without pay when facing serious criminal or PSA allegations. It remains to be seen whether this change will come about.

CHECK YOUR UNDERSTANDING

1. List the nine categories of behaviours that constitute misconduct by a chief of police or police officer as defined in O. Reg. 268/10.

2. Who can initiate an internal complaint against a police officer?

3. A chief of police may suspend a police officer (with or without pay). List the circumstances in which a chief of police may suspend a police officer.

CHAPTER SUMMARY

In this chapter, we explored the *Police Services Act* (PSA), a comprehensive statute intended to control and regulate policing in Ontario. Prior to 1946, policing in the province was poorly regulated and was inconsistent across the province. With the passing of the first *Ontario Police Act* in 1946, Ontario began to see a more consistent method of providing police services. The modern PSA was first enacted in 1990 and has received a number of amendments since then. The amendments have produced civilian oversight and investigative bodies to ensure fairness, transparency, and accountability on the part of police services and their members. The PSA of 1990 was the first policing legislation to include a declaration of principles. These principles form the basis of the Ontario philosophy of policing.

This chapter has emphasized how important it is for all police officers, especially those who are new or about to enter the profession, to understand the roles and responsibilities of various members and organizations within the policing community. We introduced the civilian bodies that oversee police services in Ontario: the Ministry of Community Safety and Correctional Services, the Ontario Civilian Police Commission (OCPC), the Office of the Independent Police Review Director (OIPRD), the Special Investigations Unit (SIU), and the Police Services Board. We discussed the duties of the chief of police and police officers as defined by the PSA and its related regulations. This definition includes a code of conduct for all police officers. This code identifies what constitutes misconduct and is tied directly to a disciplinary system. The disciplinary system creates a fair and transparent process for dealing with both internal and external complaints against police officers or against a chief of police. It defines the penalties to be imposed on those in police services who engage in unacceptable behaviour.

KEY TERMS

accountable, 32
amalgamate, 28
collective bargaining rights, 24
community-based policing, 26
core police services, 27
Crown attorney, 34

freedom of expression, 26
misconduct, 34
oversight, 32
solicitor general of Ontario, 27
unsatisfactory work performance, 34

REFERENCES

Canadian Charter of Rights and Freedoms. (1982). Part I of the *Constitution Act, 1982*, RSC 1985, app. II, no. 44.

Gillis, L. (2014, September 3). Timmins Police officer is demoted. *Timmins Times*. http://www.timminstimes.com/2014/09/03/timmins-police-officer-is-demoted.

Hotson, R. (2011). History. Peterborough Lakefield Community Police. http://www.peterboroughpolice.com.

Human Rights Code. (1990). RSO 1990, c. H.19, as amended.

McNeilly, G., & Simmonds, N. (2013). Diversity and inclusion plan: 2013-2016. Office of the Independent Police Review Director. http://www.oiprd.on.ca/EN/PDFs/Diversity-Inclusion -Strategic-Plan-2013-2016_E.pdf.

Ontario Association of Chiefs of Police (OACP). (n.d.). Constable selection system. http://www.oacp.on.ca/programs-courses/constable-selection-system.

Ontario Civilian Commission on Police Services (OCCPS). (2001). OCCPS Decision #01-07: Constable Scott Besco (appellant) and Peel Regional Police Service (respondent). http://www.ocpc.ca/files/99W52003I702N310FC136K4415457L.pdf.

Ontario Civilian Commission on Police Services (OCCPS). (2007a). INQ #07-01: In the matter of a hearing under section 65(9) of the Police Services Act R.S.O. 1990, c. P.15 as amended into the conduct of Chief Blair MacIsaac of the Pembroke Police Service. http://www.ocpc.ca/files/N6J420078K020A077U10DC59R126G1.pdf.

Ontario Civilian Commission on Police Services (OCCPS). (2007b). OCCPS Decision #07-14: Constable Imants Karklins (appellant) and Toronto Police Service (respondent). http://www.ocpc.ca/files/M3VV2008U001A6047M16D703QW51GV.pdf.

Ontario Civilian Police Commission (OCPC). (2014). Mission statement. http://www.ocpc.ca/english/index.asp.

Ottawa Police Service. (2012). In the matter of Ontario Regulation 123/89 made under the Police Services Act R.S.O. 1990, c. P.15 and the amendments thereto; and in the matter of Staff Sergeant Lyse Fournier and Ottawa Police Service.

Police Services Act. (1990). RSO 1990, c. P.15.

Police Services Act, O. Reg. 267/10. (2010). Conduct and duties of police officers respecting investigations by the Special Investigations Unit.

Police Services Act, O. Reg. 268/10. (2010). General.

Police Services Act, O. Reg. 3/99. (1999). Adequacy and effectiveness of police services.

Special Investigations Unit (SIU). (2011). What we do. http://www.siu.on.ca/en/what_we_do.php.

Victims' Bill of Rights. (1995). SO 1995, c. 6.

FURTHER READING

Blandford, S. (2004). The impact of adequacy standards on Ontario police services. *The Canadian Review of Policing Research, 1*. http://crpr.icaap.org/index.php/crpr/article/view/14/13.

Canadian Press. (2013, July 7). Police chiefs seek ability to suspend officers without pay. CBC News. http://www.cbc.ca/news/canada/toronto/police-chiefs-seek-ability-to-suspend-officers-without-pay-1.1346660.

Morris, S., & Canadian Press. (2013, November 28). Hamilton cop boss wants changes to Police Services Act. In-Depth Radio: Newstalk 1010. http://www.newstalk1010.com/news/2013/11/28/hamilton-cop-boss-wants-changes-to-police-services-act.

Office of the Independent Police Review Director. (2013). *2012-2013 Annual report*. https://www.oiprd.on.ca/CMS/oiprd/media/image-Main/PDF/OIPRD-ANNUAL-REPORT-2012-13-EN.pdf.

Ontario Civilian Police Commission (OCPC). (2014). *2013-2014 Annual report*. http://www.oiprd.on.ca/EN/PDFs/Annual-Report-2013-2014_A_E.pdf.

Police Services Act. (1990). RSO 1990, c. P.15. http://www.e-laws.gov.on.ca/html/statutes/english/elaws_statutes_90p15_e.htm.

Police Services Act, O. Reg. 3/99. (1999). Adequacy and effectiveness of police services. http://www.e-laws.gov.on.ca/html/regs/english/elaws_regs_990003_e.htm.

Police Services Act, O. Reg. 268/10. (2010). General. http://www.e-laws.gov.on.ca/html/source/regs/english/2010/elaws_src_regs_r10268_e.htm.

Special Investigations Unit. (2013). *Annual report 2012-2013*. http://www.siu.on.ca/pdfs/ar_2012_13__english___acessible.pdf.

Windsor Star. (2013, July 12). Police Services Act must be changed to withhold pay for suspended cops. *The Windsor Star*. http://blogs.windsorstar.com/2013/07/12/star-editorial-police-services-act-must-be-changed-to-withhold-pay-for-suspended-cops.

REVIEW QUESTIONS

Multiple Choice

1. The first *Police Act* was enacted in Ontario in _____

   a. 1849

   b. 1946

   c. 1959

   d. 1969

2. The philosophy of policing can be found in

   a. the six basic principles found in s. 1 of the PSA

   b. the six basic principles found in the regulations of the PSA

   c. the six basic principles found on the website of the solicitor general

   d. the six basic principles found on the website of the OPP

3. The PSA sets minimum hiring standards for police constables in Ontario. According to these standards, an individual must be at least _____ years of age.

   a. 16

   b. 18

   c. 20

   d. 21

4. When first appointed as a police constable, each police officer must serve a probationary period of

   a. six months

   b. one year

   c. eighteen months

   d. two years

5. The chief of police reports directly to

   a. city or town council

   b. the mayor

   c. the chair of the police services board

   d. the police services board

True or False

____ **1.** The PSA applies to municipal police services only.

____ **2.** Each municipality must provide adequate and effective police services. The police service must provide a minimum of five core police services.

____ **3.** The chief of police creates the service's objectives, priorities, and policies.

____ **4.** The duties of the chief of police include ensuring that the police force provides community-oriented police services.

____ **5.** The duties of a police constable include assisting victims of crime.

____ **6.** The Ontario Civilian Police Commission has been granted a broad scope of investigative and punitive capabilities to ensure that police services comply with prescribed standards of service.

_____ **7.** Management of complaints made to him or her by members of the public in accordance with Part V of the PSA and regulations is a responsibility of the director of the SIU.

_____ **8.** The PSA code of conduct defines what is unacceptable behaviour for a police officer.

_____ **9.** Police officers cannot engage in any form of political activity.

_____**10.** The chief of police initiates all internal complaints against police officers.

Short Answer

1. Looking at the photo below, consider how the six principles of the PSA may affect the policing of this situation.

Source: The Canadian Press/Patrick Dell.

2. Compare and contrast the roles of the solicitor general, the OCPC, the OIPRD, and the SIU.

3. Compare and contrast the roles of the police services board and the chief of police.

4. What restrictions does the PSA place on the off-duty activities of police officers?

5. Give an example of a circumstance in which a police officer may be suspended. Who has the authority to impose the suspension?

It's Your Move, Officer!

A. You are a member of a municipal police service and hold the rank of constable. You have been approached by a movie producer to work as a consultant on a film. This will be a temporary part-time job at which you will work only on your days off from the police service. If you accept the position, you will be required to become a member of a trade union.

1. Do you require permission from anyone in the police service to undertake this job during your time off? Explain.

2. Explain whether membership in the trade union is prohibited under the PSA.

B. As a sergeant on a municipal police service, one of your responsibilities is to assign police officers to various details. You learn that there will be a large demonstration outside a house of worship in your area. There have been reports that the protesters may try to enter the building and disrupt proceedings inside it. You detail ten officers to police the demonstration. One of the officers asks to be removed from the detail because his beliefs are similar to those of the demonstrators. You explain the assignment again, but the officer still refuses to participate.

1. List any breaches of the code of conduct this officer may have committed.

2. If convicted of a breach of the code of conduct, what penalties could be imposed?

Arrest Powers

3

LEARNING OUTCOMES

After completing this chapter, you should be able to:

- Explain where police get their powers and authority to arrest and how legislation, such as the *Criminal Code* and the *Canadian Charter of Rights and Freedoms*, limits arrest powers and authority.

- Identify the classification of offences and the rules of arrest that apply to each class.

- Describe how police decide to make an arrest without a warrant.

- List the steps for making a lawful arrest.

- Explain how police decide when not to make an arrest.

- Explain how arrest differs from voluntary accompaniment and investigative detention.

- Identify and describe different types of arrest warrants.

- Compare the treatment of adult offenders with the treatment of young offenders and of children under 12 who commit crimes.

- Describe a citizen's power of arrest and how it is different from the police power of arrest.

ON SCENE

While on foot patrol in a large downtown shopping mall, a uniform officer observes that the electronics store on the first floor has been boarded up. There is a sign on the front indicating that the store is under construction and will not be open for another three weeks. As he continues walking, the officer notices a male known to police for auto theft. As the officer watches, the man goes from one end of the construction site to the other, trying to see inside and pulling on some of the boards. The man then walks to the front of the construction site and pries open the front door, using what appears to be a screwdriver. The officer continues watching as the man goes into the construction site and, approximately one minute later, comes out carrying a power drill. The man then quickly heads toward the exit doors of the mall. The officer follows him.

Do you think the officer has the authority to make an arrest? If so, under what authority can he arrest the man?

Introduction

Canadian law gives police officers in Canada extraordinary powers, including the power to arrest and detain people they believe have committed a criminal offence or an offence under a provincial statute. But Canadian law also limits police arrest powers. In fact, police officers are discouraged from making an arrest unless the situation involves a serious offence. These restrictions were created to ensure that the rights and freedoms guaranteed to all Canadians, included suspected offenders, are respected. Under s. 9 of the *Canadian Charter of Rights and Freedoms*, "Everyone has the right not to be arbitrarily detained or imprisoned." The limitations on police arrest powers ensure that this fundamental right is protected.

In this chapter, you will learn about the scope of police arrest powers, including the limitations imposed upon these powers. You will learn about the classification of offences and how this affects the procedure for making an arrest, with and without warrants. Part of this discussion will concern how, once an officer decides to make an arrest, the law imposes restrictions on police officers in *continuing* the arrest. You will also learn about how young offenders and children under 12 who commit crimes are treated by police. Finally, you will explore the power that citizens have to arrest offenders and how this power is different from the arrest power that police have.

What is *arrest*? There are many legal definitions of *arrest*. In Canadian law, the definition is "the actual restraint on a person's liberty without the person's consent and taking physical control of a person with the intent to detain." In *R v. Therens* (1985, para. 53), detention (that is, arrest) was defined as "deprivation of liberty by physical constraint"; it was also defined as occurring "when a police officer … assumes control over the movement of a person by a demand or direction" (para. 53) and was said to involve an "element of psychological compulsion, in the form of a reasonable perception of suspension of freedom of choice" (para. 57). It follows from this definition that if a police officer takes physical control of a person for the purpose of arresting the person, or if the person believes his or her freedom to leave has been removed, then the person has in fact been arrested.

Arrest Authority: Arrest Without a Warrant

A police officer's authority to arrest a person without a warrant for a criminal act comes from s. 495 of the *Criminal Code*, as follows:

> (1) A peace [police] officer may arrest without warrant
>   (a) a person who has committed an indictable offence or who, on reasonable grounds, he believes has committed or is about to commit an indictable offence;
>   (b) a person whom he finds committing a criminal offence; or
>   (c) a person in respect of whom he has reasonable grounds to believe that a warrant of arrest or committal … is in force within the territorial jurisdiction in which the person is found.

To fully understand this section of the Code, we need to define some of the concepts and terms used in it, such as "arrest" (defined above), "reasonable grounds," and "found committing."

Reasonable Grounds

We may define **reasonable grounds** as a collection of circumstances or facts that would lead an ordinary, cautious (that is, prudent) person to form a strong belief that a person has committed an offence. An arrest made on the basis of reasonable grounds must pass two tests to qualify as lawful:

reasonable grounds
a set of facts or circumstances that would cause an ordinary and cautious (in other words, prudent) person to form a belief

1. *Subjective test*: Whether the officer believed, in the light of his or her experience in policing, that the person committed the offence.
2. *Objective test*: Whether a person other than the officer would believe that the person committed the offence. It is a question often answered by the presiding judge, who hears all the facts that contributed to the officer's belief.

The following quotation, from *R v. Storrey* (1990, p. 242), illustrates how an arrest based on reasonable grounds may be ascertained to be lawful:

> Section 450(1) [of the *Criminal Code*] requires that an arresting officer must subjectively have reasonable and probable grounds* on which to base the arrest. Those grounds must, in addition, be justifiable from an objective point of view. That is to say, a reasonable person placed in the position of the officer must be able to conclude that there were indeed reasonable and probable grounds for the arrest.

Found Committing

Found committing describes a situation in which a police officer actually witnesses an offence and clearly identifies the offender and is able to arrest the person as the offence occurs or immediately after the offence occurs. For example, a found committing arrest occurs if the offender runs from the crime location, the officer pursues without ever losing sight of him or her, and then arrests the person for the offence once he or she is caught.

found committing
a situation in which a person actually witnesses a crime taking place

---

* Note that the *R v. Storrey* decision is from 1990, so it uses terms that have changed. The term *reasonable and probable grounds* is now referred to as *reasonable grounds*.

Case law highlights two important aspects of found committing arrests. The first concerns the lawfulness of arrests made on this basis. In *R v. Biron* (1976), the Supreme Court of Canada (SCC) stated that an arrest's validity does not depend on whether the person arrested is subsequently convicted of the offence; it depends on the circumstances that were apparent to the officer at the time.

The SCC made a key distinction here, between arresting a person for an offence and convicting a person of that offence. When making an arrest, the police officer must believe the individual committed the offence for which he or she is being arrested. However, the arrest may not lead to conviction. Many variables can come into play regarding the finding of guilt or innocence in the trial process, and these variables may result in a failure to get a conviction. But this uncertainty does not negate the fact that the police officer who made the arrest believed the **criminal offence** had taken place. And it does not make the arrest unlawful.

The second important principle of found committing defined in case law comes from a case involving the drug arrest of a person in Saskatchewan. The principle relates to drug possession. In *R v. Janvier* (2007, para. 30), the Saskatchewan Court of Appeal found that an officer who observes (that is, smells) *recently smoked* marijuana cannot be said to find the person committing the offence of possession of marijuana:

criminal offence
any act or activity that violates an Act of Parliament; any offence found within the *Criminal Code* or any other federal statute that lists criminal offences

> Observation (i.e., the smell) of recently smoked marihuana is not an observation of current possession of additional unsmoked marihuana. One might *infer* the presence of more marihuana, but one is not *observing or smelling* it and one is therefore *not finding* the person committing the offence of possession of additional, unsmoked, marihuana within the meaning of s. 495(1)(b) [of the *Criminal Code*]. Section 495(1)(b) does not permit an arrest made on inference derived from the smell of burned marihuana alone.

Possession of marijuana (under 30 grams) is a summary conviction offence (discussed in the next section), so the police must find committing in order to make an arrest. This charge was dismissed because the condition for found committing was not met. It is worth noting, however, that this was a Saskatchewan Court of Appeal decision, and the Crown prosecutor *did not* appeal the decision to the SCC. As a result, judges in other provinces can use this decision in their findings, but they are not compelled to do so as they would be if the decision was made by the SCC. It is what is known as a *persuasive* decision.

CHECK YOUR UNDERSTANDING

1. List three circumstances under which a police officer may arrest an individual without a warrant.

2. In your own words, define the term *arrest*.

3. What is the difference between "found committing" and "reasonable grounds"?

Classifying Offences

To determine whether an arrest can be made without a warrant, officers must understand the different classifications of offences. Criminal offences fall into three categories depending on the severity of the offence and the nature of the wrongdoing:

1. **Summary conviction offences** are less serious crimes.
2. **Indictable offences** are more serious crimes.
3. **Dual procedure (hybrid) offences** can be treated either as summary conviction offences or as indictable offences.

Summary Conviction Offences

Summary conviction offences are generally minor offences found throughout the *Criminal Code*. Part XXVII applies to the trial of a summary conviction offence as well as to any appeal from a summary conviction trial. In Ontario, these offences are tried by the provincial Court of Justice without a jury. Section 787 of the Code sets out the maximum penalty for a summary conviction offence, which is generally a fine of $5,000 and/or six months in jail. However, there are some summary offences, such as breach of probation, that allow for higher maximum sentences. Another exception to these penalties is a case where the Crown elects to proceed summarily at trial for a charge of sexual assault. In these cases, the maximum penalty is 18 months in jail.

In order for an officer to make an arrest for a summary conviction offence, he or she must find the suspect committing the offence. Officers cannot make an arrest for this type of offence based on reasonable grounds or on evidence provided by other means—for example, statements made by the victim or eyewitnesses. If an officer does have the basis to lay a charge, the suspect is usually issued an appearance notice (Form 9, reproduced below) and released at the scene. The appearance notice directs the accused to appear before the courts on a given date. Failure to comply with the appearance notice can result in an arrest warrant and further criminal charges. Prior to the person's first court date, the arresting officer must complete a criminal information stating the criminal offence that the accused has committed, and swear to it before a justice of the peace (JP). A person is not considered to be charged with the offence until the information is signed by the JP.

There are circumstances, however, in which a person will not be released at the scene. Under s. 495(2) of the Code, an officer can arrest a person if he or she believes that arrest is required to establish the identity of the person, to secure or preserve evidence, to prevent the continuation of the offence or the commission of another offence, or to ensure the person's appearance before the courts. These conditions are often referred to by the acronym RICE, which we will discuss below.

There are instances when charges for a summary conviction offence are not laid at the scene but at a later date. For example, if an officer witnesses an offence but believes that more evidence is needed to lay a charge, he or she will release the offender pending an investigation. Generally, the officer then has six months from this time to lay a charge (this time frame varies with the statute). According to s. 786 of the Code, this six-month period can be extended if both the Crown prosecutor and the accused agree to an extension.

Indictable Offences

Indictable offences are more serious crimes, often involving violence with weapons and a degree of injury to the victim. Unlike summary conviction offences, there is no time limit

summary conviction offences
the least serious of the offences set out in the *Criminal Code*, most with a maximum penalty of $5,000 and/or six months in jail

indictable offences
the most serious types of offences, with a maximum penalty of life in prison

dual procedure (hybrid) offences
offences that can be dealt with as either summary or indictable; always treated as indictable by arresting officers

FORM 9
(Section 493)

APPEARANCE NOTICE ISSUED BY A PEACE OFFICER TO A PERSON NOT YET CHARGED WITH AN OFFENCE

Canada, Province of _____ , *(territorial division)*.

To A.B., of _____ , *(occupation)*:

You are alleged to have committed *(set out substance of offence)*.

1. You are required to attend court on _____ day, the _____ day of _____ A.D. _____ , at _____ o'clock in the _____ noon, in courtroom No. _____ , at _____ court, in the municipality of _____ , and to attend thereafter as required by the court, in order to be dealt with according to law.

2. You are also required to appear on _____ day, the _____ day of _____ A.D. _____ , at _____ o'clock in the _____ noon, at _____ *(police station)*, *(address)*, for the purposes of the *Identification of Criminals Act*. *(Ignore if not filled in.)*

You are warned that failure to attend court in accordance with this appearance notice is an offence under subsection 145(5) of the *Criminal Code*.

Subsections 145(5) and (6) of the *Criminal Code* state as follows:

"(5) Every person who is named in an appearance notice or promise to appear, or in a recognizance entered into before an officer in charge or another peace officer, that has been confirmed by a justice under section 508 and who fails, without lawful excuse, the proof of which lies on the person, to appear at the time and place stated therein, if any, for the purposes of the *Identification of Criminals Act* or to attend court in accordance therewith, is guilty of

(*a*) an indictable offence and liable to imprisonment for a term not exceeding two years; or

(*b*) an offence punishable on summary conviction.

(6) For the purposes of subsection (5), it is not a lawful excuse that an appearance notice, promise to appear or recognizance states defectively the substance of the alleged offence."

Section 502 of the *Criminal Code* states as follows:

"**502.** Where an accused who is required by an appearance notice or promise to appear or by a recognizance entered into before an officer in charge or another peace officer to appear at a time and place stated therein for the purposes of the *Identification of Criminals Act* does not appear at that time and place, a justice may, where the appearance notice, promise to appear or recognizance has been confirmed by a justice under section 508, issue a warrant for the arrest of the accused for the offence with which the accused is charged."

Issued at _____ a.m./p.m. this _____ day of _____ A.D. _____ , at _____ .

_____
(Signature of peace officer)

_____
(Signature of accused)

R.S., 1985, c. C-46, Form 9; R.S., 1985, c. 27 (1st Supp.), s. 184; 1994, c. 44, s. 84; 1997, c. 18, s. 115.

for prosecution of these offences once the identity of the suspect is known to police. There is also no general maximum penalty for indictable offences. Sentences can be 2, 5, 10, or 14 years, or life in prison. The sentences are set out within the different offence sections of the Code. For indictable offences, police officers can make arrests based on found committing or reasonable grounds.

Table 3.1 shows the major differences between summary conviction and indictable offences.

Dual Procedure (Hybrid) Offences

Dual procedure (hybrid) offences do not have a fixed or permanent initial classification and can fall into the category either of summary conviction offences or of indictable offences. Crown attorneys treat common dual procedure offences, such as assault and theft, differently from case to case, depending upon the injury the victim has sustained and the amount or value of the property involved. The offence holds "dual status" until the accused's first court appearance, at which point the Crown attorney decides how to proceed with the case.

For arrest purposes, dual procedure (hybrid) offences are treated as indictable. This has implications for arrest and release conditions. For example, an arrest for a hybrid offence can be made based on reasonable grounds, and there is no limit for prosecution once the identity of the suspect is known.

TABLE 3.1   Major Differences Between Summary Conviction and Indictable Offences

	Summary Conviction	**Indictable**
Basis for arrest	Police must find the person committing the offence	Reasonable grounds are sufficient
Time limit for laying the charge	Six months from the time the accused committed the offence	No time limitation
Level of court that handles the case	Lower court	May be handled in a lower court at the beginning, and then may be tried in a higher court
How the case is tried	By provincial court judge	By provincial court or by superior court judge (alone) or by judge with jury, with or without a preliminary hearing
Court appearance of accused	Accused does not have to appear in person; an agent may appear for him or her	Accused must appear personally in court
Preliminary hearing	Accused does not have the election to have a preliminary hearing	Accused is entitled to a preliminary hearing
Penalty	In most summary offences, maximum penalty of $5,000 and/or six-month jail sentence	From two years to life imprisonment, depending on the offence

Section 553 Offences

Police officers must be aware of offences that fall under s. 553 of the Code. These dual procedure (hybrid) offences are the most common of criminal offences, such as theft under $5,000 or mischief under $5,000. According to s. 553, provincial court judges have "absolute" jurisdiction over these cases. This means that even if the prosecution pursues the case as an indictable offence, the case is heard by a provincial judge, and the defence cannot request a trial by jury. Police officers are obligated to release individuals who have been arrested for summary conviction offences or for indictable offences that fall under s. 553 of the Code. (The exception to this is situations where risks to the public have been identified, which we will explore below in relation to RICE/PRICE.)

Table 3.2 shows some of the common offences under each category.

TABLE 3.2 Examples of Common Offences

Summary Conviction	Indictable	Dual Procedure (Hybrid)	Section 553
Cause a disturbance (s. 175(1))	Homicide (s. 222)	Carrying concealed weapon (s. 90(1))	Keeping common bawdy-house (s. 210(1))
Trespass at night (s. 177)	Infanticide (s. 233)	Personating peace officer (s. 130(1))	Theft under $5,000 (s. 334(b))
Taking motor vehicle or vessel without consent (s. 335(1))	Murder 1st or 2nd degree (s. 235(1))	Public mischief (s. 140(1))	Possession of property obtained by crime under $5,000 (s. 355(b))
Fraudulently obtaining food, beverage or accommodation (s. 364(1))	Manslaughter (s. 236)	Operation while impaired (ss. 253(1)(a), (b))	False pretenses under $5,000 (s. 362(2)(b))
Obtaining transportation by fraud (s. 393(3))	Manslaughter while using a firearm (s. 236(a))	Criminal harassment (s. 264)	Fraud under $5,000 (s. 380(1)(b))
Indecent telephone calls (s. 372(2))	Discharging firearm with intent (s. 244)	Uttering threats—to cause death or bodily harm (s. 264.1(1)(a))	Mischief under $5,000 (s. 430(4))
Harassing phone call (s. 372(3))	Administering noxious thing with intent to endanger life or cause bodily harm (s. 245)	Uttering threats—to damage property or harm an animal (s. 264.1(1)(b) or (c))	
Breach of recognizance (s. 811)	Impaired driving causing bodily harm (s. 255(2))	Assault (s. 266)	
	Aggravated assault (s. 268)	Assault with a weapon or causing bodily harm (s. 267)	
	Trafficking in persons under the age of 18 years (s. 279.011(1)(b))	Assaulting a peace officer (s. 270(1)(a))	
	Kidnapping (ss. 279(1), (1.1)(a))	Sexual assault (s. 271)	
	Robbery (s. 343)	Forcible confinement (s. 279(2))	
	Extortion (s. 346(1))	Motor vehicle theft (s. 333.1)	
	Breaking and entering with intent (dwelling) (s. 348(1))	Unauthorized use of computer (s. 342.1(1))	
	Fraud over $5,000 (s. 380(1)(a))		
	Arson (s. 434)		
	Laundering proceeds of crime (s. 462.31)		
	Conspiracy to commit murder (s. 465(1)(a))		

1. Describe each of the three classes of offences.
2. Give an example of each class of offence.
3. List the major differences between a summary conviction offence and an indictable offence.

Deciding When to Make an Arrest

There are conditions that must be met before police officers can make an arrest. Let's look at a few of these.

Establishing Facts-in-Issue

For police officers to have the authority to arrest someone for a crime, they must establish the **facts-in-issue** relating to the specific offence. The facts-in-issue include the following key components:

- day, date, time, and place;
- identity;
- *actus reus*; and
- *mens rea*.

facts-in-issue
the components that must be established by police to make an arrest—day, date, time, and place; identity; *actus reus*; and *mens rea*

Day, Date, Time, and Place

In considering whether to arrest a person, the arresting officer must be able to establish the day, date, time, and place the offence was committed. The officer may sometimes not be able to establish all of these details. Still, he or she is required to obtain as much information as possible to establish reasonable grounds to arrest a person.

Identity of the Accused

The officer must establish that the person being arrested is in fact the offender. There are many ways to establish identity. The strongest basis for establishing identity is the officer's actually witnessing the crime. A civilian eyewitness identification, on the other hand, can be the weakest basis; such identification relies on the accuracy of human memory. Although most people are honest, mistakes do occur and have resulted in wrongful convictions.

Circumstantial evidence, such as a fingerprint or DNA left at the scene, can be the key to properly identifying the perpetrator. Such evidence may not in itself positively identify the offender; in combination with other evidence, however, it can enable a police officer to infer the suspect's identity.

Actus Reus and Mens Rea

We will discuss the final two components of facts-in-issue together because they are closely related. For a crime to have been committed, the physical act of committing a crime must be combined with the mental decision to commit it. These two elements are known, respectively, as the *actus reus* and the *mens rea*. They are defined as follows:

actus reus

Latin for "a guilty act";
an *actus reus* is the
physical component of
committing a criminal act

mens rea

Latin term meaning "a
guilty mind"; an element
of criminal responsibility;
a guilty or wrongful
purpose; a criminal intent

1. The phrase **actus reus** is Latin for "a guilty act." An *actus reus* is the physical act of committing a crime.

2. The phrase **mens rea** is Latin for "a guilty mind." It is variously defined as "an element of criminal responsibility," "a guilty or wrongful purpose," "a criminal intent," or "guilty knowledge and wilfulness." *Mens rea*, in other words, is the conscious decision to commit a criminal act.

For a criminal offence to have occurred, both *mens rea* and *actus reus* must be present in the action. It must be shown, in other words, not only that the person committed the criminal act, but that he or she had intent to do so. The crime of theft, for example, according to one legal definition ("Actus Reus," n.d.), "requires physically taking something (the actus reus) coupled with the intent to permanently deprive the owner of the object (the mental state, or mens rea)." Note, however, that in some cases a person can be charged with a criminal act, regardless of intent, if it is deemed that he or she caused the offence to occur through recklessness.

Applying Facts-in-Issue

Let's look at the following scenario in order to show how to apply facts-in-issue.

On December 24, at approximately 3:00 p.m., a young male enters a busy electronics store on Yonge Street in downtown Toronto. He starts to examine the electronic games displayed on a shelf. A store security officer sees him placing a game inside his knapsack. The young man then walks around the store looking at other items as the security officer follows him. A few minutes later, the man leaves the store without attempting to pay for the game. The security officer, without losing sight of him, apprehends and arrests him outside the store. He is returned to the security office and the police are called.

Upon arrival, the responding officer is told what happened. She learns that the stolen game has a value of $90 and that the store's interior surveillance video captured the theft. The suspect says that he wanted the game, but had no money to pay for it and did not think he would get caught because the store was so busy. How will the responding officer proceed?

First, she must determine what the offence is. In this case, the offence is theft under $5,000. Section 322 of the Code defines theft as follows:

colour of right

an honestly held
belief in entitlement
to property; a defence
to a charge of theft

(1) Every one commits theft who fraudulently and without **colour of right** [emphasis added] takes, or fraudulently and without colour of right converts to his use or to the use of another person, anything, whether animate or inanimate, with intent

(a) to deprive, temporarily or absolutely, the owner of it, or a person who has a special property or interest in it, of the thing or of his property or interest in it;

(b) to pledge it or deposit it as security;

(c) to part with it under a condition with respect to its return that the person who parts with it may be unable to perform; or

(d) to deal with it in such a manner that it cannot be restored in the condition in which it was at the time it was taken or converted.

Once the police officer understands what constitutes the particular offence, she must establish

- that the suspect has no right or entitlement to the property he removed from the store; and

- that the suspect has in fact committed theft.

According to s. 322(2) of the Code, "[a] person commits theft when, with intent to steal anything, he moves it or causes it to move or to be moved, or begins to cause it to become movable."

Next, in order to make the arrest, the officer must determine whether the facts-in-issue have been established. (See Table 3.3.) (To continue the arrest—if, for example, the person had already been arrested by a citizen—the police officer would likewise have to determine whether the facts-in-issue have been established.)

TABLE 3.3   Facts-in-Issue

Category of Facts	Specific Facts
Day, date, time, and place	December 24 at 3:00 p.m. in a busy electronics store on Yonge Street in downtown Toronto
Identity	The male suspect was observed by the security officer. The security officer never lost sight of the suspect, following him as he wandered in the store looking at other items before leaving. The security officer effected a citizen's arrest. There is also video surveillance to support the security officer's identification.
Actus reus	The suspect was observed physically removing the electronic game from the store shelf, concealing the merchandise in his knapsack, and leaving the store without paying for the item.
Mens rea	The suspect without colour of right took the electronic game from the store with no intention of paying for it. By his own admission, he didn't believe he would be caught because the store was busy.

Once the facts-in-issue are established, the officer's continued arrest would be lawful and the suspect could be charged with the offence of theft under $5,000.

CHECK YOUR UNDERSTANDING

1. List the four elements needed to establish facts-in-issue.
2. What is the difference between *mens rea* and *actus reus*?
3. What is meant by the term *colour of right*?

Steps Required to Make a Lawful Arrest

For a police officer to ensure that the arrest he or she makes is legal and meets all the requirements of the Charter, certain steps must be followed. These steps cover two aspects of the arrest process: (1) the making of the arrest; and (2) the search incident to the arrest.

Making the Arrest

In making arrests, police officers must do the following:

1. *Identify themselves.* Police officers must verbally identify themselves as such to the person being arrested and show their police identification if asked. This is especially

important for officers who are not in uniform, such as detectives. Remember, too, that Canada is a very diverse nation and not everyone living or visiting Canada will recognize police uniforms. This makes it all the more crucial that police officers in Canada identify themselves.

2. *Take physical control of the person.* According to a precept from *Halsbury's Laws of England*, adopted by the SCC, the officer must touch the suspect's body during an arrest. Merely saying that the person is under arrest is not sufficient unless he or she voluntarily submits to the officer's verbal direction and goes with the officer. Taking physical control of the arrested person is also often done to protect the officers themselves.

3. *Use the appropriate amount of force.* Unfortunately for police officers, not every arrest will be peaceful or non-combative. Arrest situations are often volatile or hostile. Such arrests will require the officer to use some level of physical force. Police officers are well trained in self-defence and use of force. The amount of force used depends on the circumstances, but it must always be appropriate and justified in law.

4. *Tell the person he or she is under arrest.* Police officers are required by law to inform the suspect that he or she is under arrest. Each arrest is different, and each person being arrested will have a different understanding of the process.

5. *Tell the person why he or she is under arrest.* Officers must also tell the person being arrested the reason for the arrest, as well as the charge or charge(s). Often, people being arrested will not understand what the criminal charge means. Police officers must explain to the arrested person, in clear language, the nature of the offence they are alleged to have committed and the charge.

At times, a person who has been arrested at the crime scene for one offence will end up being charged with a different offence, or possibly with multiple offences, as a result of further investigation by the officer or detective. This does not mean that the first arrest was illegal or that the officer made a mistake. However, the officer must inform the person of any new or different charges that arise, adapting

Source: Lyle Aspinall/Calgary Sun/QMI Agency.

the language used in the initial arrest. If there is a language barrier and the person does not understand what is being said, the officer is legally bound to ensure that the person is advised about these matters in the language he or she understands.

6. *Inform the person of his or her right to counsel.* Police officers must inform the person of his or her right to speak to a lawyer.

While officers are required to inform persons under arrest of the reason for their arrest and their right to counsel, there is no specific timeline or procedure, prescribed by law, regarding when this information must be provided. The law says only that the officer must provide it as soon as is practicable. Let's look at a real-life scenario, with two versions showing how circumstances may influence the timing in this regard.

Scenario

Joe Green is thrown out of a bar for being rowdy. After he is ejected, he picks up a rock and throws it through the front window of the bar. The bar staff witness his action and call the police. The following are two possible versions of subsequent events:

- *Version A*: When police officers arrest Joe, he is remorseful and compliant, and the officers take physical control of him. Since he is being cooperative, the officers immediately tell him that, as a result of throwing the rock through the window, he is under arrest for mischief to property under $5,000. They then advise him of his right to speak to a lawyer. In doing so, the officers have arrested him according to the law and according to his Charter rights.

- *Version B*: When the officers approach Joe, he is both physically and verbally combative. The officers have to struggle to arrest him, and Joe continues to scream at them while he is being transported to the police station. Because of Green's hostility at the location of the arrest and during transport, the officers are not able to immediately advise him of the charges and of his right to counsel. They are only able to communicate this to him once he calms down at the station. However, since they communicated this information as soon as was practicable, their arrest was legal and in keeping with Joe's Charter rights, even though a certain amount of time has passed since their initial arrest of him.

Search Incident to Arrest

Upon arrest, police have the right to search the suspect in connection with the crime for which he or she has been arrested. This authority comes from common law. The arresting officer must, however, justify the level of the search being conducted. The decision to search and the extent of the search are based on considerations such as

- the arrested person's age, physical size, and gender;
- the gender of the arresting officer;
- the location of the arrest;
- any privacy issues; and
- whether the arrested person will be released at the scene or taken to the police station in a police vehicle.

The search is not limited to the person and to his or her clothing; it extends to the immediate surroundings of the arrest, including any vehicle. Because such a search is intrusive, the arresting officer must believe that the search is required for the safety of the officer, the public, and even the arrested person. The basis for a search is that it ensures that the person can't harm himself or herself or anyone else with a concealed weapon. A further search may be carried out in order to obtain evidence related to the crime and to prevent evidence from being destroyed.

The following is an important point: To conduct a search after an arrest has been made, the police do not have to have reasonable grounds for believing that the accused is in possession of weapons or evidence. The only requirement is that the search have a valid objective. However, the police must ensure that the search of an arrested person is not conducted in an abusive fashion, and any form of physical restraint must be justified by the officers conducting the search. In the case of *Cloutier v. Langlois* (1990, p. 185), the SCC has found that "a 'frisk' search is a relatively non-intrusive procedure" and "does not constitute, in view of the objectives sought, a disproportionate interference with the freedom of persons lawfully arrested."

IT'S YOUR MOVE, OFFICER!

Scenario 3.1

You are a uniform constable patrolling in your police cruiser. You see a man knock a woman down to the ground, snatch her purse, and run from the location. You quickly check to make sure the woman is not physically hurt, and then you pursue the suspect. After a short foot chase, you catch him and tackle him to the ground. He struggles, but you are able to handcuff him and take him to the police cruiser. He is now compliant and is no longer struggling, but you see what appears to be the outline of a knife in his pants pocket.

Based on what you have learned so far regarding arrest powers, what steps would you take before you transport the suspect to the police station?

CHECK YOUR UNDERSTANDING

1. List the steps for making a lawful arrest.
2. Identify three considerations that might influence the extent of a search incident to arrest.
3. Describe two reasons for a search incident to arrest.

Deciding Not to Make an Arrest

The goal of an effective justice and policing system is to protect society from those who commit crimes and harm society. However, in their efforts to meet this objective, the police and justice system need to consider and protect the rights of all individuals, including the rights of offenders. This can often be a fine balancing act.

Arrest Powers and the Charter

The Charter includes five sections concerning the rights of individuals in Canada, rights that have a direct effect on how and when police officers may arrest or charge a person for committing offences.

Section 7: The Right to Life, Liberty, and Security

Section 7 protects an individual from being held against his or her will by anyone, including the police. This section applies to every person in Canada, both citizens and non-citizens. For example, if a tourist from England is arrested for shoplifting, the person would get the same protection under the Charter as a Canadian citizen arrested for the same crime.

Section 8: The Right to Be Secure Against Unreasonable Search

This protection from unreasonable search applies not only to an individual's physical body, but also to the person's vehicles, homes, workplace, and so on.

Section 9: The Right Not to Be Arbitrarily Detained or Imprisoned

The right protected under s. 9 pertains to arrest and to any further detention or imprisonment. Police officers must balance their authority to arrest and detain an offender with the protections afforded the individual by the Charter.

Section 10: The Right upon Arrest to Be Advised of the Reason for the Arrest

Police officers must advise a person why he or she has been arrested. This must be done "promptly," at the first reasonable opportunity for the officer. Also, as soon as practicable, the officer must advise the person of his or her right to speak to a lawyer and must caution the person about answering any questions before he or she speaks to a lawyer.

Section 11(a): The Right to Be Informed of the Specific Offence

There is a difference between being arrested for an offence and being charged with an offence. Police must ensure that both measures are clearly explained to anyone who has, in fact, been arrested and is going to be charged with an offence. There are situations where a person has been arrested but, as a result of further investigation, may not be charged with an offence. There are also situations where a person is arrested for a single offence and, as a result of further investigation, is charged with another offence or with multiple offences beyond the one for which he or she was originally arrested. Section 11(a) of the Charter states that any person charged with an offence has the right "to be informed without unreasonable delay of the specific offence."

Section 12: The Right Not to Be Subjected to Cruel and Unusual Punishment

The treatment and handling of people while in police custody must be fair and professional and not cruel. All officers who interact with the accused must respect this right, from those who make the original arrest to those who later come in contact with the person.

Section 12 also has to be respected by the judiciary. Specifically, the courts sometimes have to decide whether the treatment of the arrested person, throughout the process, was cruel and unusual. Further, if punishment is required for an offence, the punishment handed out by the judiciary must be fair (that is, not cruel and unusual).

Balancing the Charter and Common Law Authority

Much of the power and authority to investigate and make arrests comes from common law and not from actual statutes. As you know from Chapter 1, common law is unwritten law based on past decisions and practices. Common law is historically based on British common law, but it is subject to change. As a society, our customs and practices change over time, so common law must also evolve to ensure that this authority remains both relevant and responsive to societal needs.

Common law authority is not an open-ended power entitling police officers to make unjustified arrests without consequences. Every arrest must be justified based on its circumstances. Police officers need to understand common law to ensure they are not infringing on a person's rights as outlined in the Charter. Most common law decisions have now been established as written rules, making decisions statutory. In many situations, however, interpretations in the area of police powers are still needed.

Section 495(2) of Canada's Criminal Code

As discussed above, s. 495(1) outlines the legal authority of Canadian police officers to make arrests without a warrant. Section 495(2) qualifies these powers, describing when an arrest *should not* be made so as to avoid violating the Charter.

Section 495(2) says that, without a warrant, officers should not make an arrest for the following types of offences:

1. less serious indictable offences, described in s. 553 of the Code;
2. dual procedure, or hybrid, offences, which may be prosecuted by indictment or punishable on summary conviction; and
3. offences punishable on summary conviction.

The decision not to arrest without a warrant assumes that conditions under ss. 495(2)(d) and (e) are met. These conditions, shown in Table 3.4, are often referred to by the acronym **RICE**, although some police services teach their cadets the acronym **PRICE**, to include the public interest factor. (*Note*: The different sections of the *Criminal Code* are referred to "out of order" in order to form the acronym.)

The only time that police officers should arrest without a warrant an individual who has committed criminal offences listed in ss. 495(2)(a), (b), and (c) is when the RICE conditions have not been met and it is necessary to meet them. For example, an arrest might be made

RICE
acronym (Repetition, Identity, Court, Evidence) for the criteria applied by police when deciding whether an arrested person should be released

PRICE
acronym for the criteria applied by police when deciding whether an arrested person should be released; the same as RICE except that it also includes "public interest" (Public interest, Repetition, Identity, Court, Evidence)

TABLE 3.4 RICE Factors

Repetition	s. 495(2)(d)(iii)	The officer believes that the offence will not continue and there is no risk of the offender repeating the offence.
Identity	s. 495(2)(d)(i)	The officer believes that he or she has accurately obtained the identity of the offender.
Court	s. 495(2)(e)	The officer has no reasonable grounds to believe that the person will fail to appear in court.
Evidence	s. 495(2)(d)(ii)	The officer has secured all necessary evidence of the offence.

to enable the officer to search for evidence, to ascertain the offender's identity, or to prevent the continuation of the offence. Meeting the RICE criteria through further investigation is preferable to meeting them through arrest. Nonetheless, an arrest may be required. If so, the suspect should be released as soon as the RICE conditions have been fulfilled.

Let's revisit our Joe Green scenario to demonstrate how RICE factors determine whether police officers decide to release or arrest an offender. As you know, Joe Green hurled a rock through a bar window and in Version A was arrested by police for mischief to property under $5,000. Mischief under $5,000 is a dual procedure (hybrid) offence that falls under s. 553 of the Code. In theory, then, if the broken window is Joe's only offence, the officer must release Joe Green at the location of arrest. But what if the RICE (or PRICE) criteria are not met?

Again, let's consider two different versions of the Joe Green arrest scenario. In each version, officers must look at the options available. Should they charge Joe Green and release him at the scene, using an appearance notice (Form 9) release to require him to go to court and to a police station for fingerprints? Or do the officers have the legal justification to continue the arrest, on the basis that they are not infringing on Joe's Charter rights?

- *Version A*: When the officers arrest Joe, he has calmed down. He apologizes to the officer, expresses remorse for his actions, and identifies himself to the officer with valid identification.

  Based on all the above factors, the officers are satisfied that the public interest has been met and that Joe can be released on an appearance notice (Form 9). Failure on the part of the officer to release Joe at the scene would be an infringement of s. 9 of the Charter.

TABLE 3.5 Applying RICE, Version A

Repetition	s. 495(2)(d)(iii)	Joe has calmed down, he is being cooperative, and there is no indication that he will go back to the bar to cause more problems.
Identity	s. 495(2)(d)(i)	Joe identifies himself to the officer and provides formal identification that verifies his name and address.
Court	s. 495(2)(e)	When Joe is informed of his obligation to attend court to answer to the charge and also to attend a police station for fingerprinting and photographs, he agrees to do so. The officer believes him.
Evidence	s. 495(2)(d)(ii)	All of the evidence has been secured or photographed, so there are no concerns that evidence will be destroyed or disappear.

- *Version B*: When the officers arrest Joe, he is combative, refuses to give his name, and warns the police officer that the bar staff had better watch out because "bad things" may happen to them.

  The officers must ensure that the RICE conditions are fulfilled and that Joe's response to being arrested is in keeping with the public interest. In light of these considerations, Joe cannot be released at the scene. He is uncooperative, refuses to identify himself, and is threatening to harm the bar's staff if he is released. *Only one RICE variable need not be met for the officer to continue the arrest.* Joe would almost certainly be arrested under these circumstances.

TABLE 3.6   Applying RICE, Version B

Repetition	s. 495(2)(d)(iii)	Joe has threatened the bar staff with "bad things." This creates a real concern that the offence will be repeated or another like it committed if the officer releases Joe at the scene.
Identity	s. 495(2)(d)(i)	Joe may not be carrying formal identification at the time of arrest, but if he verbally identifies himself to the officer, the officer must then believe the identity to be true. In this scenario, Joe refuses to identify himself to the officer, so the officer would have to continue the arrest.
Court	s. 495(2)(e)	Joe hasn't refused a request to appear, but he hasn't been cooperative on this point either. If officers have any doubt as to whether Joe will attend court and present himself to a police station to be fingerprinted and photographed, they must continue the arrest.
Evidence	s. 495(2)(d)(ii)	All of the evidence has been secured or photographed, so there are no concerns that evidence will be destroyed or will disappear.

IT'S YOUR MOVE, OFFICER!

Scenario 3.2

On Friday, February 28, 2014, a frantic mother calls 911 to report an abduction. The complainant picks up her seven-year-old daughter, Gail, every day from R.H. Smith Public School on 274 Midland Avenue, Ottawa. At approximately 3:20 p.m. on the Friday, she was waiting outside the school with three other mothers she knows. At approximately 3:30 p.m., as the children started to exit the school, a grey van entered the circular driveway, an area that is meant for school buses only and is off limits to parents. The complainant saw a male get out of the passenger side of the van and grab her daughter around the waist. Her daughter began screaming, as did other children around her. The male forced her into the van through a side sliding door and got in behind her. The van accelerated and left the school.

Schoolchildren were screaming, parents were hysterical, and the complainant was sobbing and shaking uncontrollably, while school officials tried to control the chaos. You respond to the 911 call, along with several police units, and get as much information as possible from the complainant and other witnesses. Through the investigation, you learn the licence plate number of the van from one of the witnesses and get a good description of two suspects from a teacher.

While patrolling the area of the school the next day, you see one of the suspects in a plaza, exiting what appears to be the van used in the abduction: it looks similar and has the same licence plate number. The suspect is in the company of the abducted girl.

1. Explain whether or not you can arrest this person. If you can make an arrest, what steps would you take to make the arrest lawful and not infringe on the suspect's Charter rights?

2. If you can arrest the person, do you base it on found committing or on reasonable grounds? What is the classification of the offence? What are the facts-in-issue?

3. If you do make an arrest, can the suspect be released from the scene or should he be detained and taken to the police station?

1. Explain the sections of the Charter that limit police arrest authority.

2. List and describe the four elements of RICE.

3. What is the function of RICE or PRICE?

Holding Suspects Without Arrest

There are situations in which suspects may be held voluntarily or involuntarily without being formally under arrest. These situations include **voluntary accompaniment** and **investigative detention**.

A person who chooses to accompany or remain with police for investigative purposes is not under arrest, and this must be made clear to this person. Voluntary accompaniment is different from investigative detention, as the person is not being held against his or her will by police. (We will discuss investigative detention in the next section, below.)

Police officers generally use voluntary accompaniment when there is no authority available to arrest the person for a crime. They may use this consent when they need a person to attend a police station or other location for investigative purposes, usually for questioning.

Although the person has not been arrested or detained against his or her will, police are legally required to ensure that the person is fully aware of the situation he or she faces. Police must do the following:

1. Tell the person what offence the police are investigating and why they need to ask him or her questions.

2. Inform the person that he or she may face consequences as a result of the answers that he or she gives to the police. The consequences may include laying charges against the person and using the answers against the person in any court proceeding.

3. Advise the person that he or she can at any time, without consequences, withdraw his or her consent to remain and/or answer any further questions.

The following scenario illustrates the requirements police must meet in a case of voluntary accompaniment. John is a customer in a bank when a robbery takes place. Upon reviewing the bank's security video, the police notice one of the suspects nod at John as the suspects are escaping. The police do not have enough grounds to arrest John, but they are concerned as to why the robber nodded at him. John remains in the bank when the police arrive.

Detective Monaghan of the Hold-Up Squad speaks to John. He says, "John, I'm Detective Monaghan of the Hold-Up Squad. Would you be willing to come with me to the police station to answer some questions about the robbery that took place today?"

John agrees to go to the station. Then Detective Monaghan says, "John, I just want to advise you that you don't have to go. The choice is yours." Again, John agrees to go to the station.

Detective Monaghan says, "John, at any time during our trip to the police station, and while we are asking you questions at the station about the robbery, you are free to leave with no consequences. Do you understand this?"

John acknowledges that he understands.

voluntary accompaniment
a situation where a person who is neither under arrest nor being held for investigative detention chooses to accompany or remain with police for investigative purposes

investigative detention
a situation where reasonable grounds to arrest a person are absent, but police detain the person to determine whether he or she is involved in the crime

Investigative Detention

Investigative detention is a situation in which reasonable grounds to arrest a person for a criminal offence are absent. Police can detain a person in an effort to determine whether that person is involved in the crime being investigated. The SCC decided in *R v. Mann* (2004, p. 60) that "police officers may detain an individual for investigative purposes if there are reasonable grounds to *suspect* in all the circumstances that the individual is connected to a particular crime and that the detention is reasonably necessary on an objective view of the circumstances" (emphasis added).

Investigative detention is *not* an arrest. The officer does not have reasonable grounds to conclude that the person committed the offence; otherwise, the officer would be required to arrest the person. To detain a person for investigative purposes, an officer must articulate that there is a clear connection between the individual to be detained and a recent or ongoing crime.

The overall reasonableness of the decision to detain must further be assessed in light of all of the circumstances, most notably

- the extent to which the officer, in order to perform his or her duty, needs to interfere with the person's individual liberty;
- the liberty interfered with; and
- the nature and extent of that interference.

At a minimum, the individual who is detained must be advised by the officer, in clear and simple language, of the reasons for the detention. Police need to change their phrasing from "You are under arrest" to "You are under investigative detention." They must also inform detainees of their Charter right to counsel before being questioned and their right not to make any statements. In *R v. Mann* (2004), officers were not obliged to advise detainees of these rights. However, this changed in 2009, with the SCC decisions in *R v. Grant* (2009) and *R v. Suberu* (2009).

To comply with s. 10(b) of the Charter, the detention must be brief, and there is no excuse for the police to prolong the detention either unduly or artificially.

When a police officer who has detained an individual has reasonable grounds (and not mere suspicion) to believe that his or her safety or the safety of others is at risk, he or she may conduct a proactive "pat-down" search of the detained individual. The investigative detention and proactive search power must be distinguished from an arrest and the incidental power to search on arrest.

With an individual under investigative detention, officers may only search for weapons they believe the person may be carrying and/or concealing; they may not search for evidence of a crime. Note the distinction identified by the SCC for investigative detention. To detain a person, the officers need only reasonable *suspicion* the person may be involved in a criminal offence. To search the detained individual, the officers need reasonable *grounds* to believe the person may be carrying a weapon. This is a key distinction.

The three main points to remember regarding investigative detention are that

1. police officers need reasonable *suspicion* to detain;
2. police officers need reasonable *grounds* to arrest; and
3. police officers, if they elect to search the detained individual, are not searching for *evidence*. They are searching for any *weapons* they believe the individual may have that can hurt the officer or someone else.

IT'S YOUR MOVE, OFFICER!

Scenario 3.3

You are a uniform community response officer patrolling the grounds of a college campus. A student approaches you and informs you that a man is dealing marijuana from the trunk of an old blue Dodge Neon in the northwest corner of the campus parking lot. The student provides you with a description of the suspect, including his clothing. You attend to this lot and observe a male matching the description, standing by the side of a blue Neon. When the man sees you, he immediately walks away from the car.

What do you do? Choose from one of the following options and explain your choice.

   a. Take note of the male's description and the plate number of the vehicle, but don't take proactive measures at this point. Wait for his return.

   b. Arrest the male for trafficking in marijuana and search him and his vehicle, incident to his arrest.

   c. Speak to the male and investigate him under the common law authority of investigative detention.

CHECK YOUR UNDERSTANDING

   1. What are the three obligations of a police officer in a situation involving voluntary accompaniment?

   2. Identify three important points of investigative detention.

   3. To detain a person for investigative purposes, what connection must an officer first establish? What other circumstances must he or she assess in order to establish the overall reasonableness of the decision to detain?

Arrest with Warrant

So far, we have learned about the power of police officers to arrest a person without a warrant. Let's now look at how police officers arrest individuals with a warrant. An **arrest warrant** is a court's written order for all police officers within the jurisdiction where the order is valid, authorizing them to

   • find and arrest an identified person, and

   • return the person to the court that issued the order.

To be valid or legal, the warrant must come from a justice: either a justice of the peace or a judge. Once the justice signs the order, the warrant becomes a judicial authorization for police officers to act on. A warrant is not automatically issued by the justice. A police officer must apply for the warrant, outlining his or reasons for believing there are grounds for the arrest, explaining the necessity of a warrant, and describing the steps the police have already taken in their attempt to locate and arrest the wanted person.

Warrant in the First Instance

A **warrant in the first instance** is issued for summary conviction, dual procedure, or indictable offences. It is issued when police are not able to locate the suspect or the suspect may know he or she is wanted and is evading police or other authorities. This type of warrant may also be used by citizens in private complaints, when a summons is not successful.

arrest warrant
a court's written order, directed at all police officers within the jurisdiction where the order is valid, to find and arrest an identified person and return that person to the court that issued the order

warrant in the first instance
an arrest warrant issued in circumstances where the police are unable to locate the suspect, or where the suspect, knowing that he or she is wanted, is evading police or other authorities

Bench Warrant

Sometimes, an arrested person is released on a promise to appear in court to answer to his or her charge(s). The justice presiding over the court will issue a **bench warrant** if the person fails to attend court, for either the first appearance or subsequent times. A bench warrant is a written order from the police notifying all other peace officers to arrest the person named on the warrant.

Feeney Warrant

In 1997, the SCC issued a ruling that prevents police from making arrests without a warrant in private homes (dwelling-houses). In these cases, police now have to apply for a **Feeney warrant**.

To apply for this warrant, police must establish two factors:

1. reasonable grounds to believe that the suspect is living or hiding in the dwelling-house; and
2. reasonable belief that the person in the dwelling has committed an indictable offence.

Before entering the dwelling, police must properly identify themselves. If force is needed to gain entry to the premises, police must announce their reason for entering the dwelling before any force is used.

Police do not, however, require a Feeney warrant to enter a property when the person they are physically chasing enters a dwelling. This type of active pursuit is called "fresh" or **hot pursuit**. In its decision in *R v. Macooh* (1993, p. 187), the SCC endorsed R.E. Salhany's (1989, p. 44) definition of hot pursuit: "Generally, the essence of fresh pursuit is that it must be continuous pursuit conducted with reasonable diligence, so that pursuit and capture along with the commission of the offence may be considered as forming part of a single transaction." In such a circumstance, police can enter the dwelling, using force if necessary, in continuing their pursuit to arrest the wanted person. Fresh or hot pursuit could fall under the classification of **exigent circumstances**, meaning that it is a pressing matter and needs immediate action. In such a situation, it would not be in the public's interest for police to stop and obtain a warrant when they have actively chased the wanted person into the home.

Under the authority of s. 529.3(1) of the *Criminal Code*, there are two other circumstances that fall under the classification of exigent circumstances:

1. the police have reasonable grounds to suspect that entry into the dwelling-house is necessary to prevent imminent bodily harm or death to any person; or
2. the police have reasonable grounds to believe that evidence relating to the commission of an indictable offence is present in the dwelling-house and that entry into the dwelling-house is necessary to prevent the imminent loss or imminent destruction of the evidence.

Omitting Announcement Before Entry: Section 529.4(1) of the Criminal Code

A judge or justice who authorizes a peace officer to enter a dwelling-house under s. 529 or 529.1 of the Code, or any other judge or justice, may authorize the peace officer to enter the dwelling-house without prior announcement if the judge or justice is satisfied by information on oath that there are reasonable grounds to believe that prior announcement of the entry would

> (a) expose the peace officer or any other person to imminent bodily harm or death; or
> (b) result in the imminent loss or imminent destruction of evidence relating to the commission of an indictable offence.

Time Limits and Execution of Warrants

There is no time limit for a warrant in Canada. The warrant stays active until either the accused is arrested by the police and brought before the court or the Crown attorney withdraws the warrant. Police can execute an outstanding warrant, whether a warrant in the first instance or a bench warrant, anytime and anywhere. When practical to do so, the arresting officer must either present the original warrant to the wanted person or provide a copy of the original document.

Once the accused has been arrested on the strength of the warrant, he or she must, within 24 hours of the arrest, be brought before a presiding justice for a bail hearing. The justice will then decide if the accused can be released on bail, based on RICE criteria.

In-Province Warrant

A warrant to arrest is valid within the province in which it was issued. However, when a justice or judge issues a warrant, he or she will usually identify a *return radius* on the warrant as requested by the police or the Crown attorney seeking the warrant. A **return radius** is a specified area within which a suspect, if arrested, will be returned to the police that requested the warrant.

return radius
an area, specified in an arrest warrant, within which a found suspect must be returned to the police that requested the warrant

The return radius depends on the severity of the crime. Serious crimes may have a return radius that is province-wide; it can even be Canada-wide for crimes such as murder. Less serious crimes may have a smaller return radius, such as 50 or 100 kilometres. These distances are established by the Crown attorney who requested the warrant, based on the costs of returning the prisoner from the place of arrest to the court location where the warrant was issued, and ultimately to the court where the accused will be prosecuted.

Let's look at two examples of how a return radius works.

1. An officer in Thunder Bay arrests a robbery suspect on a Kingston warrant with a province-wide return radius. The Thunder Bay police notify the Kingston police that the suspect is in their custody, and they hold the suspect in custody. The Kingston police are responsible for collecting the suspect, and the Crown in Kingston is responsible for all costs incurred in returning the suspect.

2. An Ottawa police officer arrests a person for fraud over $5,000, on a Windsor warrant that has a return radius of 200 kilometres. Ottawa is more than 200 kilometres from Windsor. The arrest of the wanted person is legal, but the crime is not very serious. In this case, the Ottawa police would contact the Windsor police, notifying them of the arrest. If the Windsor police decide that they will not go to Ottawa to pick up the wanted person because the warrant's return radius does not extend as far as Ottawa, and if the arrested person is not facing any additional charges by the Ottawa police, the Ottawa police would have to release him or her with no charges and no further detention. However, the warrant would remain in effect for the suspect and the suspect may be returned to Windsor police subsequently if he or she is arrested within the 200-kilometre radius.

1. Identify and describe different types of arrest warrants.
2. Why is a Feeney warrant not required during a hot pursuit?
3. Explain what *return radius* means.

Other Arrest Considerations

Sometimes young people, including very young children, commit crimes. Young people aged 12 to 17 are classified as young offenders, while "children" are those under 12. How should these offenders be treated by police?

Young Offenders

In theory, the powers of police officers to arrest young offenders are the same as their powers to arrest adults. However, society generally prefers that young offenders be dealt with differently than adult offenders are. Police need to be aware of this. In 2003, the *Youth Criminal Justice Act* replaced the *Young Offenders Act* in Canada. With this new Act came new principles regarding how the police, courts, and communities should deal with young offenders, as shown in ss. 6-8.

Warnings, Cautions and Referrals

6(1) A police officer shall, before starting judicial proceedings or taking any other measures under this Act against a young person alleged to have committed an offence, consider whether it would be sufficient, having regard to the principles set out in section 4, to take no further action, warn the young person, administer a caution, if a program has been established under section 7, or, with the consent of the young person, refer the young person to a program or agency in the community that may assist the young person not to commit offences.

(2) The failure of a police officer to consider the options set out in subsection (1) does not invalidate any subsequent charges against the young person for the offence.

7. The Attorney General, or any other minister designated by the lieutenant governor of a province, may establish a program authorizing the police to administer cautions to young persons, instead of starting or continuing judicial proceedings under this Act.

8. The Attorney General may establish a program authorizing prosecutors to administer cautions to young persons instead of starting or continuing judicial proceedings under this Act.

Children Under Twelve Years of Age

What happens when a person under the age of 12 commits a crime? In Ontario, these very young offenders are dealt with not by the *Youth Criminal Justice Act* but by the provincial *Child and Family Services Act*. If the police deem the offence to be minor, such as a theft of a chocolate bar from a store, the police will apprehend rather than arrest the child. The officer may then return the child to his or her parents.

However, children may sometimes commit more serious crimes, such as setting a house on fire. Furthermore, the parent(s) in some cases either has encouraged the acts or has not provided sufficient supervision to discourage them. In these cases, the police or the Children's Aid Society could start legal proceedings to find the child "in need of protection" under the law, in which case the child may be apprehended and removed from the parents.

CHECK YOUR UNDERSTANDING

1. Give an account of (in other words, paraphrase) two provisions in the *Youth Criminal Justice Act* that are concerned with the treatment of young offenders.

2. How do police generally deal with offenders under the age of 12?

Citizens' Powers of Arrest

Police officers are not the only ones who can make arrests. Citizens can do so, too, under the authority of s. 494(1) of the Code, which provides as follows:

> (1) Any one may arrest without warrant
>   (a) a person whom he finds committing an indictable offence; or
>   (b) a person who, on reasonable grounds, he believes
>   (i) has committed a criminal offence, and
>   (ii) is escaping from and freshly pursued by persons who have lawful authority to arrest that person.

Citizens have the same search authority when making an arrest as police have. In other words, citizens who make an arrest have the common law authority to search a person and their immediate area incident to the lawful arrest. However, like the police, citizens who make arrests are also restricted in that the conduct toward the accused must not violate his or her Charter rights. The responsibility to comply with the Charter when carrying out a citizen's arrest was described in *R v. Lerke* (1986, para. 23); the court stated that "when one citizen arrests another, the arrest is the exercise of a governmental function to which the Canadian Charter of Rights and Freedoms applies."

Once citizens make an arrest, they must turn the arrested person over to a police officer. Section 494(3) of the Code states the following: "Any one other than a peace officer who arrests a person without warrant shall forthwith deliver the person to a peace officer."

Defence of Property

Section 494(2) of the Code states the following: "The owner or a person in lawful possession of property, or a person authorized by the owner or by a person in lawful possession of property, may arrest a person without a warrant if they find them committing a criminal offence on or in relation to that property."

In 2012, the *Citizen's Arrest and Self-Defence Act* was passed, primarily to protect owners of property. Its more specific goal was to protect small store owners who are victims of repeated crimes of theft, often involving the same offenders. According to the Department of Justice (2013a), this Act allows a person who is in "peaceable possession" of property, or anyone who is assisting him or her, "to commit a reasonable act" to protect the property. Such an act may include the justified use of force to protect the property from "being taken, damaged, or trespassed upon."

There is a restriction on defence of property. To claim the right to defend a property, the person must have *peaceable* possession of it. The courts' interpretation of "peaceable possession" is "possession that is not likely to lead to a breach of the peace" (Department of

Justice, 2013a). Consider a situation in which a person steals a cellphone from a store and is apprehended by the owner of the store. The thief cannot claim defence of property in his or her effort to resist the store owner's attempt to take back the property. The thief does not have colour of right to the property.

The *Citizen's Arrest and Self-Defence Act* was also passed in response to the limitations placed on citizens' powers of arrest under s. 494 of the Code. Section 494 provided that citizens could only arrest a person at the time when they witnessed the person committing the crime on their property. The problem with this restriction was that, in a small retail outlet, the owner of the store, or the operator in charge, is often the only person working at the store at the time he or she witnesses the crime. A person in this situation can't leave the store unattended to apprehend the offender at precisely the time the crime is taking place. Also, police can't always attend the theft calls quickly enough to catch the offenders on scene, with the result that the offenders escape. The Act's changes to citizens' powers of arrest were aimed at assisting small-store owners. The Act now allows for a reasonable window of time in which the citizen can arrest the offender. However, the Act stipulates that a citizen is only authorized to make such an arrest when he or she has reasonable grounds to believe that a police officer is not available to make the arrest.

The new Act still requires citizens to deliver the arrested person to a police officer as soon as possible. Failing to do so can make the arrest illegal, and the citizen who made the arrest could face civil or criminal consequences.

Self-Defence

Under the Code, citizens can take reasonable actions to protect themselves or others. This rule means that citizens are protected from being charged with a criminal offence if, at the time when they took the self-protective action, they had reasonable belief that either they or others were being threatened with force, and if the actions they took were strictly to defend themselves or others.

However, a citizen can't simply state that he or she felt threatened or felt that another person was threatened. The courts will look closely into the circumstances of the perceived threat of force and consider questions such as the following:

- Was the actual threat of force imminent, and could the citizen have done anything to remove himself or herself or others from the threat?
- Did the person the citizen was arresting have a weapon?
- What were the physical characteristics of the person being arrested (for example, the evident physical capabilities) compared with those of the citizen making the arrest?

Reasonable Use of Force

Although citizens can legally use reasonable force during an arrest, the law places limits (as with police) on how much force can be used. Any force that is used during an arrest must be justified. The force that is applied must not be excessive and must be in keeping with the compliancy of the person being arrested.

Steps for Making a Citizen's Arrest

Although the Code authorizes citizens to make arrests, it does not outline what citizens should actually do when making an arrest. The Department of Justice (2013b) provides the following guidelines:

If you do decide to make a citizen's arrest, you should:

- Tell the suspect plainly that you are making a citizen's arrest and that you are holding him or her until police arrive.
- Call the police.
- Ask explicitly for his or her cooperation until police arrive.
- Avoid using force, if at all possible, and use it to the minimum possible otherwise.
- Do not question or search the suspect or his or her possessions. Your purpose is only to temporarily detain him or her until police arrive.
- When police arrive, state the plain facts of what happened.

Situations Where Citizen's Arrests Cannot Be Made

There are times when citizens cannot make an arrest even if they believe a crime has been committed. Consider the following example.

Thirteen-year-old Jennifer has been very depressed and has been acting out in school. Jennifer's parents are concerned, but they believe it's just a teenage phase. Still, they decide to speak with Jennifer. After much prodding, she finally reveals that Gord, her babysitter, has been molesting her for the past three years. The furious parents immediately confront Gord at his workplace. When he confesses to molesting Jennifer, her parents arrest him and hold him for the police.

Did Jennifer's father have the legal authority to arrest Gord on the spot? The confession gives Jennifer's parents reasonable grounds to believe that Gord committed the dual procedure (hybrid) offence of sexual offence. However, they did not see him committing the offence, so they cannot arrest him. They could arrest him only if they walked in on him as he was committing the offence. They can certainly call the police, who can arrest Gord based on reasonable grounds.

Private Security Guards' Powers of Arrest

Private security guards in Ontario are not police officers, peace officers, or special constables, so they do not have the powers afforded to those in these positions. However, s. 494 of the Code grants security guards the same arrest authority as citizens.

Security guards are primarily hired to protect private or public buildings or property. In Ontario, they must receive proper training and be licensed. As part of this training, security guards are required to properly identify and categorize criminal offences as being summary conviction, indictable, or dual procedure (hybrid) offences.

According to s. 494, if a security guard has been hired to guard a property, then the guard is acting on the authorization of the property owner. If the security guard witnesses a criminal offence on or against the property, the guard can carry out a citizen's arrest. Then, like any other citizen, the guard must deliver the arrested person to a police officer as soon as possible.

Let's look at an example of a situation where a security guard may make an arrest. Susan, the owner of a florist shop, gets into a dispute with a female customer, Donna, who claims that the shop sent the wrong order to her birthday party. Donna now wants her money back, but Susan refuses to comply. Donna angrily leaves the store. Outside, she throws a flowerpot against the glass door of the shop, breaks it, and walks away. A security guard hired by the owner of the plaza witnesses Donna's actions. The guard grabs her, physically holds her, and arrests her. Donna states that "Susan had it coming to her."

In this scenario, the security guard can arrest Donna for the offence of mischief under $5,000. Even though it might be tried in court as a summary conviction offence, it is actually a dual procedure (hybrid) offence and, therefore, is treated as indictable for arrest purposes.

CHECK YOUR UNDERSTANDING

1. Where do citizens, including private security guards, get their powers of arrest?

2. To what restrictions in the *Criminal Code* was the *Citizen's Arrest and Self-Defence Act* a response?

3. List the steps for making a citizen's arrest.

CHAPTER SUMMARY

In this chapter, we learned that the powers of arrest in Canada are some of the most important powers available to police in their daily interactions with the public. These powers involve rules, limitations, and Charter provisions that aim to ensure that police, when making arrests, act legally, professionally, and according to procedure. Much of this chapter was focused on the rights of the individual in Canada. Regardless of whether a person has been detained for questioning or for investigative detention or has been arrested, he or she has legal rights. If the police violate these rights, the arrest can be deemed unlawful and the case dismissed in court. This is why police officers need to thoroughly understand their powers of arrest, the classification of criminal offences, and the rights of the individual.

This chapter has explored not only how police make arrests without warrants, but also how they arrest *with* warrants. There are different types of arrest warrants, each with its own rules that police must follow. We have also discussed how police treat young offenders and children who commit crimes. These offenders are viewed and treated differently from adult offenders. Police must be aware of these differences.

Finally, we learned that citizens in Canada can also, under certain circumstances, arrest those committing criminal offences. However, citizens' powers of arrest are much more restricted than the powers held by police.

KEY TERMS

actus reus, 56
arrest warrant, 67
bench warrant, 68
colour of right, 56
criminal offence, 50
dual procedure (hybrid)
   offences, 51
exigent circumstances, 68

facts-in-issue, 55
Feeney warrant, 68
found committing, 49
hot pursuit, 68
indictable offences, 51
investigative detention, 65
mens rea, 56
PRICE, 62

reasonable grounds, 49
return radius, 69
RICE, 62
summary conviction offences, 51
voluntary accompaniment, 65
warrant in the first instance, 67

REFERENCES

Actus Reus. (n.d.). In *Nolo law for all: Nolo's plain-English law dictionary*. Retrieved from http://www.nolo.com/dictionary/actus-reus-term.html.

Biron, R v. (1976). [1976] 2 SCR 56, 23 CCC (2d) 513 (5:3).

Canadian Charter of Rights and Freedoms. (1982). Part I of the *Constitution Act, 1982*, RSC 1985, app. II, no. 44.

Child and Family Services Act. (1990). RSO 1990, c. C.11.

Citizen's Arrest and Self-Defence Act. (2012). SC 2012, c. 9.

Cloutier v. Langlois. (1990). [1990] 1 SCR 158.

Criminal Code. (1985). RSC 1985, c. C-46.

Department of Justice. (2013a). Backgrounder: Citizen's power of arrest and self-defence and defence of property. http://news.gc.ca/web/article-en.do?mthd=index&crtr.page=1&nid =832699&_ga=1.15676158.911418053.1421006582.

Department of Justice. (2013b). What you need to know about making a citizen's arrest. http://www.justice.gc.ca/eng/rp-pr/other-autre/wyntk.html.

Feeney, R v. [1997] 2 SCR 13.

Fuhr, R v. (1975). [1975] 4 WWR 403 (Alta. SC (AD)).

Grant, R v. (2009). 2009 SCC 32, [2009] 2 SCR 353.

Janvier, R v. (2007). 2007 SKCA 147, [2008] 3 WWR 1.

Lerke, R v. (1986). 1986 ABCA 15, 25 DLR (4th) 403.

Macooh, R v. (1993). [1993] 2 SCR 802, 1993 CanLII 107.

Mann, R v. (2004). 2004 SCC 52, [2004] 3 SCR 59.

Salhany, R.E. (1989). *Canadian Criminal Procedure* (5th ed.). Aurora, ON: Canada Law Book.

Storrey, R v. (1990). [1990] 1 SCR 241, 1990 CanLII 125.

Suberu, R v. (2009). 2009 SCC 33, [2009] 2 SCR 460.

Therens, R v. (1985). [1985] 1 SCR 613, 1985 CanLII 29.

Young Offenders Act. (1985). RSC 1985, c. Y-1 [repealed].

Youth Criminal Justice Act. (2002). SC 2002, c. 1.

FURTHER READING

Biron, R v. (1976). [1976] 2 SCR 56, 23 CCC (2d) 513 (5:3).

Cloutier v. Langlois. (1990). [1990] 1 SCR 158.

Feeney, R v. (1997). [1997] 2 SCR 13.

Grant, R v. (2009). 2009 SCC 32, [2009] 2 SCR 353.

Janvier, R v. (2007). 2007 SKCA 147, [2008] 3 WWR 1.

Lerke, R v. (1986). 1986 ABCA 15, 25 DLR (4th) 403.

Mann, R v. (2004). 2004 SCC 52, [2004] 3 SCR 59.

Storrey, R v. (1990). [1990] 1 SCR 241, 1990 CanLII 125.

Suberu, R v. (2009). 2009 SCC 33, [2009] 2 SCR 460.

Therens, R v. (1985). [1985] 1 SCR 613, 1985 CanLII 29.

REVIEW QUESTIONS

Multiple Choice

1. According to what you have read in this chapter, the authority for a Canadian police officer to arrest a person is found in

    a. s. 489(2) of the *Criminal Code*

    b. British common law and s. 495(1) of the *Criminal Code*

    c. the *Statute of Westminster* of 1285

    d. British common law only

2. A citizen has authority to make an arrest under s. 494 of the *Criminal Code*. In which of the following situations can the person identified *not* arrest?

    a. A citizen finds someone committing a murder.

    b. A security officer finds someone causing damage on the property that he or she has been hired to protect.

    c. A security officer at a nightclub is told by a witness that another person has been scratching the doors of cars parked across the street.

    d. A store owner is given a counterfeit $50 bill.

3. According to s. 494(3) of the *Criminal Code*, a citizen must surrender the person he or she has arrested to

    a. a special constable, whom the citizen knows and who is on his or her way to work

    b. a security guard who is a neighbour of the citizen

    c. the citizen's father, who is a retired RCMP officer

    d. a peace officer

4. From the list below, select the terms that best describe two arrest warrants:

   a. surety warrant and revocation of bail

   b. warrant in the first instance and bench warrant

   c. bench warrant and default-of-payment warrant

   d. flight risk and warrant in the first instance

5. When does the time limit for a warrant expire?

   a. six months for a summary conviction offence

   b. one year from the date of issue

   c. five years for all offences

   d. indefinitely; the warrant remains valid until it is executed or withdrawn by the Crown.

True or False

_____ **1.** Police cannot detain persons for investigative purposes; they must arrest the individual first and then question the person after giving him or her the appropriate caution.

_____ **2.** A citizen may arrest a person for a criminal offence when he or she finds the person committing a crime on or near public property.

_____ **3.** A bench warrant is a written order from the police notifying all other peace officers to arrest the person named on the warrant.

_____ **4.** A police officer decides to arrest William for having committed theft under $5,000 for the third time in a month. William has no means of support and is living on handouts from people on the street. He stays in a known rooming house when he can afford it. RICE has not been fulfilled.

_____ **5.** The accused must be released at the scene by the arresting officer if the offence is a summary conviction offence and RICE is met.

_____ **6.** The police must find a person committing an indictable offence in order to arrest that person.

_____ **7.** The maximum penalty for first degree murder is 25 years in prison.

_____ **8.** Because Canada is such a diverse country, it is especially important that police in this country identify themselves when making an arrest.

_____ **9.** When considering making an arrest, police officers must establish the facts-in-issue, one element of which is the suspect's identity.

_____**10.** *Actus reus* is defined as having a guilty mind and knowledge of committing a criminal offence.

Short Answer

1. Does a police officer have to arrest a person who has committed a summary conviction offence? Explain.

2. Why do you think that police require only reasonable grounds to arrest someone for a dual procedure or indictable offence, but need to find the person committing the criminal offence in order to arrest them for a summary conviction offence?

3. Why is it important that ordinary citizens have powers of arrest?

4. Why must police, in order to make an arrest, prove *mens rea* as part of the facts-in-issue? Do police always have to do this?

5. Why must police advise the person they have arrested of his or her right to speak to a lawyer?

It's Your Move, Officer!

A. Sally Brown is alone at home watching television. At 11:00 p.m., she gets up for a glass of water and sees a man peering in through her kitchen window. Sally immediately calls the police. You are one of the responding officers. Upon your arrival, you check around the house, but you can't find the suspect. Sally gives you a good description of the suspect before you leave.

Approximately one hour later, in a 24-hour doughnut shop, you and your partner see a male who matches the description of the suspect. You approach the man, who is cooperative when you ask him his name and other particulars.

What can you do in this situation? Can you arrest this person? Why or why not?

B. While out on patrol in the downtown core of a major city, you receive a call about a fight outside a bar. Upon arrival at the bar, you see two men fighting on the sidewalk outside. Pedestrians have to step off the sidewalk onto the roadway to avoid the two men. You and your partner break up the fight, but the two continue to swear at each other. You and your partner establish that the two men agreed to the fight.

What will you do next? Why?

Location of Arrest and Feeney Laws

4

LEARNING OUTCOMES

After completing this chapter, you should be able to:

- Describe the two locations of arrest.
- Explain how laws concerning the rights of individuals in a dwelling-house have evolved.
- Describe current laws concerning the protection of the rights of individuals in a dwelling-house.
- Describe current laws concerning the authority of officers to enter a dwelling-house to make an arrest.
- Identify the steps an officer should take to protect a person's rights when making an arrest in a dwelling-house.

ON SCENE

One morning, police are called to a local residence to investigate the death of an 85-year-old male.* Officers determine that the victim died after being struck on the head multiple times with an iron bar or similar object. The victim was last seen the evening prior to the morning his body was discovered.

Police learn that the victim's pickup truck had been involved in an accident about half a kilometre west of his home address. When they attend the scene of the accident, two local residents tell them they saw the truck in the ditch at about 6:45 a.m., and a male, known to them as Michael, walking away from the truck in an easterly direction. The witnesses say they think the man had a beer or a coffee cup in his hand. They also tell investigators where this man lives.

Police officers arrive at the address and speak with the owner of the property. The owner tells them Michael returned home at about 7 a.m. that morning, after a night of drinking, and is now asleep in the trailer behind the residence. The trailer is a construction trailer where Michael has been permitted to live.

The officers knock on the door and announce "Police!" They receive no answer. The officers open the unlocked door and enter the trailer. Once inside the windowless trailer, the officers can see, with the aid of flashlights, a male sleeping on a bed. They observe what appears to be a bloodstain on his shirt.

The officers wake the male and begin questioning him about the murder. On the basis of his answers and their own observations, the officers arrest the man for murder.

What do you think? Do police have—and should they have—the authority to enter a residence to arrest someone? Should there be restrictions on when police are authorized to enter a residence to arrest someone?

Introduction

In this chapter, we will discuss the locations of arrests and under what conditions these arrests may be made. We will explore the history and court rulings relating to entry into a home to arrest an individual. This discussion will cover the rights of individuals protected under the *Charter of Rights and Freedoms*, as well as pre- and post-Charter rulings, and it will consider situations where it is legal for police officers to enter a home without a warrant to make an arrest. Finally, to reinforce all the information in the chapter, we will provide a systematic method of determining the most appropriate course of action when it comes to entering a home to make an arrest.

Location of Arrest

Before making an arrest, police officers must consider the suspect's location. For the purposes of police, a suspect may be found in one of two types of locations: (1) a dwelling-house; or (2) any place other than a dwelling-house. The definition of a dwelling-house is found in s. 2 of the *Criminal Code*:

---

*   This scenario is based on *R v. Feeney* (1997).

"dwelling-house" means the whole or any part of a building or structure that is kept or occupied as a permanent or temporary residence, and includes

(a) a building within the curtilage [that is, the surrounding area] of a dwelling-house that is connected to it by a doorway or by a covered and enclosed passage-way, and

(b) a unit that is designed to be mobile and to be used as a permanent or temporary residence and that is being used as such a residence.

In most cases, a dwelling-house is simply a physical structure used, either temporarily or permanently, as a residence. A place other than a dwelling-house is everywhere outside a dwelling-house, and includes both private and public property. Table 4.1 provides examples of dwelling-houses and of places other than dwelling-houses.

TABLE 4.1 Examples of Locations of Arrest

Dwelling-House	Places Other Than a Dwelling-House
• house • apartment • occupied hotel room • recreational vehicle (RV) parked in trailer park • tent	• shopping mall • front lawn of private home • school • business premises

Lawful Entry into a Dwelling-House

We must distinguish between a dwelling-house and a place that isn't a dwelling-house because common law has long held that a person's home is to be considered a place of safety and privacy. Unauthorized violation of this space by anyone, including police, is unlawful. The Code recognizes the sanctity of this space and authorizes individuals to use force to defend their homes. Section 35(1)(b) states that, in defending his or her property, a person "is not guilty of an offence" if

(b) they believe on reasonable grounds that another person

(i) is about to enter, is entering or has entered the property without being entitled by law to do so,

(ii) is about to take the property, is doing so or has just done so, or

(iii) is about to damage or destroy the property, or make it inoperative, or is doing so.

Under the circumstances listed in s. 35(1)(b), the only restriction on the individual protecting his or her home is that, as s. 35(1)(d) stipulates, "the act committed is reasonable in the circumstances."

Consider the implications of this provision for police who wish to enter or are in the process of entering a dwelling-house for the purpose of preventing an offence, or stopping an offence that is in progress, or protecting an occupant's safety, or securing evidence that might be destroyed. Without further refinement, s. 35 of the Code might prevent police from protecting the public interest in cases where doing so required entering and taking action inside a dwelling-house. The courts, however, recognized that there are times when public-safety considerations outweigh the individual's privacy considerations. In 1975, the Supreme Court of Canada (SCC) found, in *Eccles v. Bourque et al.* (1975, p. 743), that the criminal "is not immune from arrest in his own home nor in the home of one of his friends." In its decision, the court cited (1975, p. 743) a 1604 English case, called *Semayne's Case*, in which the following was stated:

> In all cases when the King is party, the Sheriff (if the doors be not open) may break the party's house, either to arrest him, or to do other execution of the K.'s process, if otherwise he cannot enter. But before he breaks it, he ought to signify the cause of his coming, and to make request to open doors …

The ruling in *Eccles v. Bourque* gives police the authority to enter a dwelling-house under certain limited circumstances. In the 1986 case of *R v. Landry*, the SCC again upheld the right of peace officers to enter a dwelling-house for the purpose of arresting an individual. In this case, however, the court set out specific criteria that must be met by the peace officer. The court ruled (1986, p. 147) that, for an arrest to be lawful when it involves the peace officer's entering the offender's dwelling-house, each of the following questions must be answered with "yes":

1. Is the offence in question indictable?
2. Has the person who is the subject of arrest committed the offence or does the peace officer believe on reasonable and probable grounds* that the person has committed or is about to commit the offence in question?
3. Are there reasonable and probable grounds to believe that the person sought is within the premises?
4. Was proper announcement made before entry?

At the time of the ruling, it was thought that these conditions reasonably balanced the interests of the individual and the interests of the public. In effect, the *Landry* case simply reaffirmed previous court rulings while clearly defining the restrictions on peace officers' entry of a dwelling-house to make an arrest.

CHECK YOUR UNDERSTANDING

1. According to the Code, a person does not commit an offence in protecting his or her home if he or she has reasonable grounds to believe what?
2. Define *dwelling-house*.
3. In the *Landry* case, the SCC defined four questions that must be answered in the affirmative for an arrest to be lawful. What are these questions?

The Charter and Bill C-16

It is important to note that even though *Landry* was a 1986 case, the ruling relied on precedents and processes that existed prior to the passing of the Charter. One might wonder, then, what the Charter itself says about the rights of the individual in his or her home. Has it had any effect on individual rights in relation to homes? While the Charter does not specifically define a person's right to privacy within a dwelling-house, and certainly does not prohibit a person's arrest within a dwelling-house, it *does* guarantee an individual's reasonable expectation of privacy and—as s. 8 provides—the right to be secure against unreasonable search and seizure. To explore the implications of the Charter, we will look more closely at the case of *R v. Feeney* (1997), which provided the basis of our chapter's opening scenario.

---

* At the time of the *Landry* ruling in 1986, "reasonable and probable grounds" was the term that was used. Today, the term has changed to "reasonable grounds," but the meaning remains the same.

R v. Feeney: Search Within Dwelling-Houses Redefined

In 1997, the SCC overturned the murder conviction of a British Columbia man. The court's decision would have a profound effect on the way peace officers deal with individuals within a dwelling-house. This case is known as *R v. Feeney* (1997).

In 1991, police officers who were investigating the murder of an 85-year-old man entered an equipment trailer that was the home of Michael Feeney. Witnesses had identified Feeney as the person they saw walking away from a vehicle accident that involved a truck owned by the murder victim. When the police arrived at Feeney's trailer and knocked on his door, they did not receive an answer to their knock. They then entered the trailer, without permission, and awoke the sleeping Feeney. When they saw blood on the shirt he was wearing, they arrested Feeney on suspicion of murder. The police later obtained a search warrant based on the search they conducted of the trailer at the time of the arrest. As a result of the investigation, Feeney was convicted of second degree murder.

Feeney was convicted of the offence, but he appealed the murder decision to the British Columbia Court of Appeal. He claimed that the entry of the officers into his home and the subsequent search were unconstitutional. This appeal was dismissed, so Feeney took his case to the SCC. The court examined a number of issues arising from Feeney's arrest.

One issue was whether the accused's right to be secure from unreasonable search and seizure had been violated. In seeking to determine this, the court applied the pre-Charter criteria for warrantless arrest, as described in *Eccles v. Bourque* (1974) and *R v. Landry* (1986). The court determined that the subjective requirements for a lawful arrest were *not* met because, prior to seeing the blood on Mr. Feeney's shirt, the officers did not have reasonable grounds to arrest him. Without these grounds, officers did not have the authority to enter the dwelling-house, so the entry and the arrest were unlawful.

In its ruling, the SCC declared that the *Landry* test for warrantless searches did not provide an individual with sufficient protection against unreasonable search and seizure. The court pointed out (1997, p. 15) that, while the *Landry* test created a balance between "aiding the police in their protection of society on the one hand, and the privacy interests of individuals in their dwellings on the other," the test needed to be adjusted to support the Charter. Even if the warrantless search were authorized by law, the search *must* respect s. 8 of the Charter, and both the law and the manner in which the search was conducted must be reasonable.

The court ruled that, with certain exceptions, police require a warrant to enter a dwelling-house. When considering whether to issue the warrant, a judge or justice would apply the test from *R v. Landry*. In this respect, the court did not actually change the requirements for police to enter a dwelling-house. However, the court's ruling did establish that it would no longer be up to the police to determine whether the requirements for entry had been met. This determination must henceforward be made by a justice; it would be a justice who would authorize entry.

Bill C-16: Entrance into a Dwelling-House with an Arrest Warrant

The court ruled that, to protect privacy rights guaranteed by the Charter, police must in general obtain judicial authorization to enter a dwelling-house to arrest a person. The SCC's decision in *Feeney* also recognized that the Code failed to provide an adequate process whereby police could obtain such authorization. In response, Bill C-16 was introduced in 1997.

Bill C-16 tabled amendments to the Code, creating "Powers to Enter Dwelling-Houses to Carry Out Arrests" under s. 529. The amendments included the following rules:

- A peace officer must obtain authorization from a judge or justice—in other words, a warrant—to enter the dwelling-house to make an arrest. This type of warrant is often called the Feeney warrant.

- A judge or justice will issue this warrant if he or she is satisfied, based on information provided under oath, that there are reasonable grounds for the arrest and reasonable grounds to believe that the person will be found in the dwelling-house. This authorization protects the privacy rights of the individual through a prior analysis of the reasonableness of the entry and arrest.

- This warrant must stipulate that the peace officer may not enter the dwelling-house unless he or she has reasonable grounds to believe, immediately before entry, that the person is in the dwelling-house.

- Police must properly announce themselves before entering the dwelling-house to make an arrest unless it is a case of *hot pursuit*—in other words, the immediate and direct pursuit of a suspect. (The court did not address exigent circumstances in this case, but the federal government did when it amended the Code to address the SCC's concerns. We will look further at exigent circumstances below.)

It is interesting to note that the SCC's suggested criteria for entry into a dwelling-house to arrest did not differ from common law criteria based on the 1604 *Semayne's Case* or the 1986 *Landry* case. The difference introduced by this ruling was that police now needed, in most cases, confirmation by a judge or justice of the grounds for entry. Requiring judicial authorization before entry and arrest precluded the after-the-fact analysis of whether the intrusions and invasive arrests by police were based on reasonable grounds.

Section 529.1 of the Code was created to address cases in which an arrest warrant had been previously issued and the police were now seeking to enter a dwelling-house to make the arrest. Like the warrant issued under s. 529, the Feeney warrant is issued on the basis of sworn information allowing the judge or justice to determine that there are reasonable grounds to believe the person named in the warrant is or will be found in the dwelling-house.

POWERS TO ENTER DWELLING-HOUSES TO CARRY OUT ARRESTS

529(1) A warrant to arrest or apprehend a person issued by a judge or justice under this or any other Act of Parliament may authorize a peace officer, subject to subsection (2), to enter a dwelling-house described in the warrant for the purpose of arresting or apprehending the person if the judge or justice is satisfied by information on oath in writing that there are reasonable grounds to believe that the person is or will be present in the dwelling-house.

(2) An authorization to enter a dwelling-house granted under subsection (1) is subject to the condition that the peace officer may not enter the dwelling-house unless the peace officer has, immediately before entering the dwelling-house, reasonable grounds to believe that the person to be arrested or apprehended is present in the dwelling-house.

529.1 A judge or justice may issue a warrant in Form 7.1 authorizing a peace officer to enter a dwelling-house described in the warrant for the purpose of arresting or apprehending a person identified or identifiable by the warrant if the judge or justice is satisfied by information on oath that there are reasonable grounds to believe that the person is or will be present in the dwelling-house and that

(a) a warrant referred to in this or any other Act of Parliament to arrest or apprehend the person is in force anywhere in Canada;

(b) grounds exist to arrest the person without warrant under paragraph 495(1)(a) or (b) or section 672.91; or

(c) grounds exist to arrest or apprehend without warrant the person under an Act of Parliament, other than this Act.

FORM 7
(Sections 475, 493, 597, 800 and 803)
WARRANT FOR ARREST

Canada, Province of .... , (*territorial division*).

To the peace officers in the said (*territorial division*):

This warrant is issued for the arrest of A.B., of .... , (*occupation*), hereinafter called the accused.

Whereas the accused has been charged that (*set out briefly the offence in respect of which the accused is charged*);

And whereas:*

(*a*) there are reasonable grounds to believe that it is necessary in the public interest to issue this warrant for the arrest of the accused [507(4), 512(1)];

(*b*) the accused failed to attend court in accordance with the summons served on him [512(2)];

(*c*) (an appearance notice *or* a promise to appear *or* a recognizance entered into before an officer in charge) was confirmed and the accused failed to attend court in accordance therewith [512(2)];

(*d*) it appears that a summons cannot be served because the accused is evading service [512(2)];

(*e*) the accused was ordered to be present at the hearing of an application for a review of an order made by a justice and did not attend the hearing [520(5), 521(5)];

(*f*) there are reasonable grounds to believe that the accused has contravened or is about to contravene the (promise to appear *or* undertaking *or* recognizance) on which he was released [524(1), 525(5), 679(6)];

(*g*) there are reasonable grounds to believe that the accused has since his release from custody on (a promise to appear *or* an undertaking *or* a recognizance) committed an indictable offence [524(1), 525(5), 679(6)];

(*h*) the accused was required by (an appearance notice *or* a promise to appear *or* a recognizance entered into before an officer in charge *or* a summons) to attend at a time and place stated therein for the purposes of the *Identification of Criminals Act* and did not appear at that time and place [502, 510];

(*i*) an indictment has been found against the accused and the accused has not appeared or remained in attendance before the court for his trial [597];

(*j*) **

This is, therefore, to command you, in Her Majesty's name, forthwith to arrest the said accused and to bring him before (*state court, judge or justice*), to be dealt with according to law.

(*Add where applicable*) Whereas there are reasonable grounds to believe that the accused is or will be present in (*here describe dwelling-house*);

This warrant is also issued to authorize you to enter the dwelling-house for the purpose of arresting or apprehending the accused, subject to the condition that you may not enter the dwelling-house unless you have, immediately before entering the dwelling-house, reasonable grounds to believe that the person to be arrested or apprehended is present in the dwelling-house.

Dated this .... day of .... A.D. .... , at ....

_____
Judge, Clerk of the Court, Provincial Court Judge *or* Justice

* *Initial applicable recital.*
** *For any case not covered by recitals (a) to (i), insert recital in the words of the statute authorizing the warrant.*

FORM 7.1
(Section 529.1)
WARRANT TO ENTER DWELLING-HOUSE

Canada, Province of .... , *(territorial division)*.

To the peace officers in the said *(territorial division)*:

This warrant is issued in respect of the arrest of A.B., or a person with the following description ( ), of .... , *(occupation)*.

Whereas there are reasonable grounds to believe:*

(a) a warrant referred to in this or any other Act of Parliament to arrest or apprehend the person is in force anywhere in Canada;

(b) grounds exist to arrest the person without warrant under paragraph 495(1)*(a)* or *(b)* or section 672.91 of the *Criminal Code*; or

(c) grounds exist to arrest or apprehend without warrant the person under an Act of Parliament, other than this Act;

And whereas there are reasonable grounds to believe that the person is or will be present in *(here describe dwelling-house)*;

This warrant is issued to authorize you to enter the dwelling-house for the purpose of arresting or apprehending the person.

Dated this .... day of .... A.D. .... , at ....

_____
Judge, Clerk of the Court, Provincial Court Judge *or* Justice

* *Initial applicable recital.*

CHECK YOUR UNDERSTANDING

1. Police officers were still authorized to enter a dwelling-house after Bill C-16 passed. What was Bill C-16 and what additional requirement was added with the passing of the Bill?

2. What is the difference between a warrant issued under s. 529 and one issued under s. 529.1?

3. Every warrant authorizing a peace officer to enter a dwelling-house to make an arrest must include what restriction on the peace officer?

Entry into a Dwelling-House Without an Arrest Warrant

At times, it will be impracticable for a police officer to obtain a warrant before entering a dwelling-house. The principle that no person can avoid arrest simply by seeking refuge in a dwelling-house still holds true despite the Charter.

Exigent Circumstances

Section 529.3 of the Code grants police the authority, under specific circumstances, to enter a dwelling-house to make an arrest without a warrant. One such circumstance is when an officer believes on reasonable grounds that the person is within the dwelling-house and the conditions exist to obtain a warrant under s. 529.1, but it would be impractical to do so owing to exigent circumstances. Exigent circumstances are circumstances in which a police officer believes on reasonable grounds that he or she must enter the dwelling-house immediately and must arrest a person either (1) to prevent physical harm or death; or (2) to prevent evidence of an indictable offence from being lost or destroyed.

EXIGENT CIRCUMSTANCES

529.3(1) Without limiting or restricting any power a peace officer may have to enter a dwelling-house under this or any other Act or law, the peace officer may enter the dwelling-house for the purpose of arresting or apprehending a person, without a warrant referred to in section 529 or 529.1 authorizing the entry, if the peace officer has reasonable grounds to believe that the person is present in the dwelling-house, and the conditions for obtaining a warrant under section 529.1 exist but by reason of exigent circumstances it would be impracticable to obtain a warrant.

(2) For the purpose of subsection (1), exigent circumstances include circumstances in which the peace officer

(a) has reasonable grounds to suspect that entry into the dwelling-house is necessary to prevent imminent bodily harm or death to any person; or

(b) has reasonable grounds to believe that evidence relating to the commission of an indictable offence is present in the dwelling-house and that entry into the dwelling-house is necessary to prevent the imminent loss or imminent destruction of the evidence.

IT'S YOUR MOVE, OFFICER!

Scenario 4.1

You and your partner respond to a call regarding a domestic assault. You speak with a woman who is standing outside the house and has very visible injuries on her face and arms. She informs you that her husband assaulted her during an argument over his drinking. She tells you that after her husband assaulted her, he forced her out of the house and locked all the doors. The victim's two-year-old daughter is still in the house, sleeping in the second-floor bedroom. The woman is fearful for her daughter's safety because her husband is very drunk; she suspects he is continuing to drink as they speak. She says that her husband is violent to almost everyone when he has been drinking.

What do you think you should do? Justify your course of action.

Hot Pursuit

Police officers have long had the authority, granted through common law, to follow a pursued individual into a dwelling-house to make an arrest. In *R v. Macooh* (1993), the SCC confirmed this common law authority. In a unanimous decision, the court stated (1993, p. 822) the following:

> It goes without saying that a person who enters his house or that of someone else to get away from the police who are pursuing him in connection with an offence he has just committed and for which there is a power of arrest without a warrant cannot expect his privacy to be protected in such circumstances so as to prevent the police from making an arrest.

Four years later, in the *Feeney* case, the court again recognized this common law authority, stating that, in cases of hot pursuit, the individual's privacy interest must give way to the interest of society for adequate police protection. However, it is important to remember that, as in entrance with a warrant, the pursuing officer must have reasonable grounds to believe that he or she has the authority to arrest the person being pursued.

911 Calls

A third exception to the requirement that police must obtain a warrant before entering a dwelling-house comes with the investigation of 911 calls. Police have a common law duty as well as a statutory duty to protect lives. The statutory duties incumbent on police officers in Ontario are set out in s. 42 of the *Police Services Act*. To perform them, police officers may under certain circumstances enter a dwelling-house to ensure no one is in distress.

The SCC upheld this authority in *R v. Godoy* (1999). In this case, police officers responded to a 911 call that got disconnected. When police arrived at the apartment door, a man answered and indicated that everything was fine. However, the officers requested permission to enter and investigate further. The man refused and began to close the door. The officers forced their way into the apartment and discovered the man's common law wife crying in a bedroom, with injuries to her face. The officers arrested the man for assault. The trial judge dismissed the case on the grounds that the officers' entry into the apartment was unauthorized and so their actions after entry were illegal. The Ontario Court of Appeal and the SCC disagreed. Both courts found that the officers' forced entry into the accused's apartment was justified because the police had a duty to ascertain the reason for the 911 call. In other words, the police had authority under common law to enter the apartment to verify that there was no emergency. This meant that their actions in the apartment were legal. They formed reasonable grounds that the accused had committed assault and arrested him.

CHECK YOUR UNDERSTANDING

1. Define *exigent circumstances*.

2. Describe three circumstances under which a peace officer may enter a dwelling-house without a warrant to effect an arrest.

3. Where do police officers in Ontario get the statutory duty to protect life?

Gaining Entry into a Dwelling-House

Police may gain entry into a dwelling-house by several prescribed means, depending on the circumstances. The law prescribes these methods to ensure that individuals' Charter rights are not violated.

Implied Invitation to Knock

Common law recognizes that anyone, police or citizen, may approach and knock at a dwelling-house with a lawful purpose without the resident's explicit consent. This common law principle is known as "implied invitation to knock." Police officers may use this common law principle and their duty to investigate crime to authorize their entering the outer perimeter of residential property and knocking on its door to conduct an investigation or to determine if an individual is in the dwelling-house. The resident of the dwelling-house may refuse them permission to enter or may revoke the implied invitation to knock.

Consent

The most obvious and simplest method of gaining entrance to a dwelling-house to make an arrest is simply to ask for consent. Police officers may enter a dwelling-house with the consent of the owner or occupant. Simple though it seems, this method can be the most complicated to justify in court.

Consent may be either expressed or implied. With **expressed consent**, the owner or occupant specifically invites the police into the dwelling-house. The individual's words leave no question as to his or her intentions. He or she might say, for example, "Hello, officer, please come in." **Implied consent** is less clear and may be misinterpreted. It is the person's actions rather than their words that provide consent. Let's say, for example, that the occupant answers the door but says nothing. He or she then walks back into the house without saying a word, leaving the door open. Does the police officer interpret this as an implied invitation to enter or is the person just walking away?

And it is not sufficient merely to obtain consent from the individual; the consent must be **informed consent**. The SCC applies a stringent test in cases where the Crown contends that an accused waived his or her constitutional rights during a police investigation. The Crown must prove that the accused gave up his or her constitutional rights with full knowledge of the existence of the rights and an appreciation of the consequences of waiving them (*R v. Willis*, 2003). In *R v. Borden* (1994), the SCC found that voluntarily giving up one's constitutional rights wasn't the issue. At issue was whether the accused had sufficient information to truly waive his or her right to be secure from unreasonable search and/or seizure. The court determined that, for the accused to have sufficient information, an officer seeking consent to enter a home must

expressed consent
direct and specific permission

implied consent
a person's actions that are inferred by a police officer to be permission

informed consent
voluntary consent, revocable at any time, from a person who is fully aware of the intent of the police and the consequences he or she may face if consent is given

- inform the occupant of the reason for the request and the possible consequences he or she faces for granting permission;

- ensure that the occupant understands that the consent is voluntary and that there are no consequences for refusing consent; and

- make it clear to the individual that he or she may revoke consent at any time.

Source: Derek Ruttan / The London Free Press / QMI Agency.

Police knocking on the door of a home.

Given the previous rulings of the SCC, and given the Code provision requiring officers to obtain a warrant to enter a dwelling-house to make an arrest, it would be unwise for an officer to use consent as a basis for entry when he or she already has reasonable grounds to arrest the occupant. However, it is reasonable for an officer, once he or she has knocked on the door and determined that the suspect is in the dwelling-house, to invite the suspect to voluntarily leave the dwelling-house. Once outside, the suspect is in a place other than a dwelling-house and can be legally arrested without a warrant.

Who May Give Consent?

It is not always clear who may give consent to enter a dwelling-house. The SCC provided guidance in *R v. Edwards* (1996). As with all Charter rights, the right to be secure against unreasonable search or seizure protects people and not places. When determining an individual's expectation of privacy, the totality of the circumstances must be considered, including the ownership and use of the dwelling-house (*R v. Edwards*, 1996). Often, police are confronted with conflicting privacy rights. For example, a husband and wife share ownership in a home, yet do not jointly consent to police entering. Faced with this situation, police should seek consent from the individual facing the most serious consequences.

Forcible Entry

Police officers sometimes need to use force to enter a dwelling-house to make an arrest. Under s. 25 of the Code, the use of force is justified when a peace officer, in administering or enforcing the law, acts on reasonable grounds and uses only as much force as necessary. To avail themselves of the protection afforded by s. 25, officers must be able to prove—see *Chartier v. Greaves* (2001)—that these conditions were met during forcible entry. Simply put, a warrant to enter a dwelling-house does not give an officer the authority to use any level of force to enter the dwelling-house.

IT'S YOUR MOVE, OFFICER!

Scenario 4.2

You have an arrest warrant endorsed to enter a specific dwelling-house. The dwelling-house has been under surveillance, so there is no doubt that the individual named in the warrant is in the home.

You attempt to communicate with the person in the dwelling-house, but you receive no response. All the doors and windows are locked. A relative of the individual sought by the police offers to provide you with a key to unlock the front door, but she has to pick it up at another location. It will be about ten minutes before she can return with the key. You have a hand-held battering ram on scene that you might use to break open the door right now.

Should you use the ram to open the door or wait for the key? Justify your decision.

CHECK YOUR UNDERSTANDING

1. Explain the difference between implied and expressed consent.
2. What is the meaning of informed consent?
3. Explain the common law concept of "implied invitation to knock."

A Systematic Approach

To ensure that individual rights are protected and that the proper course of action is taken when entering a dwelling-house, follow the step-by-step approach shown in Figure 4.1.

FIGURE 4.1   A Systematic Approach to Entering a Dwelling-House to Make an Arrest: A Decision-Making Chart

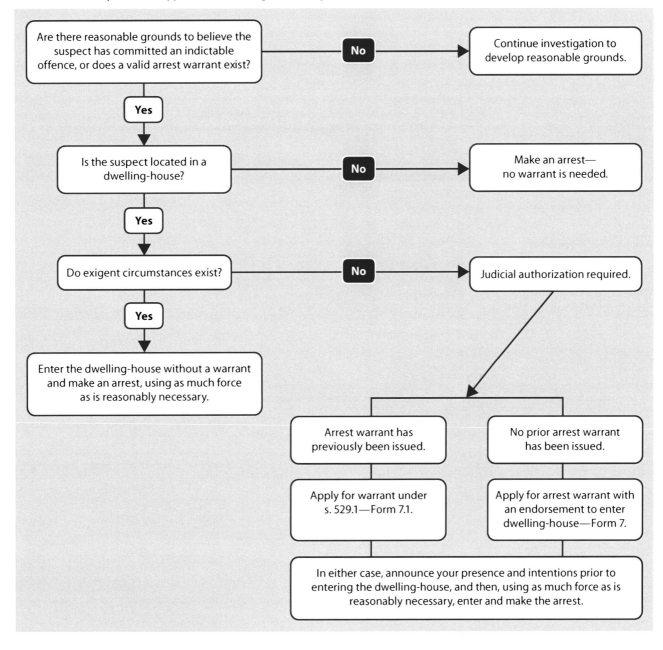

CHECK YOUR UNDERSTANDING

1. Describe the steps you should take if you have reasonable grounds to believe that someone has committed an indictable offence.

2. What should you do if you do not have reasonable grounds to form this belief?

CHAPTER SUMMARY

It has long been recognized that an individual has a right to privacy within his or her own home. However, it has also been recognized that no one should expect to avoid arrest simply by being in his or her home. Following several SCC rulings and the enactment of the Charter, the Parliament of Canada amended the Code to ensure both that individuals' rights are protected and that police have the authority to arrest suspects regardless of their location.

Amendments to the Code created a process whereby police may obtain judicial authorization prior to entering a dwelling-house to make an arrest. The amendment also defined the circumstances—namely, exigent circumstances—in which police are not required to obtain judicial authorization before entering a dwelling-house to make an arrest.

There are many questions for police to consider before they make an arrest in a dwelling-house. One concerns whether judicial authorization is required. For this reason, it is important to have a systematic approach, with clear steps. Following these steps will help you both to make lawful arrests and to protect the rights of the suspect and of the community.

KEY TERMS

expressed consent, 89
implied consent, 89
informed consent, 89

REFERENCES

Adams, R v. (2001). 2001 CanLII 16024 (Ont. CA).

Borden, R v. (1994). [1994] 3 SCR 145, 1994 CanLII 63.

Chartier v. Greaves. (2001). [2001] OJ No. 634 (Sup. Ct. J) (QL).

Criminal Code. (1985). RSC 1985, c. C-46.

Eccles v. Bourque et al. (1975). [1975] 2 SCR 739, 1974 CanLII 191.

Edwards, R v. (1996). [1996] 1 SCR 128, 1996 CanLII 255.

Evans, R v. (1996). [1996] 1 SCR 8, 1996 CanLII 248.

Feeney, R v. (1997). [1997] 2 SCR 13, 1997 CanLII 342; 1995 CanLII 1016.

Godoy, R v. (1999). [1999] 1 SCR 311, 1999 CanLII 709.

Landry, R v. (1986). [1986] 1 SCR 145, 1986 CanLII 48.

Macooh, R v. (1993). [1993] 2 SCR 802, 1993 CanLII 107.

Willis, R v. (2003). 2003 SCC 12, [2003] 1 SCR 127.

FURTHER READING

Crampton v. Walton. (2005). 2005 ABCA 81.

Duong, R v. (2002). 2002 BCCA 43.

Feeney, R v. (1997). [1997] 2 SCR 13, 1997 CanLII 342.

Phillips, R v. (2006). 2006 NSCA 135.

REVIEW QUESTIONS

Multiple Choice

1. An individual may be arrested in two types of locations. These locations are
   a. private property and public property
   b. private residence and public place
   c. dwelling-house and place other than a dwelling-house
   d. dwelling-house and public place

2. In the *Feeney* case, the SCC ruled that police had violated the right of the accused to be secure against unreasonable search and seizure; this ruling was made on the basis that
   a. the officers entered the trailer without a warrant
   b. the officers did not announce their intention to enter the trailer
   c. the officers should have left the trailer once they saw the accused was sleeping
   d. the officers had not formed reasonable grounds for believing that the occupant had committed an indictable offence prior to entering the trailer

3. For a judge or justice to issue an arrest warrant with an endorsement to enter a dwelling-house, he or she must be satisfied on reasonable grounds that
   a. the named person may be in the dwelling-house
   b. the named person is or will be in the dwelling-house
   c. the named person lives in the dwelling-house
   d. the named person owns the dwelling-house

4. A police officer forcibly entering a dwelling-house to make an arrest may use
   a. as much force as he or she wants
   b. the least level of force required
   c. as much force as is reasonably necessary
   d. the force of the body only

5. You have conducted a criminal investigation and developed reasonable grounds to believe that Harold Wall has committed an assault causing bodily harm. You learn that Harold is now working at an auto repair shop. You should
   a. apply for a Feeney warrant before arresting Harold
   b. ask Harold or his boss for consent to enter the repair shop
   c. enter the repair shop and arrest Harold; no warrant is required
   d. wait for Harold to leave work and then arrest him

True or False

_____ 1. Police must always obtain a warrant prior to entering a dwelling-house to make an arrest.

_____ 2. An emergency 911 call cannot provide police with grounds to enter a dwelling-house without a warrant.

_____ 3. Once informed consent is given, it cannot be revoked.

_____ 4. A police officer must have the power to arrest an individual prior to obtaining a Feeney warrant.

_____ 5. The onus of proving that consent is voluntary and that informed consent was obtained rests on the accused.

_____ **6.** An arrest warrant allows a police officer to enter a dwelling-house to make an arrest.

_____ **7.** Before entering a dwelling-house under the authority of a Feeney warrant, police must have reasonable grounds to believe that the person being sought is in the dwelling-house.

_____ **8.** A police officer entering a dwelling-house under the authority of a warrant to enter a dwelling-house (Form 7.1) may use force to enter provided the amount of force is reasonable.

_____ **9.** There are two types of warrants commonly referred to as Feeney warrants.

_____**10.** An occupied hotel room is considered a dwelling-house.

Short Answer

1. Explain the concept of exigent circumstances and how it applies to a police officer's powers of arrest.

2. A police officer wishes to enter an apartment to arrest a robbery suspect. The officer knows a Feeney warrant is required to enter the apartment. Explain the information the officer must provide to the judge or justice to obtain the warrant.

3. A police officer is investigating a domestic assault. The officer has been informed by the female victim that her husband, the suspect, is alone in their home. The officer has developed reasonable grounds to believe that the suspect is responsible for the assault. The victim has given the officer consent to enter her home to arrest her husband. Explain the best course of action the officer should take.

4. While on patrol, a police officer sees a female she knows. The officer also knows there is a valid arrest warrant in effect for the female. The female is standing on the driveway of the house speaking with another female. Explain the best course of action the officer should take.

5. Explain the circumstances in which a police officer may forcibly enter a dwelling-house with intent to make an arrest, and explain what amount of force can be used.

It's Your Move, Officer!

A. As part of the investigation of a home invasion, you are assigned to canvass the homes in the area near the home to identify potential witnesses. When you knock on the door of one home, a male opens the door. As the door opens, you feel a rush of warm, humid air, and you smell marijuana in two forms—both burning and growing. You conclude from your observations and from the man's demeanour that there is a marijuana grow operation inside the home.

What do you do now?

B. Following an investigation, you have reasonable grounds to arrest a male for trafficking in a narcotic. (_Note_: This scenario is based on the Ontario case of _R v. Adams_ (2001).) You, along with other police officers, attend the rooming house the accused lives in. You locate the accused in the laundry room of the rooming house and arrest him. A search incident to the arrest finds narcotics in his pocket. At trial, the accused concedes that you had reasonable grounds to arrest him for the earlier offence of trafficking in a narcotic. The sole issue at trial is whether the arrest was unlawful, in which case the search would constitute a violation of the accused's right to be secure against unreasonable search and seizure.

Discuss whether you should have applied for a Feeney warrant in this situation.

Use of Force and Officer Safety

5

LEARNING OBJECTIVES

After completing this chapter, you should be able to:

- Explain the concepts of reasonable and unreasonable force.
- Explain police rights and duties with regard to the use of force.
- Identify and explain federal and provincial legislation regarding the use of force.
- Describe the Use-of-Force Continuum model and its role in public and police safety.
- Describe alternative approaches to use of force with mentally ill subjects.

ON SCENE

On a warm Saturday evening, Constable Savard is patrolling in her assigned area with her partner. They are dispatched to a report of a disturbance at a wedding reception. When they arrive, they find many of the partiers engaged in fistfights. A woman runs up to them, claiming to have been assaulted by the bride. She has a bloody nose and her clothes are disorderly.

Constable Savard approaches the bride and asks about the alleged assault. The bride, who is about 1.6 metres (5'2") and 50 kilograms, admits to punching the complainant. She says that the woman used to date the groom and was not invited to the wedding and is trespassing. Constable Savard decides to place the bride under arrest, though she has no prior history of violence or arrest. The bride begins to resist as the constable attempts to place her in handcuffs. Savard removes her pepper spray canister from its holster, at which point several of the partygoers start toward her and the suspect.

Do you agree with Constable Savard's response to the situation? Is she justified in placing the bride in handcuffs and in unholstering her pepper spray when the woman resists? What should she do next? Would your answers to these questions be different if Constable Savard were dealing not with the bride but with the groom, a heavy-set 1.9-metre (6'2") martial arts expert who has been drinking throughout the evening?

Introduction

The job of a law enforcement officer sometimes involves force. In order for police officers to perform their duties, they need to be able to touch people—to physically manage them with varying degrees of intentional force. In many cases, managing people means subduing them for the safety of the officer, the public, and the subject.

What is meant by *force*? Under what circumstances can it be applied? An officer must be confident in his or her answers to these questions; his or her use of force will be scrutinized by police administration, by the public, and by the media, and it will be scrutinized in courtrooms. In this chapter, we look at the special powers afforded to police and other law enforcement agents authorizing them to use force in the performance of their duties.

What Is Force?

force
psychological or physical contact with another person, used by officers in the course of performing their duties

For our purposes, the term **force** applies to any touching of a person without their consent. Any contact with another person, regardless of the degree, is force. Force can also be psychological in basis; the mere presence of police officers often produces submissive behaviour from a suspect. Police officers use force to meet their professional responsibilities. Sometimes they need to coerce a subject to do their bidding; they often use force to arrest and apprehend suspects. Let's take a closer look at what this means.

Protections and Constraints

Use of force is described in many sections of the *Criminal Code* as well as in provincial legislation and in case law. Section 25 of the Code, in particular, outlines the basic authority of law enforcement representatives to use force. It states that everyone "required or authorized by law to do anything in the administration or enforcement of the law" is, "if he acts on reasonable grounds, justified in doing what he is required or authorized to do and in using as much force as is necessary for that purpose." In other words, a person authorized to enforce the law is justified in using whatever force is necessary to fulfill that purpose.

Note the qualifications and restrictions in s. 25; the person authorized (or required) by law to use force is justified in doing so as long as he or she *acts on reasonable grounds*. An officer using force must perform a delicate balancing act and must always be prepared to explain and justify his or her use of force.

Reasonable Grounds for Use of Force

The concept of reasonable grounds, as we have seen, is significant to many areas of law related to police powers, including arrest, search and seizure, and the use of force. In 1990, the Supreme Court's ruling in *R v. Storrey* contributed significantly to the definition of police powers and the nature of reasonable grounds. The ruling was made in relation to arrest powers, but the definition it offers for reasonable grounds extends to all other areas of police powers. The court (1990, p. 242) said that the Code "requires that an arresting officer must subjectively have reasonable and probable grounds on which to base the arrest" and that these grounds "must, in addition, be justifiable from an objective point of view."

The suggestion here, and an important point to keep in mind, is that reasonable grounds are an **objective standard** against which an officer's actions can be judged. Those assigned the task of judging an officer's actions will measure his or her actions in relation to what the average, objective, reasonable person would have concluded in the same situation. An officer establishes reasonable grounds by gathering evidence, through interview and/or observation, from one or more sources in a criminal investigation. Officers are frequently called upon to present this evidence and to present their reasonable grounds both to their supervisors and to a court of law.

The assessment of an officer's actions will be based on objective criteria, but this does not mean that the officer's own subjective perception of the situation has no weight and will not be considered. The assessment of an officer's actions will also take into account **subjective elements**—in other words, those elements that constitute the officer's own point of view. Those in charge of reviewing the officer's actions will ask the officer what he or she subjectively believed to be reasonable or necessary in the given situation.

In arriving at its conclusions, the court or other reviewer will not (and should not) give weight to information that was unknown to the officer at the time. For example, if an officer was facing a suspect whom he or she believed to be armed with a real firearm, the reviewer needs to consider the officer's actions in light of that belief. That the firearm turned out to be a fake should not be a factor in the reviewer's judgment, unless such information would have been available to the officer had he or she taken reasonable steps to obtain it. In this respect, there is no clear rule, and each situation must be assessed according to the facts available at the time of the event.

objective standard
a standard based on how an ordinary person would have behaved in the same circumstances; used in determining whether an officer had *reasonable grounds* for his or her actions

subjective elements
elements composing the officer's personal interpretation of the situation, used in determining whether he or she had *reasonable grounds* for his or her actions

IT'S YOUR MOVE, OFFICER!

Scenario 5.1

There has been a rash of break-and-enters into small businesses in the neighbourhood where you patrol. These have been occurring weeknights, primarily between midnight and 5:00 a.m. Nighttime security guards have noticed a general increase in pedestrian traffic during this time frame, though they have witnessed no break-and-enters. Your platoon sergeant has directed you to stop and obtain the identity of anyone you see walking around the district during these hours.

One Wednesday night at 2:00 a.m., you observe two young men walking through the area, each carrying backpacks. You stop to question them. "Good evening, gentlemen. Can I ask you a couple of questions?" The men look at you warily, and then respond, "We're not doing anything. We're just walking home." You begin to question them further, asking for their names, dates of birth, and their reason for being in the area. One of them looks directly at you and says, "Look, man, I've had it with this crap and I'm not answering any more of your questions. I'm outta here." With that, he begins to walk away. The other male follows.

At the same time, dispatch broadcasts that another pair of officers has responded to a report of a break-and-enter at a small auto body repair shop approximately one block away. A security guard observed two males with backpacks leaving the area about 30 minutes prior to the officers' arrival at the scene. You return your attention to the two young men, now walking away, and ask them to stop for further questioning. They refuse and continue to walk away.

What would you do? Would you use force to detain these individuals? How would you justify your choice, based on the requirements of s. 25(1) of the Code?

CHECK YOUR UNDERSTANDING

1. Under what circumstances is a person justified in using force in law enforcement?
2. Explain the concept of *reasonable grounds*.
3. What is the objective perspective in relation to the concept of reasonable grounds?

Source: Darren Makowichuk/Calgary Sun/QMI Agency.

Police officers use force in apprehending a suspect.

Reasonable, Excessive, and Lethal Force

If a situation requires a police officer to use force, how does he or she decide what degree of force is necessary? What circumstances in a situation affect the amount of force that is required?

Reasonable Force

The use of force is intended to allow the police to carry out their duties effectively and to protect the general public from criminal behaviour. However, there are legal constraints on when and how much force can be used. In *R v. Nasogaluak* (2010, para. 32), the Supreme Court stated that "the allowable degree of force to be used remains constrained by the principles of proportionality, necessity and reasonableness." As a police officer, when you find your-self in a situation where force is necessary, you will need to decide what degree of force is proportional, necessary, and reasonable under the circumstances.

The concept of using the "necessary" amount of force is echoed in s. 25(1) of the Code. Again, the word *necessary* suggests an objective measure. And again, as we discussed above, the objective measure of what is reasonable and necessary will be what a person operating with ordinary common sense would consider necessary under the circum-stances. Therefore, **reasonable force** may be defined as the force that any person with ordinary common sense would exercise when put in the same position as the officer.

Excessive Force

Any use of force in any given situation that goes beyond what "ordinary common sense" would dictate is considered **excessive force**. Any use of excessive force comes with conse-quences. Section 26 of the Code says the following: "Every one who is authorized by law to use force is criminally responsible for any excess thereof according to the nature and qual-ity of the act that constitutes the excess." This means that law enforcement officers are not protected from liability if it is determined that the force they have used is excessive. Even in a case where some force seems justifiable, police are open to charges, ranging from assault to murder, if the force used is found to be excessive.

The challenge for police officers is distinguishing between the proper use of force (rea-sonable force) and the improper use of force (excessive force). Decisions in this regard often have to be made in the heat of the moment, in potentially dangerous or even life-threatening situations. Later in the chapter, we will look at the factors that come into this decision-making process.

Lethal Force

Lethal force is a last resort, and its use is very closely monitored by police organizations, by the courts, and by the public. Lethal force is not necessarily excessive. By definition, the word *excessive* means something that exceeds what is necessary. Unfortunately, police of-ficers are sometimes put into situations where the use of lethal force is necessary.

Section 25(3) of the Code states that a person is not justified

> in using force that is intended or is likely to cause death or grievous bodily harm unless the person believes on reasonable grounds that it is necessary for the self-preservation of the person or the preservation of any one under that person's pro-tection from death or grievous bodily harm.

Section 25(4) goes on to outline the conditions under which use of such force would be defensible:

> 25(4) A peace officer, and every person lawfully assisting the peace officer, is justified in using force that is intended or is likely to cause death or grievous bodily harm to a person to be arrested, if
>
> (a) the peace officer is proceeding lawfully to arrest, with or without war-rant, the person to be arrested;
>
> (b) the offence for which the person is to be arrested is one for which that person may be arrested without warrant;
>
> (c) the person to be arrested takes flight to avoid arrest;
>
> (d) the peace officer or other person using the force believes on reasonable grounds that the force is necessary for the purpose of protecting the peace officer,

reasonable force
the force that any person with ordinary common sense would exercise if placed in the officer's position

excessive force
force whose use in the given situation does not accord with ordinary common sense

lethal force
force that is intended or is likely to cause death or grievous bodily harm

the person lawfully assisting the peace officer or any other person from imminent or future death or grievous bodily harm; and

(e) the flight cannot be prevented by reasonable means in a less violent manner.

HOW MUCH FORCE CAN A PRIVATE INDIVIDUAL USE?

Private citizens can find themselves in situations where they, too, have to use a degree of force to prevent or stop a criminal activity. In very specific instances, the Code provides use-of-force authorization for people who are not peace officers:

- Section 27(a) states that everyone is justified in using as much force as is reasonably necessary "to prevent the commission of an offence." This includes an offence for which a person might be arrested without a warrant or any action that threatens the safety of people. (Section 27.1(1) specifies these use-of-force authorities for private citizens with respect to the safety of people on an airplane.)

- Section 34 sets out the law regarding the use of force in relation to self-defence or defending another person. The person resorting to such force must believe on reasonable grounds that there is force, or the threat of force, being used against him or her or another person. He or she must also be acting solely for the purpose of defending himself or herself, or another person, and he or she must be acting reasonably for the situation.

The circumstances under which a person's use of force may be considered reasonable, which are listed in s. 34(2), are similar to the circumstances under which a police officer's use of force may be considered reasonable:

(2) In determining whether the act committed is reasonable in the circumstances, the court shall consider the relevant circumstances of the person, the other parties and the act, including, but not limited to, the following factors:
(a) the nature of the force or threat;
(b) the extent to which the use of force was imminent and whether there were other means available to respond to the potential use of force;
(c) the person's role in the incident;
(d) whether any party to the incident used or threatened to use a weapon;
(e) the size, age, gender and physical capabilities of the parties to the incident;
(f) the nature, duration and history of any relationship between the parties to the incident, including any prior use or threat of force and the nature of that force or threat;
(f.1) any history of interaction or communication between the parties to the incident;
(g) the nature and proportionality of the person's response to the use or threat of force; and
(h) whether the act committed was in response to a use or threat of force that the person knew was lawful.

In exercising the power to use force, private individuals are still subject to the limitations set out in s. 26, which says that anyone using force is criminally responsible for the use of excessive force.

IT'S YOUR MOVE, OFFICER!

Scenario 5.2

It is 8:00 a.m. on a Sunday, the start of your day shift. You are dispatched to 549 Mapleview Drive to respond to a report of a break-and-enter. Dispatch advises that the resident has the suspect in custody. Upon arrival, you are met by Francis Erdman, the homeowner. He explains that at 11:00 p.m. the night before, he found a 14-year-old teenager in his garage. The offender had broken in through the window and was trying to hotwire the homeowner's car.

When the homeowner confronted the teenager, the teen attacked him with his fists and attempted to flee from the garage. Erdman defended himself, overpowering the teenager. He tied the boy up with bungee cords that he had hanging in the garage, and then went inside the house, intending to call the police. He started to call 911, but then hung up, deciding that it could wait until morning because the offender needed to be taught a lesson. On questioning the offender, you determine that he has been sleeping and has not sustained any injuries.

Like the homeowner, you believe the teenager needs to be taught a lesson. So, without advising the teen that he is under arrest, you leave him in the garage and shut the doors while you speak further with Erdman. He decides he does not want to provide a statement. After about 40 minutes, you release the teenager with a warning.

1. What would you do in this situation?

2. Did the homeowner, in tying up the teenager, act in self-defence? Why or why not?

3. Has the officer used excessive force?

CHECK YOUR UNDERSTANDING

1. Define the term *reasonable force*.

2. What is meant by the term *excessive force*?

3. What consequences are set out in the Code for an officer or civilian who uses excessive force?

Use of Force and Provincial Statutes

Provincial statutes are enforced by many kinds of law enforcement officers, including police officers, bylaw officers, conservation officers, and liquor inspectors. These officers are authorized to use force to perform their duties. In Ontario, for example, these powers are described in s. 146(1) of the *Provincial Offences Act* (POA), in terms that are almost identical to those in s. 25 of the Code: "Every police officer is, if he or she acts on reasonable and probable grounds, justified in using as much force as is necessary to do what the officer is required or authorized by law to do."

Section 146(1) of the POA provides a general use-of-force authority to Ontario police. Some statutes, however, have their own use-of-force provisions, authorizing both law enforcement officers and private citizens to use force in certain situations. Here are two examples of use-of-force provisions from other statutes:

- From the Ontario *Liquor Licence Act* (LLA): Under s. 34(2), the holder of a licence or permit may use whatever force is necessary (but no more than is necessary) to remove a person from the premises if they are there illegally or if they are there for an unlawful purpose.

- From the Ontario *Child and Family Services Act* (CFSA): Under ss. 40(6), 44(1), and 44(2), any person authorized by a warrant to bring a child to a place of safety is authorized to use any force necessary to search for and remove the child.

These two statutes, while they describe specific circumstances in which police or other authorities are authorized to use force, do not provide use-of-force authority to enforce *all* of their provisions. For example, s. 31(4)(a) of the Ontario LLA makes it illegal to be intoxicated in a public place. This statute contains no provision authorizing officers to use force in enforcing this law against public intoxication. In situations like this, officers rely on s. 146(1) of the POA for their authority to use force. This provision applies to all situations, and gives officers a general authority to use reasonable force to perform their duties.

Most provincial statutes, such as the *Highway Traffic Act* (HTA), the *Trespass to Property Act*, the *Mental Health Act*, and the *Family Law Act*, do *not* have their own use-of-force provisions. To use reasonable and necessary force in enforcing these statutes' laws, police officers are authorized by s. 146(1) of the POA. This provision applies to all situations, and gives officers a general authority to use reasonable force to perform their duties.

IT'S YOUR MOVE, OFFICER!

Scenario 5.3

You are on patrol with your partner when you witness the driver of a 2010 Mazda 3 talking on a cellphone. This is an offence under the Ontario HTA, so you decide to pull over the driver. As you and your partner approach the vehicle, you observe the driver slip the cellphone into her shirt pocket. You advise the woman of your reason for pulling her over, and you ask for her licence, ownership documents, and insurance papers. You then ask her to produce the cellphone, which she refuses to do. What is your next step?

1. Is there a use-of-force authority in the HTA related to this offence?
2. Should you use force to obtain the evidence of the infraction? Why or why not?
3. Would you be protected by the POA if you used force?

CHECK YOUR UNDERSTANDING

1. Does the POA provide authority for use of force for all provincial legislation? Explain.
2. Identify two pieces of provincial legislation that do not have their own use-of-force authority.
3. Where does the use-of-force authority for most provincial offences reside?

Weapons and the Use of Force

Every province has its own police services legislation concerning weapons and the use of force. In Ontario, it is RRO 1990, Reg. 926 ("Equipment and Use of Force"), under the *Police Services Act* (PSA). This regulation does not describe any new authority to use force; rather, it describes the equipment (that is, firearms) that officers are permitted to carry and the guidelines for their use. This regulation also describes the training that is required before officers are issued weapons. This requirement and the nature of the training are described in ss. 14.2 and 14.4 of Reg. 926. Officers are also required to receive ongoing training, with s. 14.3 prescribing the training's frequency and specifying any exceptions to the schedule. Officers in Ontario must requalify annually, with the possibility of a 60-day extension if, for example, an officer is ill or unavailable to participate on the prescribed training dates.

Types of Weapons

Sections 3-13 of Reg. 926 deal specifically with firearms. These sections contain very specific technical specifications concerning the kind of weapon and type of ammunition that may be issued to and carried by police officers in Ontario. Officers are not allowed to modify any handgun issued to them or to use ammunition other than the kind officially supplied to them.

Sections 14 and 14.1 of Reg. 926—together composing a section entitled "Other Weapons"—describe other types of weapons that police may require in use-of-force situations. Section 14 says that any other weapon that a police officer uses must be of a type approved by the solicitor general, must meet the technical standards set by the solicitor general, and must be used in accordance with any standards established by the solicitor general. Section 14.1(1) forbids the use of "any gas, chemical or aerosol weapon," while s. 14.1(2) permits the use of tear gas "if it is not applied intentionally in concentrated form directly to the person" and the use of aerosol weapons that do not have an active ingredient that is a gas or chemical.

Use of Weapons

Though officers are issued handguns, police officers in Ontario are not meant to use, or even unholster, that weapon except in exceptional circumstances. According to s. 9 of Reg. 926, an officer "shall not draw a handgun, point a firearm at a person or discharge a firearm unless he or she believes, on reasonable grounds, that to do so is necessary to protect against loss of life or serious bodily harm." Section 12 states that if an officer does discharge a firearm for any reason, intentionally or unintentionally, except on the firing range or during ordinary maintenance, the chief or a commissioner must immediately order an investigation into the circumstances.

In cases where an officer uses force, regardless of the circumstances, he or she is required to complete a Form 1: Use of Force Report. The report is required when a gun is drawn, when a weapon is used on another person, or when an officer uses physical force causing injury that requires medical attention. It is also required if police use their firearms to put down or destroy a dangerous or injured animal, an action that is authorized under s. 10(b). A police officer need not fill out a Form 1 when a firearm is discharged in training, when it is cleaned or used on the practice range, or when it is used to signal for help in an emergency situation. Otherwise, he or she must fill one out.

Provincial legislation tightly controls the use of weapons by police officers, but it also acknowledges that there are cases when the use of force involving weapons is required. The legislation is clear that the use of a weapon may be defended if the officer can satisfy the requirement that reasonable grounds were met. What this legislation means, in combination with s. 25(1) of the Code, is that reasonable grounds must meet both the subjective requirement (that is, what was in the officer's mind) and the objective one (that is, what a reasonable person would have done in the same situation).

Form 1: Use of Force Report

(Check more than one box in each section, where appropriate)

Police Service	Location Code (If applicable)

Part A

Date (day/month/year)	Time Incident Commenced (24 hr)	Time Incident Terminated (24 hr)

☐ Individual Report	Length Of Service (years completed)	Rank	☐ Team Report	Type of Team	# of Police Officers Involved

Type Of Assignment
- ☐ General Patrol
- ☐ Foot Patrol
- ☐ Traffic
- ☐ Investigation
- ☐ Drugs
- ☐ Off-duty
- ☐ Other (specify)

Type Of Incident
- ☐ Robbery
- ☐ Break and Enter
- ☐ Domestic Disturbance
- ☐ Other Disturbance
- ☐ Traffic
- ☐ Suspicious Person
- ☐ Serious Injury
- ☐ Homicide
- ☐ Weapons Call
- ☐ Alarm
- ☐ Other (specify)

Police Presence At Time Of Incident
- ☐ Alone
- ☐ Police Assisted (specify #) _____

Attire
- ☐ Uniform ☐ Civilian Clothes

Number of Subject(s) Involved In Incident
- ☐ One ☐ Two ☐ Three ☐ Other (specify #) _____

Type Of Force Used (include all options used during incident & rank in sequence of use)	**Was Force Effective?** Yes / No	**Reason For Use Of Force**	**Alternative Strategies Used** (If Applicable)
Firearm - discharged ___	☐ ☐	☐ Protect Self	☐ Verbal Interaction ☐ Cover
Firearm - pointed at person ___	☐ ☐	☐ Protect Public	☐ Concealment ☐ Other (specify)
Handgun - drawn ___	☐ ☐	☐ Effect Arrest	
Aerosol Weapon ___	☐ ☐	☐ Prevent Commission of Offence	**Type Of Firearm Used** (If Applicable) / **No. Of Rounds Discharged** (If Applicable)
Impact Weapon - Hard ___	☐ ☐	☐ Prevent Escape	☐ Revolver ___
Impact Weapon - Soft ___	☐ ☐	☐ Accidental	☐ Semi-automatic ___
Empty Hand Techniques - Hard ___	☐ ☐	☐ Destroy an Animal	☐ Rifle ___
Empty Hand Techniques - Soft ___	☐ ☐	☐ Other (specify)	☐ Shotgun ___
Other (specify) ___	☐ ☐		☐ Other (specify) ___

Distance (Between you & subject at the time the decision was made to use force)
- ☐ Less than 2 metres
- ☐ 2 to 3 metres
- ☐ 3 to 5 metres
- ☐ 5 to 7 metres
- ☐ 7 to 10 metres
- ☐ Greater than 10 metres

Weapons Carried By Subject(s) — 1 2 3
- ☐ ☐ ☐ Unknown
- ☐ ☐ ☐ None
- ☐ ☐ ☐ Revolver
- ☐ ☐ ☐ Semi-automatic
- ☐ ☐ ☐ Rifle
- ☐ ☐ ☐ Shotgun
- ☐ ☐ ☐ Knife/Edged Weapon
- ☐ ☐ ☐ Baseball Bat/Club
- ☐ ☐ ☐ Other (specify)

Location Of Subject's Weapon (at time decision was made to use force) — 1 2 3
- ☐ ☐ ☐ In-hand
- ☐ ☐ ☐ At hand
- ☐ ☐ ☐ Concealed on person

Number Of Rounds Fired By Subject(s) (If Applicable)
Total Number: ___

Location Of Incident

Outdoors
- ☐ Roadway
- ☐ Laneway
- ☐ Yard
- ☐ Park
- ☐ Rural
- ☐ Motor Vehicle
- ☐ Other (specify)

Indoors

Private Property
- ☐ House
- ☐ Apartment
- ☐ Hallway

Public Property
- ☐ Financial Institution
- ☐ Commercial Site
- ☐ Public Institution
- ☐ Other (specify)

Weather Conditions
- ☐ Clear
- ☐ Sunny
- ☐ Cloudy
- ☐ Rain
- ☐ Snow/sleet
- ☐ Fog
- ☐ Other (specify)

Lighting Conditions
- ☐ Daylight
- ☐ Dusk
- ☐ Dark
- ☐ Good Artificial Light
- ☐ Poor Artificial Light
- ☐ Other (specify)

Person Injured	Medical Attention Required — Yes / No	Nature Of Injuries — Minor / Serious / Fatal / Unknown
1. Self	☐ ☐	☐ ☐ ☐ ☐
2. Other Police Officer	☐ ☐	☐ ☐ ☐ ☐
3. Subject	☐ ☐	☐ ☐ ☐ ☐
4. Third Party	☐ ☐	☐ ☐ ☐ ☐

Narrative: (if no occurrence report) - *Do not include personal names or information.*

If more space is required please continue on back of form.

Reviewed by Supervisor ☐ Yes ☐ No	Reviewed by Training Analyst ☐ Yes ☐ No	Recommended Post Traumatic Incident Counseling ☐ Yes ☐ No	Recommended Other Training ☐ Yes ☐ No	Date (day/month/year)

Part B

Officer involved (name, rank & badge #)

Date of last use of force refresher training	Would you like to participate in an interview with a training sergeant/analyst to discuss this incident and/or use of force training? ☐ Yes ☐ No

Additional training recommended by: ☐ training analyst ☐ supervisor	Type of training recommended:

This is an unofficial version of Government of Ontario legal materials.

CHECK YOUR UNDERSTANDING

1. How often do police officers in Ontario have to requalify to carry a firearm?
2. When must an officer submit a use-of-force report?
3. Are police limited to using force on human subjects only? Explain.

Determining the Appropriate Response

At what point do officers resort to force when performing their duties? Which level of force is the right one?

Factors Considered When Using Force

A police officer must consider many factors when trying to determine whether force should be used and what level of force is appropriate. For example, the physical attributes of the people involved can be a consideration. An officer weighing 63 kilograms may need to resort to a greater degree of force than a bigger, heavier officer does, especially if the party being dealt with is a male kick-boxer weighing 125 kilograms. On the other hand, a large, physically fit police officer may need to exercise restraint when trying to restrain an elderly hospital patient who is flailing about wildly. Evidence shows (Toronto Police Service, 2013, p. 19) that officers mostly resort to force when they are protecting themselves or effecting an arrest. And it is front-line constables who most often have to use force because they are the ones usually facing incidents that involve physical confrontations or interventions.

The Toronto Police Service (2013, p. 19) lists several categories of factors that affect an officer's response to a situation and whether he or she uses force:

> **situational factors**
> environmental factors in a situation that are beyond the officer's control; can include time, place, and the suspect's characteristics

*   **Situational factors** are those environmental factors that are beyond the control of an officer, and can include time, place, and the characteristics of the suspect.

> **tactical factors**
> skills and resources available to an officer in helping him or her manage an incident

*   **Tactical factors** are the officer's skills, as well as the resources that are available to help the officer manage an incident.

> **behavioural factors**
> attributes of the responding officer(s) that affect how he or she manages an incident

*   **Behavioural factors** refer to those personal attributes of the responding officer(s) that affect how an incident is managed.

Some of these factors are listed in Table 5.1.

TABLE 5.1   Situational, Tactical, and Behavioural Factors in Police Response

Situational Factors	Tactical Factors	Behavioural Factors
• Perceived cues	• Available officers	• Overall fitness
• Use of alcohol or drugs	• Available weapons	• Personal experience
• Perceived knowledge of subject (i.e., information in police or CPIC databases)	• Available expertise (e.g., negotiator, crisis expert)	• Skills
• Time and distance	• Training	• Fatigue
• Location of incident		• Injuries
• Number of subjects		• Training
• Abilities of subject (e.g., mixed martial arts)		• Officer's policing experience

SOURCE: Toronto Police Services (2013, p. 19).

Police agency policies and guidelines also contribute to the dynamic interplay of factors affecting police response. Officers' perceptions vary, but when they are considered in connection with the behaviour of the subject and the tactical considerations of the situation, the results of any incident involving the use of force can be better understood.

The Use-of-Force Continuum Model

Use-of-Force Continuum model
a model, used by police, that aligns the suspect's behavioural responses and profiles with suggested police responses

A great deal of effort has been put into developing use-of-force models over the past several decades. In Canada, there is a National Framework for Use of Force that each province has adapted for its own police officers. Ontario has its own **Use-of-Force Continuum model**, which is taught to all recruits at Ontario Police College and is reinforced through service training with individual police services throughout the province. The purpose of the Continuum is to provide a guideline to officers regarding various levels of threat and resistance. It is meant to enable them to arrive rapidly at a logical response to a volatile situation.

The Use-of-Force Continuum model is not meant to give officers justification for a particular level of force, but rather to help them explain why they chose a particular response. This is important: an officer must always be prepared to justify the level of force he or she applied. The Continuum is not prescriptive, either. The strategies identified for controlling a subject are suggestions, not requirements. For example, sometimes the best move an officer can make is to disengage or wait for support, rather than to move to the next reactive phase identified in the model. It is worth noting that the model's shape—circular rather than linear—is meant to convey this discretionary element. Linear models, drawn step by step, imply a steady increase in the level of aggression involved in any encounter. A circular model suggests the possibility of some movement back and forth between the different levels of response. (See Figure 5.1.)

The Use-of-Force Continuum model is a visual diagram of suggested responses. It is not meant to provide precise guidelines; it is an "at-a-glance" learning aid. One training officer commented that, when officers are faced with a situation that may require the use of force, the model's simplicity can help them. That is the point of the Continuum—to provide a reference point that an officer can quickly use to formulate a strategic response.

Applying the Use-of-Force Continuum

Now let's interpret the Use-of-Force Continuum. Consider the very centre of the diagram to represent the officer's arrival at the scene of a situation. Officers must, as the first ring outside the centre indicates, immediately assess the situation, make a plan of action, and then act. (Keep in mind that the officer's choice of action, on arriving at the site of an incident, might be simply to disengage or wait for backup.) It has been noted (Osborne, 2013, p. 2) that officers have three goals at this point:

1. to prevent escalation of the incident,
2. to de-escalate the incident, and
3. to maintain public and personal safety while achieving the first two goals.

behavioural profile
one measure of the risk posed by a subject, categorized as either cooperative, passive or active resistant, assaultive, or threatening grievous bodily harm or death

The first thing that the officer must assess is the level of threat. This assessment is based on the **behavioural profiles** of the individuals involved. The range of possible behaviours is shown in the second ring of the continuum figure:

1. *Cooperative*: There is no threat and the person is compliant.
2. *Passive resistant*: The person is not acting aggressively toward police, but is noncompliant. This level also applies to someone who may be completely inactive, possibly even lying rigid or limp.

FIGURE 5.1   Ontario Use-of-Force Continuum Model

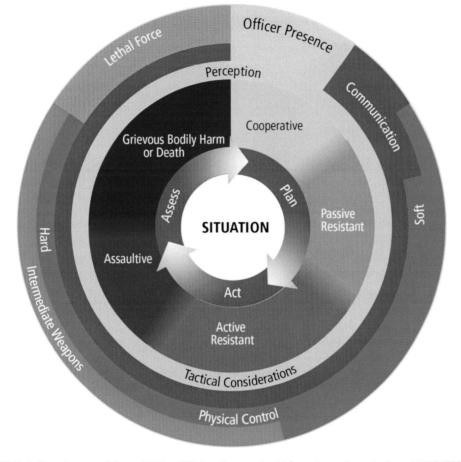

SOURCE: Hoffman, Lawrence, & Brown (2004, p. 132). http://www.policechiefmagazine.org/magazine/issues/102004/PDFS/page132_fig3.pdf. Canadian Association of Chiefs of Police. Used with permission.

3. *Active resistant*: The person is not exhibiting assaultive behaviour toward the officer, but uses words and/or the body to avoid cooperating, is refusing to comply, and may even be issuing verbal threats.

4. *Assaultive*: This person is using intentional physical force, directly or indirectly. His or her actions may include spitting, biting, punching, kicking, or other physical manoeuvres.

5. *Grievous bodily harm or death*: The person is using physical force, possibly involving a weapon, in an effort to seriously injure or kill the officer.

There are patterns in day-to-day human behaviour, but individuals in crisis function much less predictably. Their behaviour could begin at any level of the Continuum and then progress from one level to the next. Or, quite possibly, it could move in the opposite direction. Good police training provides officers with the tools to assess an individual's movement within this continuum of behaviours. It also provides officers with the skills—physical, communicative, and psychological—to effectively respond to and manage difficult situations.

Officers attending a situation have six possible responses, according to the use-of-force framework. Which of these responses is appropriate depends on the level of threat. The possible responses, presented in the outer ring of Figure 5.1, are as follows:

1. *Officer presence*: Often the mere presence of police will stop negative behaviours, including behaviours that involve all levels of threat.

2. *Communication*: This may include calming the situation. Officers can use encouraging words, warnings, or negotiation tactics, or can communicate possible consequences.

3. *Soft physical control*: These tactics, which would include handcuffing the person in order to control him or her, are less likely to cause injury.

4. *Hard physical control*: This level of force includes the use of empty hand strikes to stop a subject's behaviour. These tactics are more likely to cause injury, but are not likely to be lethal or cause grievous injury.

5. *Intermediate weapons*: This level of action involves the use of aerosol sprays, conducted energy weapons (for example, tasers), or impact weapons (for example, batons) to incapacitate a subject and stop his or her resistance or assaultive behaviour. While these tactics can cause injury and discomfort, there is still little risk of serious injury or death.

6. *Lethal force*: This level represents the last resort and the least preferred tactic. The death of a subject is never a goal, but the use of lethal force is sanctioned when there is a genuine threat to the life of a member of the public or of an officer (Pelley, 2009).

Criticism of the Continuum and an Alternative Approach

The Use-of-Force Continuum model is not without its critics. Officers appreciate its concrete logic, but some observers have noted that it focuses entirely on behavioural threat. This seems sensible when you think about physical safety, but different circumstances call for different responses. For example, the Canadian Mental Health Association (Ontario) has recommended (CMHA, 2008) that when police are dealing with people who are psychologically disordered or distressed, they should consider alternatives to tasers. The CMHA report states the following:

> Ontario's Use-of-Force Model does not make allowance or offer guidance to police officers when encountering individuals who may be experiencing a mental health crisis and by virtue of their condition may not appear cooperative, due to hallucinations, delusions or other symptoms. However, other options are available, and mental health crisis intervention is the preferred approach for police to de-escalate such encounters.

The CMHA has made recommendations for alternative crisis management with mentally ill and distressed subjects. Significantly, they recommend that police work directly with the mental health system in first-response situations. The CMHA endorses the models described in Table 5.2.

Many police services, such as those in Ottawa, Toronto, and London, have begun to implement these models. The officers in these services are strong proponents of the programs, but they cite the need for increased resources, including more money and staffing. In addition, the Canadian Association of Chiefs of Police has developed guidelines for police programs and services with a goal of "effective and compassionate crisis response" (CMHA, 2008).

TABLE 5.2 Models for Crisis Intervention Involving People with Mental Illness

Model	Description
Comprehensive advanced response	Police receive in-service training in managing situations that involve mental health crisis
Mental health professionals co-response	Police automatically have mental health workers assisting at mental health calls
Mobile crisis team co-response	Interdisciplinary deployment of mental health workers and police; police working in mental health agencies and mental health workers working at police services
Crisis intervention team (CIT)	Team of specially trained officers designated to duties from which they may be easily freed as required
Telephone consultation	24/7 access, by telephone, to a staffed psychiatric unit of a hospital or mental health facility

SOURCE: Mental Health Association (2008, p. 4).

IT'S YOUR MOVE, OFFICER!

Scenario 5.4

While on foot patrol in your patrol area, you and your partner are approached by a distraught woman. She asks the two of you to come to her apartment. Her boyfriend has locked himself in her bedroom and is threatening to hang himself. They have just had a big fight and she has a split lip; she claims he hit her.

When you enter the apartment, you attempt to speak to the boyfriend. He swears at you and tells you that his life is his own business. After some time, you learn that he is about to lose his job, and that he believes he has evidence that his girlfriend is cheating on him. Snooping through her cellphone, he found sexual messages.

As you try to determine whether he has a weapon, you learn that he has just come home from work and that he is an off-duty security guard. He came home in uniform, which, according to the girlfriend, means he has a baton and handcuffs. After about 15 minutes, he decides to come out of the bedroom. He still has his baton on his duty belt. You decide to arrest him for the assault on his girlfriend. He turns to go back into the bedroom.

1. How would you classify his response?
2. What use-of-force option is available to you according to the Use-of-Force Continuum?
3. If you decide to use force, are your actions justified under the *Criminal Code*? Explain.

CHECK YOUR UNDERSTANDING

1. Identify the six responses available to officers when they are using the Use-of-Force Continuum model as a response guideline.
2. Identify the five potential reactions that subjects may have to police presence, according to the Use-of-Force Continuum.
3. The Use-of-Force Continuum model provides rules for officers to follow when dealing with a member of the public. Is this statement true or false? Explain.

CHAPTER SUMMARY

In this chapter, we have considered the role of force in law enforcement. Police officers must sometimes use force, because some subjects are not cooperative or compliant. Force is required to arrest offenders, to ensure their attendance in court, or to ensure the public's safety. Section 25 of the *Criminal Code* authorizes police officers to use force, thus providing them with legal protection in the event force is needed. To qualify for this protection, however, the officer must always be acting in the lawful performance of his or her duty and must be acting on reasonable grounds. Section 26 of the Code prohibits the use of excessive force and makes officers and civilians criminally liable for using excessive force. In addition, the Code provides use-of-force authority for self-defence (s. 34) and for preventing an offence (s. 27).

Provincial statutes also provide some use-of-force authority. While Ontario's *Provincial Offences Act* provides a general authority in s. 146(1), officers need to be familiar with the use-of-force authorities that certain other acts provide. Examples of statutes that provide their own use-of-force authorities are the *Liquor Licence Act* and the *Child and Family Services Act*. The Ontario *Police Services Act*, though it does not provide use-of-force authority, prescribes the training that officers must undergo in order to use force. The PSA also describes the weapons that can be used, their specifications, and the training and requalification rules that apply to them. The PSA also identifies when an officer may use a firearm and provides a standardized use-of-force report for submission under prescribed circumstances.

The final section of the chapter dealt with the Ontario Use-of-Force Continuum model, and we looked at the factors that could affect the outcome of a police–subject interaction. Officer perceptions, subject behaviour, and tactical considerations create a dynamic environment for police response. In addition, we considered the Canadian Mental Health Association recommendations on police response to crises involving mental health or psychiatric factors. The CMHA suggests a separate intervention approach when police officers are dealing with mentally ill subjects who are in crisis.

To summarize, force is a tool for law enforcement to use in order to gain compliance with the law and in order to keep the public and the police safe. It must be used judiciously.

KEY TERMS

behavioural factors, 105
behavioural profile, 106
excessive force, 99
force, 96

lethal force, 99
objective standard, 97
reasonable force, 99
situational factors, 105

subjective elements, 97
tactical factors, 105
Use-of-Force Continuum model, 106

REFERENCES

Canadian Mental Health Association (CMHA), Ontario. (2008, June 1). Conducted energy weapons (tasers). *Public Policy*. Retrieved from http://ontario.cmha.ca/public_policy/conducted-energy -weapons-tasers/.

Child and Family Services Act. (1990). RSO 1990, c. C.11.

Criminal Code. (1985). RSC 1985, c. C-46.

Hoffman, M.A., Lawrence, C., & Brown, G. (2004). Canada's national use-of-force framework for police officers. *The Police Chief, 71*(10), 125-126. Retrieved from http://www.policechiefmagazine .org/magazine/index.cfm?fuseaction=display_arch&article_id=1397&issue_id=102004.

Liquor Licence Act. (1990). RSO 1990, c. L.19.

Nasogaluak, R v. 2010 SCC 6, [2010] 1 SCR 206.

Osborne, R.F. (2013, February 11). Re: 2012 Annual use of force report [Memorandum to Chief P. Nelson]. Sarnia Police Service. Retrieved from http://www.sarniapolice.com/wp-content/ uploads/2011/01/2012-use-of-force.pdf.

Pelley, L. (2009, October 22). Forced to react: Police officers explain "Use of Force" continuum. *The Western Gazette*. Retrieved from http://www.westerngazette.ca/2009/10/22/forced-to-react -police-officers-explain-%E2%80%9Cuse-of-force%E2%80%9D-continuum/.

Police Services Act, RRO 1990, Reg. 926. (1990). Equipment and use of force.

Provincial Offences Act. (1990). RSO 1990, c. P.33.

Storrey, R v. (1990). [1990] 1 SCR 241, 1990 CanLII 125.

Toronto Police Service. (2013). *Professional standards: Annual report 2013*. Retrieved from http://www.torontopolice.on.ca/publications/files/reports/prs2013annualreport.pdf.

FURTHER READING

Butler, C. (2009). The use of force model and its application to operational law enforcement— Where have we been and where are we going? Retrieved from http://www.cacole.ca/ resource%20library/conferences/2009%20Conference/Chris%20Butler.pdf.

Canadian Mental Health Association (CMHA), Ontario. (2008, June 1). Conducted energy weapons (tasers). *Public Policy*. Retrieved from http://ontario.cmha.ca/public_policy/conducted-energy -weapons-tasers/#.VDkqMPlSZLO.

Pelley, L. (2009, October 22). Forced to react: Police officers explain "Use of Force" continuum. *The Western Gazette*. Retrieved from http://www.westerngazette.ca/2009/10/22/ forced-to-react-police-officers-explain-%E2%80%9Cuse-of-force%E2%80%9D-continuum/.

Toronto Police Service. (2013). *Professional standards: Annual report 2013*. http://www.torontopolice.on.ca/publications/files/reports/prs2013annualreport.pdf.

The Police Policy Studies Council. (2010). A research-based, interdisciplinary, training and consultation corporation. Retrieved from http://www.theppsc.org.

REVIEW QUESTIONS

Multiple Choice

1. The Use-of-Force Continuum model includes six possible police responses. These include

   a. officer presence, communication, soft physical control

   b. officer presence, communication, hard physical control

   c. communication, hard physical control, intermediate weapons, lethal force

   d. all of the above

2. Police and other law enforcement personnel are legally authorized to use force if

   a. they are doing something required by law

   b. they are doing something regarding law enforcement only

   c. they are acting on reasonable grounds

   d. all of the above

3. Section 146 of the *Provincial Offences Act* is not the primary source of use-of-force authority for the following statute:

   a. the *Highway Traffic Act*

   b. the *Child and Family Services Act*

   c. the *Trespass to Property Act*

   d. a and c

4. The *Child and Family Services Act* use-of-force protection applies to

   a. a person authorized to bring a child to a place of safety

   b. child protection workers only

   c. peace officers only

   d. none of the above

5. If a police officer believes, on reasonable grounds, that doing so is necessary to protect against loss of life or serious bodily harm, then he or she is justified, under the Ontario PSA, in

   a. drawing, pointing, or discharging a firearm

   b. drawing, pointing, or using any weapon

   c. instructing a civilian to draw, point, or discharge a firearm

   d. instructing a civilian to draw, point, or use any weapon

True or False

1. Section 26 of the *Criminal Code* provides legal protection for persons in authority when they need to use excessive force.

2. A police officer is criminally responsible if he or she uses excessive force.

3. The presence of a uniform officer is in itself a level of force according to the Use-of-Force Continuum model.

4. The CMHA believes the Use-of-Force Continuum model is adequate and effective in dealing with mentally ill subjects in crisis.

5. A police officer is not required to submit a use-of-force report if he or she merely unholsters his or her firearm in the course of his or her duties.

6. Reasonable grounds require only that an officer's subjective view of a situation be considered.

7. A subject in a police response situation will move predictably and progressively through the steps of the behavioural profile set out in the Use-of-Force Continuum.

8. A subject offering passive resistance requires hard physical control in every situation.

9. The principal reason for police to use force, according to one large urban police service, is to euthanize injured or dangerous animals.

10. Only police officers and security guards are authorized by law to use force.

Short Answer

1. Discuss the subjective and objective components of reasonable grounds.

2. What would be the role of a crisis intervention team, as identified in the CMHA recommendations, in responding to the mentally ill in crisis?

3. How is the Use-of-Force Continuum model used by police in responding to incidents?

4. Under what circumstances may lethal force be justified?

5. What are the categories of factors that an officer needs to consider in responding to an incident?

It's Your Move, Officer!

A. You are working one night when you receive a call from the dispatcher regarding a subject with mental health issues. The dispatcher informs you that a mother has called about her son. He is destroying the house, smashing and breaking glass and furniture. You and your partner arrive at the house. The mother lets you in and informs you that the son is upstairs. As you and your partner proceed toward the stairs, you see the subject approaching you, carrying a gun. You issue the standard police challenge: "Police, don't move!" The subject drops the gun, but continues to walk toward you and your partner.

1. Which category of behaviour on the Use-of-Force Continuum reflects the actions of this subject?
2. What would be a suitable response by police?

B. One Sunday morning, you and your partner respond to a dispatch to a possible threat of suicide. When you arrive at the house, you speak to a young man who tells you that his mother, who is in the living room, is quite depressed. He believes she may be suicidal. Upon speaking with the woman, you are able to determine that she is thinking of killing herself, possibly with insomnia medication. She resists the idea of accompanying you to a hospital for evaluation.

1. Which behaviour profile reflects the actions of the subject?
2. What would be a suitable response by police?

Releasing and Charging a Suspect

6

LEARNING OUTCOMES

After completing this chapter, you should be able to:

- Explain the concepts of interim and judicial interim release.

- Explain how the *Canadian Charter of Rights and Freedoms* and the *Criminal Code* relate to interim release.

- Identify the individuals responsible for determining if an accused will be released.

- Identify the documents used to release and compel an accused to attend court, and explain when and how they are used.

- Explain circumstances under which release may be denied.

- Describe the process of charging a suspect.

A police officer is walking his beat when he observes a teenage girl. She is familiar to him. He has encountered her a number of times over the past year and knows where she lives and goes to school. She used to hang out with a group of teenagers known for committing minor theft and causing damage to local homes and businesses. The officer previously arranged for the girl to receive assistance from a community group. Though he hasn't seen her for several weeks, he has heard that she is no longer hanging out with the problem teenagers.

The officer is watching the girl from a short distance away when suddenly she picks up a rock and throws it through the window of a bakery. After a short foot pursuit, the officer detains the girl. He learns from her that she worked in the bakery for several weeks. Her employment there ended recently when the bakery owner accused her of stealing from the cash register and fired her. The girl denied the accusation and tried to prove her innocence. The owner refused to listen to her explanation.

The owner of the bakery wants the teenager charged for smashing his window. The officer determines that it is not in the public interest to arrest her, but he feels it is important to charge her with mischief and have her attend court to answer the charge. The girl tells the officer that she wants to go to court to tell her side of the story to a judge.

What process will the officer use to bring the girl to court to answer the charge? How can he release the girl at the scene, but still compel her appearance at court? What are the consequences if the girl does not attend court?

Introduction

As a police officer, what do you do after you have arrested an individual under the authority of s. 495 of the *Criminal Code*? Or what do you do if you have detained an individual who was in the process of committing or had just committed an offence? As you have seen, policing in Canada is a delicate balance; it requires protecting the public interest while respecting and protecting the rights of the accused, which are guaranteed under the *Canadian Charter of Rights and Freedoms*.

To respect individual rights while protecting the public interest, our laws favour the pre-trial release of an accused person rather than his or her pre-trial detention. The police and courts are required to justify continued detention of an accused person and to justify any release conditions that have been imposed on release. Barring exceptional circumstances, persons charged with a criminal offence must be released from custody during the period between original detention or arrest and their appearance in court. The Code provides specific details on when, how, and by whom an accused person will be released. In this chapter, we will explore release requirements, with particular attention to the requirements imposed on peace officers.

Interim Release Defined

interim release
releasing an accused person from custody with a document compelling his or her appearance in court

The term **interim release** refers to the pre-trial release of a suspect. This must occur, except in very specific circumstances, as soon as certain conditions are fulfilled. The issue of interim release arises as soon as a police officer takes active steps to detain an individual whom he or she suspects of having committed (or of being in the process of committing) an offence against the Code.

Generally speaking, there are three categories of locations from which an accused person may be released: street level, station level, and court level. Which person is responsible for releasing an accused person depends on the location of the release (see Table 6.1).

TABLE 6.1   Individuals Responsible for Release

Level	Who Makes the Release?	Description of the Releaser
Street level	Arresting officer	Generally the officer who detained or arrested the accused
Station level	Officer in charge at the police station	Officer at the police station who has responsibility for the accused and is authorized by law to release the accused
Court level	Justice	Justice of the peace or a judge of a provincial court

Interim Release, the Charter, and the Criminal Code

There are several sections of the Charter that are particularly relevant to the discussion of interim release. They are the following:

- Section 9—Everyone has the right not to be arbitrarily detained or imprisoned.
- Section 11(d)—Any person charged with an offence has the right to be presumed innocent until proven guilty according to law in a fair and public hearing by an independent and impartial tribunal.
- Section 11(e)—Any person charged with an offence has the right not to be denied reasonable **bail** without just cause. (*Bail* is any form of interim release that is authorized by law.)

bail
any form of interim release authorized by law

These sections of the Charter are closely related. For example, denying an individual bail may cause the accused person to appear guilty prior to his or her conviction.

An individual's Charter rights are protected under the Code and under other laws. For example, the presumption of innocence is outlined in s. 6(1)(a) of the Code, which states that "a person shall be deemed not to be guilty of the offence until he is convicted or discharged." Sections 494 through 523 of the Code describe the conditions under which an accused person can be held or released.

The Code also ensures that an accused person is not "arbitrarily detained." The general principle is that the accused must be released as soon as possible. The actual rules governing interim release, however, are somewhat complex; they differ according to the position of the person responsible for the accused's release. Section 503(1) of the Code is very specific about what must happen to an accused person following arrest:

503(1) A peace officer who arrests a person with or without warrant or to whom a person is delivered under subsection 494(3) or into whose custody a person is placed under subsection 163.5(3) of the *Customs Act* shall cause the person to be detained in custody and, in accordance with the following provisions, to be taken before a justice to be dealt with according to law:

(a) where a justice is available within a period of twenty-four hours after the person has been arrested by or delivered to the peace officer, the person shall be taken before a justice without unreasonable delay and in any event within that period, and

(b) where a justice is not available within a period of twenty-four hours after the person has been arrested by or delivered to the peace officer, the person shall be taken before a justice as soon as possible,

unless, at any time before the expiration of the time prescribed in paragraph (a) or (b) for taking the person before a justice,

(c) the peace officer or officer in charge releases the person under any other provision of this Part, or

(d) the peace officer or officer in charge is satisfied that the person should be released from custody, whether unconditionally under subsection (4) or otherwise conditionally or unconditionally, and so releases him.

To summarize, the peace officer or officer in charge will release the accused either unconditionally or with the condition to attend court at a later date. If the accused is not released, he or she is to be brought before a justice without delay, if possible within 24 hours of the arrest. Section 503(1) of the Code states that if a justice is not available within 24 hours (rarely the case in urban areas of Canada, but it does happen in less populous, rural areas), the person is to be brought before a justice as soon as possible. The police and the courts are required to justify continued detention of an accused person, as well as any release conditions that have been imposed.

CHECK YOUR UNDERSTANDING

1. There are three categories of persons responsible for the release of an accused person. Name these three persons.

2. Which section of the Charter is best reflected in s. 6.1 of the Code, which provides that a person shall be deemed not to be guilty of the offence until he is convicted or discharged?

3. Explain the restrictions on how long a person can be detained before appearing before a justice. What part(s) of the Code describes this limitation?

The Decision to Release

As we discussed in Chapter 3, Arrest Powers, a police officer, except in certain circumstances, is not required to arrest a suspect. In fact, the Code specifically identifies the circumstances in which an officer *shall not* arrest. Whether imposed by the Code or based on the officer's own discretion, the decision not to arrest a suspect is itself a form of release. Rather than detaining the suspect for any period of time, the officer simply allows the suspect to continue to enjoy his or her liberty.

Mandatory Release

mandatory release
compulsory release of the accused from custody by a peace officer or the officer in charge

There are circumstances where a police officer *must* release an accused person if doing so is in the public interest. This is referred to as **mandatory release**. Release is mandatory for certain types of offences and under certain conditions, as shown in Table 6.2.

TABLE 6.2   Mandatory Release

Releasing Officer	Offences	Conditions
Arresting officer	• Summary conviction offences • Dual procedure offences • Indictable offences listed in s. 553	• The arrest was without a warrant • PRICE fulfilled before the accused person arrives at the station
Officer in charge	• Summary conviction offences • Dual procedure offences • Indictable offences listed in s. 553 • Offences punishable by imprisonment for 5 years or less	• The arrest was without a warrant or with a warrant endorsed by a justice to allow release • PRICE fulfilled after the accused person arrives at the station

Discretionary Release

With offences that do not involve mandatory release, police are able to use discretion regarding release. Circumstances under which **discretionary release** occurs include those where release is made with no intention of charging the individual. The following factors must be considered when police are deciding whether to release a suspect:

- the type of offence,
- public interest, and
- specific facts about the case and the accused.

discretionary release release of the accused by a peace officer or the officer in charge that is not mandatory, but is done on the basis of the officer's own judgment

Type of Offence

For the purpose of release, the Code divides criminal offences into three categories.

1. Summary conviction offences, dual procedure (hybrid) offences, and indictable offences listed in s. 553. (Offence categories are discussed in more detail in Chapter 3.)
2. The offences listed above (summary conviction offences, dual procedure (hybrid) offences, and indictable offences listed in s. 553), plus those offences that have a maximum punishment of five years or less.
3. Offences listed in s. 469. Section 469 lists very serious offences, such as treason, murder, seditious offences, and piracy. These offences fall within the absolute jurisdiction of the superior court of criminal jurisdiction. Police officers have no authority to release a person accused of a s. 469 offence.

For offences in the first category, an officer at the street level may make the decision to release. For offences in the second category, the officer in charge at the station may make this decision. As you progress through this chapter, it will become clearer to you how the type of offence affects the release decision and who makes this decision.

Public Interest

Public interest, as we saw in Chapter 3, is a consideration for an officer trying to decide whether to arrest a suspect without a warrant. It is similarly a consideration in an officer's decision whether to release a suspect. Various sections of the Code describe *public interest* and the conditions that must be met to preserve it. Section 497(1.1) states the following:

(1.1) A peace officer shall not release a person ... if the peace officer believes, on reasonable grounds,

(a) that it is necessary in the public interest that the person be detained in custody or that the matter of their release from custody be dealt with under another provision of this Part, having regard to all the circumstances including the need to

(i) establish the identity of the person,

(ii) secure or preserve evidence of or relating to the offence,

(iii) prevent the continuation or repetition of the offence or the commission of another offence, or

(iv) ensure the safety and security of any victim of or witness to the offence; or

(b) that if the person is released from custody, the person will fail to attend court in order to be dealt with according to law.

Section 498(1.1) outlines these same conditions for an officer in charge.

These release conditions are often represented with the acronym PRICE, which we introduced in Chapter 3. To reiterate, it stands for the following:

- *Public interest.* Ensure the safety and security of any victim of or witness to the offence.

- *Repetition.* Prevent the continuation or repetition of the offence or the commission of another offence.

- *Identity.* Establish the identity of the accused person.

- *Court.* Ensure that the person will attend court to answer the charges.

- *Evidence.* Secure or preserve evidence of or relating to the offence.

The PRICE criteria can be applied to release at both the street and the station levels. Generally, if the PRICE criteria are met, a suspect should be released. Conversely, if any of the conditions under PRICE are not met, the accused person should *not* be released. For example, an accused person would not be released, or his or her release would be delayed, in the following situations:

- *Public interest.* The accused represents a threat to the victim, witnesses, or any other person.

- *Repetition.* The officer believes the accused person will repeat or continue the offence—for example, in a case where an intoxicated person has been arrested for causing a disturbance and is likely to continue causing a disturbance if released at the scene.

- *Identity.* The accused person refuses to give his or her full name, or his or her identity cannot be established to the satisfaction of the releasing officer.

- *Court.* The person has given the police officer reason to believe that he or she will leave the jurisdiction and fail to attend court if released.

- *Evidence.* There is reason to believe that the person will destroy evidence if released, so the person should not be released until that evidence has been secured.

Here are a couple of examples of how PRICE might be applied:

- *Example 1*: A police officer has arrested an individual for a domestic-related offence. The accused and the victim are husband and wife, respectively, and live in the same home. In a case like this, the officer would not release this arrested individual because if he is released and returns home, reasonable grounds exist to believe that he would threaten or harm the victim. Reasonable grounds also exist to believe that the accused would repeat the offence. Research shows that domestic assault involves a pattern of repetition; it will likely have occurred many times before the police are called, and it will likely continue unless police intervene. In this example, therefore, two conditions of PRICE—both the public interest element and the repetition element—have not been met.

- *Example 2*: A police officer has been called to a local department store because shoplifting has occurred. The accused was lawfully arrested by store security and held for police. The accused has satisfactorily identified himself to the police. It is the first time he has committed theft or any other criminal offence. All of the stolen property has been recovered and returned to the store. The accused has indicated that he will attend court as required. In this case, all aspects of PRICE have been met, so the accused should be released.

Specific Facts About the Case and the Accused

Before deciding whether to release the suspect, police officers often need to consider certain facts about the case and the release order. For example, if the accused was arrested on the authority of a warrant, the police officer cannot release the accused person without a justice's permission. This permission may come in the form either of an endorsement on the warrant or of an order from a justice after a bail hearing.

There are other factors concerning the accused that need to be considered. For example, the location of the accused's residence must be considered. In Alberta, for example, the accused should be released if the person is a resident of that province who lives within 200 kilometres of the location where he or she is being held in custody. If the person is not a resident of Alberta or lives outside the 200-kilometre radius, the release conditions are more stringent.

CHECK YOUR UNDERSTANDING

1. For the purpose of release, the Code divides criminal offences into three categories. List the types of offences that are included in each category.

2. Suspects accused of less serious offences should be released unless it is not in the public interest. What does s. 497(1.1)(a) of the Code include in its definition of public interest?

3. Name and describe the five elements of PRICE.

Compelling Appearance in Court: Forms

Specific steps must be taken to ensure that a person released from custody attends court to answer the charge(s) against him or her. The process of releasing an accused person involves issuing one of several kinds of documents that compel the accused person to attend court on a certain date, time, and place to answer to the charges against him or her. These are called **compelling documents**.

Each of these documents contains, at a minimum, the following information:

- the name of the accused;
- the offence(s) the accused is facing; and
- a requirement that the accused attend court at the date, time, and location specified in the document and thereafter, as required by the court.

compelling document
a document that compels an individual to attend court to answer a criminal charge (for example, a summons, an appearance notice, a promise to appear, a recognizance to officer in charge or justice, or an undertaking entered into before a justice)

Compelling documents may call for other information required by law, or may list conditions or promises to which the accused person is required to agree as a condition of his or her release.

Street-Level Release

At the street level, officers immediately serve an accused person with a notice that obligates the accused to attend court. Alternatively, the officer can release the person with the intention of later serving him or her with a document that will compel a court appearance.

Appearance Notice

There is one form available to an officer on the street to release and compel the accused to attend court. This form is the **appearance notice** (Form 9). (For an example, see the Appendix at the end of this chapter.) The appearance notice is used by the arresting/detaining officer when

- the offence the person is suspected of committing is a summary conviction offence, a hybrid offence, or an indictable offence listed in s. 553, and the officer has chosen not to arrest the individual, but wants to compel him or her to attend court to answer the charge; or
- the officer has chosen to arrest the individual without a warrant, and all elements of PRICE have been fulfilled.

The requirements of a Form 9 are defined in the Code. In addition to the information mentioned above (that is, name, offence, and court date), a Form 9 must contain the text of the following provisions from the Code:

- Sections 145(5) and 145(6)—the offence of failing to comply with an appearance notice; and
- Section 502—failure to appear in court.

Also, if the suspect is accused of an indictable offence, the appearance notice (Form 9) will contain a clause requiring the accused to appear at a stated date, time, and place to have his or her fingerprints and photograph taken under the authority of the *Identification of Criminals Act*.

Summons

An arresting officer may release the accused unconditionally with the intention of serving a summons on him or her later. A **summons** (Form 6—see the Appendix at the end of this chapter) is issued by a justice after receiving an **information** under oath (we will discuss an information later in the chapter). Once issued, a summons must be personally served on the accused (that is, given directly to the accused by an officer). The summons will contain the same information as the appearance notice and will compel the accused to attend court and, in the case of an indictable offence, compel his or her attendance for fingerprinting and photographing.

A summons is used when the following four conditions are met:

- The accused is charged with a summary conviction offence, a hybrid offence, or an indictable offence listed in s. 553.
- The officer has arrested the person without a warrant.

appearance notice
a notice in Form 9, issued by a peace officer (street level), that compels an accused person to appear in court at a specific date, time, and location

summons
a summons in Form 6, issued by a justice or judge, requiring an accused person to appear in court at a specific date, time, and location (the document is later served on the accused person personally)

information
a document that begins all criminal proceedings and that contains the charge (counts) against the accused

TABLE 6.3   Release Options at the Street Level (Officer in the Field)

Offences	Options	Forms	Purpose of Form
Summary conviction, hybrid, and indictable offences listed in s. 553	Unconditional release	None	
	Unconditional release with intent to summons	Summons (Form 6)	Compel attendance in court
	Release and compel attendance in court	Appearance notice (Form 9)	Release from custody, compel attendance in court, and compel attendance for fingerprinting and photographing
	Continue custody	None	

- All elements of PRICE have been fulfilled and the officer has released the accused person unconditionally.
- An information will be laid as soon as possible thereafter with respect to the charges.

If the accused cannot be released at the scene due to the nature of the offence(s) that he or she is charged with, or due to the fact that one of the elements of PRICE has not been met, then the officer will take the accused to a police station.

IT'S YOUR MOVE, OFFICER!

Scenario 6.1

You are a police officer in the city of St. John's. You have been called to a local drugstore to deal with a shoplifter. At the scene you meet the store's loss prevention officer, who tells you that a young female has taken a quantity of makeup without paying for it, all of which has been recovered. The loss prevention officer tells you that the female has been arrested for theft under $5,000. She is refusing to identify herself.

You ask the female suspect to identify herself and she replies, "I don't have to tell you anything." At this point, you arrest the female for theft under $5,000 and advise her of her right to speak with counsel. You then inform her that she will be taken to the police station and that if she continues to refuse to identify herself, she will be taken to court for a hearing. The female suddenly has a change of heart, apologizes, and tells you her name, address, and date of birth. When you perform a check on the woman's information, you learn that she lives in St. John's and has no criminal record.

1. Is it mandatory for you to release this female? What must you consider in order to determine the answer to this question? How will you compel her to attend court?

Station-Level Release

Once an accused is arrested and brought to a police station, the responsibility of determining whether to release him or her falls on the officer in charge. The range of release options available to the officer in charge is broader than those available to the officer in the field.

Source: The Canadian Press Images/Lee Brown.

At the station level, police may release the accused on the basis of a promise to appear—in other words, a promise that he or she will appear in court. In other cases, the accused may be held.

Promise to Appear

promise to appear
a promise in Form 10, issued by an officer in charge (station level), requiring the accused person to attend court at a specific date, time, and location

The first option for the officer in charge is to issue a **promise to appear** (Form 10). (For an example of a Form 10, see the Appendix at the end of this chapter.) This document serves the same purpose as the appearance notice and contains the same information. The requirements of a Form 10 are defined in the Code. In addition to the information mentioned above (that is, name, offence, and court date), a Form 10 must contain the text of the following provisions of the Code:

- ss. 145(5) and (6), which create the offence of failing to comply with an appearance notice; and
- s. 502, which creates the offence of failure to appear in court.

If the offence for which the suspect is accused is an indictable offence, Form 9 will also contain a clause requiring the accused to appear at a stated date, time, and place to have his or her fingerprints and photograph taken under the authority of the *Identification of Criminals Act*.

Recognizance

recognizance
a document, issued by the officer in charge or by a justice, that requires an accused person to agree to meet certain obligations in exchange for being released from custody, and that also requires the accused person to appear in court at a specific date, time, and location

According to s. 503(2), the second option available to the officer in charge is a **recognizance** (Form 11—see the Appendix at the end of this chapter). The recognizance may be used under the same circumstances as the promise to appear and has the same effect: it releases the accused from custody and compels his or her appearance in court. The difference between these two methods is that the recognizance involves the use of **sureties**. When using a recognizance, the accused agrees that he or she will owe the Queen (that is, the government) an amount not exceeding $500 if he or she fails to attend court. Under s. 498(1)(c) of the Code, the accused is not required to deposit a surety. However, as s. 498(1)(d) prescribes, the officer in charge can require a surety in an amount not exceeding $500 if the accused is not ordinarily a resident in the province or does not ordinarily reside within 200 kilometres of the place in which the individual is in custody.

sureties
the deposit of something of value with the police or court to ensure that the accused person will attend court

Consider the following example. An Alberta resident has been arrested for impaired driving in Ontario, and meets the requirements of PRICE. The officer in charge has the option of requiring him to deposit up to $500 when being released on a recognizance. If the accused appears at court as required, the money will be returned. If the accused fails to appear in court as required, the money is forfeited to the Crown and, in addition, the accused can be charged with failing to appear.

Undertaking

A third option that an officer in charge has is the use of an **undertaking** (Form 11.1—see the Appendix at the end of this chapter) in conjunction with the promise to appear or a recognizance. This option is described in s. 503(2.1) of the Code. An undertaking does not compel an accused to attend court in the way that an appearance notice, a promise to appear, and a recognizance do. The undertaking allows the officer in charge to require further promises from the accused as a requirement of release. These can include any combination of the following promises:

- to remain in the territorial jurisdiction specified in the undertaking;
- to notify the police of any change of address, employment, or occupation;
- to abstain from communicating with specified persons or from going to specified places;
- to deposit his or her passport with the police;
- to abstain from possessing a firearm and to turn over to the police any firearm that he or she may already possess, along with any documents in his or her possession that enable him or her to acquire or possess a firearm;
- to report to the police at specified times; and
- to abstain from consumption of alcohol or illicit drugs.

undertaking
an undertaking in Form 11.1 or 12, used in conjunction with a promise to appear or with a recognizance (if issued by the officer in charge), that requires an accused person to meet certain obligations in exchange for being released from custody and that may also require (if issued by a justice) the accused person to attend court at a specific date, time, and place

TABLE 6.4 Release Options at the Station Level (Officer in Charge)

Offences	Options	Forms	Purpose of Form
Summary conviction, hybrid, and indictable offences listed in s. 553, and offences punishable by a maximum of 5 years	Unconditional release	None	
	Unconditional release with intent to summons	Summons (Form 6)	Compel attendance in court
	Release and compel attendance in court	Promise to appear (Form 10), with or without Form 11.1	Release from custody, compel attendance in court, and compel attendance for fingerprinting and photographing
		Recognizance to officer in charge (Form 11) with or without Form 11.1, with or without surety	Release from custody, compel attendance in court, and compel attendance for fingerprinting and photographing
		Undertaking to officer in charge (Form 11.1) (Note: Form 11.1 must be used with a Form 10 or a Form 11.)	Impose restrictions on accused as a condition of release

For example, it is often the case that the accused will have met all the requirements of PRICE, but has a relationship with the victim or witness that raises the risk of his or her repeating the offence. Under these circumstances, a release may be granted, but it is granted under the condition that the accused is prohibited from contacting the victim or witness directly or indirectly, or from going to an address where the victim or witness lives or works.

The use of conditions through the undertaking cannot be a form of punishment imposed on the accused. The conditions must be reasonable in light of the totality of the circumstances of the accused and the offence he or she is accused of. Unreasonable conditions may constitute denying the accused the right to reasonable bail, which is a violation of his or her Charter rights.

The accused must agree to the conditions listed in the undertaking and must sign the undertaking document. Failure to agree or to sign can indicate that one of the elements of PRICE has not been met, and on that basis the officer in charge may refuse to release the accused before a hearing. In this case, the accused will be detained until he or she is presented in front of a justice, which should take place within 24 hours or as soon as a justice is available.

Summons

The final options available to the officer in charge are similar to the options available to the officer in the field: the accused can be released unconditionally or can be released unconditionally with the intention of having him or her served with a summons at a later date. These options can be exercised under the following circumstances:

- The accused is charged with a summary conviction offence, a hybrid offence, an indictable offence listed in s. 553, or any other offence with a maximum punishment of imprisonment for five years or less.
- There was no warrant for the arrest.
- All elements of PRICE have been fulfilled.
- An information will be laid as soon as possible thereafter with respect to the charge.

IT'S YOUR MOVE, OFFICER!

Scenario 6.2

You are the officer in charge of a police station in Toronto. A young male has been brought to your station; he is under arrest for a break-and-enter with intent into a dwelling-house. The accused has been speaking to members of the major crime unit and has indicated that if he can be released before attending court, he will provide officers with information about an individual who is selling guns.

An officer from the major crime unit speaks to you and requests that you release the man so that the unit can get the information about the gun dealer. The officer provides you with the following information about the case and the accused person: he broke into a single-family home, causing a very small amount of damage to a back door, and stole nothing because police attended very quickly after receiving the alarm call. The accused person has a very short criminal record—two convictions for fraud, the last five years ago. He is also known to the officer because he has supplied information in the past, and he has indicated to the officer that he will attend court and will likely plead guilty at the first opportunity.

1. What will you do? Will you release the male as the officer requested or send him to court for a hearing before a justice?

2. What document could you use to release the accused from custody and compel his attendance at court? Are there any other options available to you?

1. List the offences for which a police officer *on the street* must release an offender if PRICE is met.

2. List the offences for which an officer in charge must release an offender if PRICE is met.

3. List the documents used by police officers to release an accused person and compel that person to attend court.

Court-Level Release (Judicial Interim Release)

As we have mentioned, an accused person who has not been released by a peace officer or officer in charge must be taken before a justice within 24 hours, if a justice is available, or—if a justice is not available during that time frame—as soon as a justice can be made available. The justice may then ask for a plea. If the accused person pleads not guilty, the justice must decide whether to release the individual. Judicial interim release is outlined in great detail in s. 515 of the Code. A full account of judicial interim release is beyond the scope of this text. The following is a brief, partial discussion of the topic.

Court-Level Release: Forms

As with street-level release and station-level release, there are release options available to the justice:

- release on an undertaking (Form 12),
- release on an undertaking with conditions (Form 12),
- release on a recognizance (Form 32), and
- release on a recognizance with sureties (Form 32).

See the Appendix at the end of this chapter for examples of these forms.

In most cases, it is the Crown's responsibility to "show cause" why the accused person should not be released on an undertaking. In fact, the Crown has to show cause for each level of release. For example, if the Crown wishes to release the accused person on a recognizance with sureties, it must first show cause why the accused person should not be released on a simple undertaking, then show cause why the accused person should not be released on an undertaking with conditions, and then show cause why the accused person should not be released on a recognizance. The justice must order only that level of release for which the Crown has successfully shown cause.

The Decision Not to Release

In some cases, the prosecutor may seek to have the accused individual detained in custody, which means that the accused is not released until he or she is dealt with according to the law. A justice is restricted as to when he or she may detain an accused person in custody. According to s. 515(10) of the Code, detention of the accused person is justified only if one or more of the following conditions exist:

- Detention is required to ensure his or her appearance in court.
- Detention is required to protect the public, including the victim or a witness or a person under the age of 18 years.
- Detention is required to maintain confidence in the administration of justice.

When considering the final ground for detention—to maintain confidence in the administration of justice—the Code states in s. 515(10) that the justice must consider four factors:

1. the strength of the prosecution's case;
2. the severity of the crime;
3. the circumstances under which the offence was committed, such as whether a firearm was involved; and
4. the length of the sentence that the accused is facing.

Whether the maintenance of confidence in the administration of justice should be grounds for detention was challenged in 2002, in *R v. Hall*. In that case, the court was considering the man accused in the brutal murder of a Sault Ste. Marie, Ontario woman, in 1999. The lower court, while allowing that detention of the accused was not needed to ensure his appearance in court or to protect the safety of the public, had ordered the detention in order to maintain confidence in the administration of justice. The defence challenged the constitutionality of these grounds, but the Supreme Court of Canada (SCC) upheld the lower court's decision. In its ruling, the SCC justices wrote (2002, pp. 311-312) the following:

> Although the circumstances in which recourse to this ground for bail denial may not arise frequently, when they do it is essential that a means of denying bail be available because public confidence is essential to the proper functioning of the bail system and the justice system as a whole. … Parliament has hedged the provision with important safeguards: a judge can only deny bail if satisfied that, in view of the four specified factors and related circumstances, a reasonable member of the community would be satisfied that denial of bail is necessary to maintain confidence in the administration of justice. The provision is not overbroad but strikes an appropriate balance between the rights of the accused and the need to maintain justice in the community.

A justice may also order the accused to be detained in custody if the accused person meets any of the criteria outlined in s. 515(6) of the Code. These criteria include the following:

- The accused is charged with an indictable offence (other than those listed in s. 469) while on interim release for another offence.
- The accused is charged with an indictable offence (other than those listed in s. 469), but is not ordinarily resident in Canada.
- The accused is charged with a terrorism offence or a serious offence alleged to have been committed for the benefit of, at the direction of, or in association with, a criminal organization.

Details of these and other criteria can be found in s. 515(6) of the Code. In these situations, the onus shifts to the accused person to show cause why he or she should not be detained and then, if he or she is successful in that regard, why he or she should not be subject to the more onerous release conditions.

Mandatory Detention in Custody

According to s. 515(11), the justice, in cases involving offences listed under s. 469 of the Code, must order that the accused be detained in custody and must issue a warrant for the committal of the accused person to trial. Only a judge of the superior court of criminal

TABLE 6.5   Release Options at the Court Level (Justice)

Offences	Options	Forms	Purpose of Form
All criminal offences with the exception of s. 469 offences (Justice)	Release and compel attendance in court	Undertaking given to a justice, with or without conditions (Form 12)	Release the accused from custody, compel attendance in court
		Recognizance, with or without surety, and with or without deposit, with or without conditions (Form 32)	Release the accused from custody, compel attendance in court
Section 469 offences	No release, remand in custody		

jurisdiction can authorize release in such cases. This exception is set out in s. 522(1) of the Code:

> 522(1)   Where an accused is charged with an offence listed in section 469, no court, judge or justice, other than a judge of or a judge presiding in a superior court of criminal jurisdiction for the province in which the accused is so charged, may release the accused before or after the accused has been ordered to stand trial.

CHECK YOUR UNDERSTANDING

1. On what three grounds can the justice order the detention of an accused person?

2. Describe two of the conditions, outlined in s. 515(6) of the Code, under which a justice may order the detention of an accused person.

3. A justice must order detention in custody if the person is charged under which section of the *Criminal Code*?

Charging the Offender

So far we have discussed the arrest, detention, and release of the accused. You may be surprised to learn that, up to this point, the accused has not been charged with an offence. A criminal charge is laid through the use of an information. An information (Form 2—see the Appendix at the end of this chapter) is a document sworn before a justice, and it contains the following details:

- the name of the territorial jurisdiction,
- the name and occupation of the person swearing to the information (the **informant**),
- the name of the accused,
- a statement of the allegations being made against the accused, and
- the signature of the informant.

informant
the person laying an information under oath before a justice

Police officers are not the only persons who may charge an individual with a criminal offence. Under s. 504 of the Code, any person may lay an information when the offence alleged is indictable. It is common for security officers or private investigators to lay an information without involving the police. Under s. 504, a private citizen may lay an information, although this is uncommon.

When the accused has been issued an appearance notice or has been released by way of a promise to appear or a recognizance, the information must be laid as soon as possible, and it must be laid prior to the accused person's first appearance in court. The justice receiving the information must conduct a hearing to consider the informant's allegations. Section 507 of the Code states that the justice may hear sworn evidence from the informant or from any witness he or she chooses to hear from. This hearing is an ***ex parte* hearing**, which means that the accused is not present during the hearing.

ex parte **hearing**
a court proceeding held in the absence of the accused person

If the justice determines, after the hearing, that there is sufficient evidence to force the accused to answer to the charge(s), he or she may compel the accused person to attend court. To do this, the justice may use one of the following means:

- issue a summons to the accused person;
- issue a warrant for the arrest of the accused person (must be in the public interest);
- if issuing a warrant, endorse the warrant authorizing a police officer to release the accused person;
- if an appearance notice, promise to appear, or recognizance has been issued or entered into by the accused person, confirm that document and endorse the information (this ties the information and the release document together); or
- if an appearance notice, promise to appear, or recognizance has been issued or entered into by the accused person, cancel that document and issue either a summons or a warrant for the accused person's arrest.

It is at this point that the accused person is formally charged with an offence. Of course, under s. 507 of the Code, the justice, at this point, also has the option of refusing to sign the information if he or she deems that there is not enough evidence to force the accused to answer the charge.

CHECK YOUR UNDERSTANDING

1. Name the document that is used to charge an accused.
2. List the options available to a justice who has received an information and has conducted a hearing.
3. Who may lay an information?

CHAPTER SUMMARY

Interim release is a balance between the rights of the accused person—including that person's right to be free from arbitrary detention and his or her right to reasonable bail—and the protection of society and of the public from those who commit criminal offences. Deciding whether to release the accused can be a complex process; the decision must take into account the offence he or she is alleged to have committed, and it must take into account the public interest. The Code provides specific rules concerning the release of an accused person, and these rules vary according to whether the person determining that release is an officer on the street, an officer in charge, or a justice. The process of charging an individual with a criminal offence is not complete until a justice has received an information and held a hearing where sworn evidence is received. You are better equipped to do your job as a police officer when you understand these aspects of release.

KEY TERMS

appearance notice, 122

bail, 117

compelling document, 121

discretionary release, 119

ex parte hearing, 130

informant, 129

information, 122

interim release, 116

mandatory release, 118

promise to appear, 124

recognizance, 124

summons, 122

sureties, 124

undertaking, 125

REFERENCES

Canadian Charter of Rights and Freedoms. (1982). Part I of the *Constitution Act, 1982*, RSC 1985, app. II, no. 44.

Criminal Code. (1985). RSC 1985, c. C-46.

Hall, R v. (2002). 2002 SCC 64, [2002] 3 SCR 309.

FURTHER READING

Hall, R v. (2002). 2002 SCC 64, [2002] 3 SCR 309.

Morales, R v. (1992). [1992] 3 SCR 711.

Pearson, R v. (1992). [1992] 3 SCR 665.

REVIEW QUESTIONS

Multiple Choice

1. Which of the following people may be responsible for determining whether an accused person should be released before a hearing?

    a. a police officer on the street or a member of the public

    b. a police officer on the street or an officer in charge

    c. a police officer on the street or an officer in charge or a justice

    d. a justice

2. The existence of which of the following conditions requires a police officer on the street to release an accused person?

    a. The arrest was made without a warrant.

    b. PRICE has been fulfilled.

    c. The offence for which the person was arrested was a summary conviction offence, a dual procedure offence, or an indictable offence listed in s. 553.

    d. all of the above

3. An officer in charge may release and compel an accused person's attendance in court by using which of the following documents?

   a. appearance notice (Form 9)

   b. recognizance (Form 32)

   c. promise to appear (Form 10)

   d. undertaking (Form 11.1)

4. Which of the following conditions may be included in an undertaking?

   a. The accused must remain in the territorial jurisdiction specified in the undertaking.

   b. The accused must deposit his or her passport with the police.

   c. The accused must report to the police at specified dates and times.

   d. all of the above

5. Which of the following is not required in an information?

   a. the name of the officer who released the accused person

   b. the name and occupation of the informant

   c. a brief statement of the allegation(s) against the accused person

   d. the signature of the informant

True or False

_____ 1. A police officer on the street may release and compel an accused person to court using a promise to appear (Form 10).

_____ 2. An accused person is considered "charged" once he or she has been released from custody.

_____ 3. Canadian law favours releasing individuals from custody rather than detaining them prior to trial.

_____ 4. It is mandatory for an officer in charge, provided the PRICE criteria have been met, to release a person accused of an indictable offence punishable by five years or less.

_____ 5. An officer in charge may release an individual accused of a s. 469 offence, because these offences are less serious than others.

_____ 6. It is only in cases where an alleged offence is indictable that anyone may lay an information.

_____ 7. An undertaking (Form 11.1) must be used in conjunction with another document compelling the accused person to attend court.

_____ 8. A summons is issued either by an officer on the street or by an officer in charge.

_____ 9. Police officers or officers in charge, when they are trying to decide whether to release an accused person, need not consider the type of offence alleged to have been committed.

_____10. The Charter provides everyone with the right to be presumed innocent until proven guilty.

Short Answer

1. Explain PRICE, and explain how it is used to determine whether to release an accused person.

2. What options are available to a justice who is seeking both to compel an accused person to attend court and to release that person from custody?

3. For each of the following law enforcement officials, which types of offences call for mandatory release if PRICE criteria are met?

   a. an officer on the street

   b. an officer in charge

4. As an officer on the street, you have detained an individual for an offence listed in s. 495(2) of the Code. RICE is met, so you cannot arrest this person. What are your options when it comes to compelling this person's attendance in court?

5. A person has been arrested under the authority of an arrest warrant. Explain what circumstances must exist in order for an officer in charge to release this person.

It's Your Move, Officer!

You are the officer in charge of 46 Division. Police Constable Singh has brought a male into the station under arrest. He has legally arrested this man for assault causing bodily harm. The male has been identified to your satisfaction. He has a short criminal record, but has not been convicted of any offences in the last ten years. He has never been convicted of an offence involving violence. The male lives and works in your city. He does not know the victim of the assault.

It is your responsibility to determine whether this male should be released. Explain the basis on which you will make this decision.

APPENDIX: SAMPLE FORMS

FORM 2
(Sections 506 and 788)
INFORMATION

Canada, Province of _____ , (*territorial division*).

This is the information of C.D., of _____ , (*occupation*), hereinafter called the informant.

The informant says that (*if the informant has no personal knowledge state that he believes on reasonable grounds and state the offence*).

Sworn before me this _____ day of _____ , A.D. _____ , at _____ .	_____ (*Signature of Informant*)

_____
A Justice of the Peace in and for _____ .

Note: The date of birth of the accused may be mentioned on the information or indictment.

R.S., 1985, c. C-46, Form 2; R.S., 1985, c. 27 (1st Supp.), s. 184.

FORM 6
(Sections 493, 508 and 512)
SUMMONS TO A PERSON CHARGED WITH AN OFFENCE

Canada, Province of _____ , *(territorial division).*

To A.B., of _____ , *(occupation)*:

Whereas you have this day been charged before me that (*set out briefly the offence in respect of which the accused is charged*);

This is therefore to command you, in Her Majesty's name:

(*a*) to attend court on _____ , the _____ day of _____ A.D. _____ , at _____ o'clock in the _____ noon, at _____ or before any justice for the said (*territorial division*) who is there, and to attend thereafter as required by the court, in order to be dealt with according to law; and

(*b*) to appear on _____ , the _____ day of _____ A.D. _____ , at _____ o'clock in the _____ noon, at _____ , for the purposes of the *Identification of Criminals Act*. (*Ignore, if not filled in*).

You are warned that failure without lawful excuse to attend court in accordance with this summons is an offence under subsection 145(4) of the *Criminal Code*.

Subsection 145(4) of the *Criminal Code* states as follows:

"(4) Every one who is served with a summons and who fails, without lawful excuse, the proof of which lies on him, to appear at a time and place stated therein, if any, for the purposes of the *Identification of Criminals Act* or to attend court in accordance therewith, is guilty of

(*a*) an indictable offence and is liable to imprisonment for a term not exceeding two years; or

(*b*) an offence punishable on summary conviction."

Section 510 of the *Criminal Code* states as follows:

"**510.** Where an accused who is required by a summons to appear at a time and place stated therein for the purposes of the *Identification of Criminals Act* does not appear at that time and place, a justice may issue a warrant for the arrest of the accused for the offence with which he is charged."

Dated this _____ day of _____ A.D. _____ , at _____ .

_____   _____

A Justice of the Peace in and for _____ *or* Judge

R.S., 1985, c. C-46, Form 6; R.S., 1985, c. 27 (1st Supp.), s.184.

FORM 9
(Section 493)
APPEARANCE NOTICE ISSUED BY A PEACE OFFICER TO A PERSON NOT YET CHARGED WITH AN OFFENCE

Canada, Province of _____ , (*territorial division*).

To A.B., of _____ , (*occupation*):

You are alleged to have committed (*set out substance of offence*).

1. You are required to attend court on _____ day, the _____ day of _____ A.D. _____ , at _____ o'clock in the _____ noon, in courtroom No. _____ , at court _____ , in the municipality of _____ , and to attend thereafter as required by the court, in order to be dealt with according to law.

2. You are also required to appear on _____ day, the _____ day of _____ A.D. _____ , at _____ o'clock in the _____ noon, at _____ (*police station*), (*address*), for the purposes of the *Identification of Criminals Act*. (*Ignore if not filled in.*)

You are warned that failure to attend court in accordance with this appearance notice is an offence under subsection 145(5) of the *Criminal Code*.

Subsections 145(5) and (6) of the *Criminal Code* state as follows:

"(5) Every person who is named in an appearance notice or promise to appear, or in a recognizance entered into before an officer in charge or another peace officer, that has been confirmed by a justice under section 508 and who fails, without lawful excuse, the proof of which lies on the person, to appear at the time and place stated therein, if any, for the purposes of the *Identification of Criminals Act* or to attend court in accordance therewith, is guilty of

(*a*) an indictable offence and liable to imprisonment for a term not exceeding two years; or

(*b*) an offence punishable on summary conviction.

(6) For the purposes of subsection (5), it is not a lawful excuse that an appearance notice, promise to appear or recognizance states defectively the substance of the alleged offence."

Section 502 of the *Criminal Code* states as follows:

"**502.** Where an accused who is required by an appearance notice or promise to appear or by a recognizance entered into before an officer in charge or another peace officer to appear at a time and place stated therein for the purposes of the *Identification of Criminals Act* does not appear at that time and place, a justice may, where the appearance notice, promise to appear or recognizance has been confirmed by a justice under section 508, issue a warrant for the arrest of the accused for the offence with which the accused is charged."

Issued at _____ a.m./p.m. this _____ day of _____ A.D. _____ , at _____.

_____
(*Signature of peace officer*)

_____
(*Signature of accused*)

R.S., 1985, c. C-46, Form 9; R.S., 1985, c. 27 (1st Supp.), s. 184; 1994, c. 44, s. 84; 1997, c. 18, s. 115.

FORM 10
(Section 493)
PROMISE TO APPEAR

Canada, Province of _____ , *(territorial division)*.

I, A.B., of _____ , *(occupation)*, understand that it is alleged that I have committed (*set out substance of offence*).

In order that I may be released from custody,

1. I promise to attend court on _____ day, the _____ day of _____ A.D. _____ , at _____ o'clock in the _____ noon, in courtroom No. _____ , at _____ court, in the municipality of _____ , and to attend thereafter as required by the court, in order to be dealt with according to law.

2. I also promise to appear on _____ day, the _____ day of _____ A.D., at _____ o'clock in the _____ noon, at _____ (*police station*), (*address*), for the purposes of the *Identification of Criminals Act*. (*Ignore if not filled in.*)

I understand that failure without lawful excuse to attend court in accordance with this promise to appear is an offence under subsection 145(5) of the *Criminal Code*.

Subsections 145(5) and (6) of the *Criminal Code* state as follows:

"(5) Every person who is named in an appearance notice or promise to appear, or in a recognizance entered into before an officer in charge or another peace officer, that has been confirmed by a justice under section 508 and who fails, without lawful excuse, the proof of which lies on the person, to appear at the time and place stated therein, if any, for the purposes of the *Identification of Criminals Act* or to attend court in accordance therewith, is guilty of

(*a*) an indictable offence and liable to imprisonment for a term not exceeding two years; or

(*b*) an offence punishable on summary conviction.

(6) For the purposes of subsection (5), it is not a lawful excuse that an appearance notice, promise to appear or recognizance states defectively the substance of the alleged offence."

Section 502 of the *Criminal Code* states as follows:

"**502.** Where an accused who is required by an appearance notice or promise to appear or by a recognizance entered into before an officer in charge or another peace officer to appear at a time and place stated therein for the purposes of the *Identification of Criminals Act* does not appear at that time and place, a justice may, where the appearance notice, promise to appear or recognizance has been confirmed by a justice under section 508, issue a warrant for the arrest of the accused for the offence with which the accused is charged."

Dated this _____ day of _____ A.D., at _____.

_____
(*Signature of accused*)

R.S., 1985, c. C-46, Form 10; 1994, c. 44, s. 84; 1997, c. 18, s. 115.

FORM 11
(Section 493)
RECOGNIZANCE ENTERED INTO BEFORE AN OFFICER IN CHARGE OR OTHER PEACE OFFICER

Canada, Province of _____ , *(territorial division)*.

I, A.B., of _____ , *(occupation)*, understand that it is alleged that I have committed *(set out substance of offence)*.

In order that I may be released from custody, I hereby acknowledge that I owe $ *(not exceeding $500)* to Her Majesty the Queen to be levied on my real and personal property if I fail to attend court as hereinafter required.

(or, for a person not ordinarily resident in the province in which the person is in custody or within two hundred kilometres of the place in which the person is in custody)

In order that I may be released from custody, I hereby acknowledge that I owe $ *(not exceeding $500)* to Her Majesty the Queen and deposit herewith *(money or other valuable security not exceeding in amount or value $500)* to be forfeited if I fail to attend court as hereinafter required.

1. I acknowledge that I am required to attend court on _____ day, the _____ day of _____ A.D., at _____ o'clock in the _____ noon, in courtroom No. _____ , at _____ court, in the municipality of _____ , and to attend thereafter as required by the court, in order to be dealt with according to law.

2. I acknowledge that I am also required to appear on _____ day, the _____ day of _____ A.D. _____ , at _____ o'clock in the _____ noon, at _____ *(police station)*, *(address)*, for the purposes of the *Identification of Criminals Act*. *(Ignore if not filled in.)*

I understand that failure without lawful excuse to attend court in accordance with this recognizance to appear is an offence under subsection 145(5) of the *Criminal Code*.

Subsections 145(5) and (6) of the *Criminal Code* state as follows:

"(5) Every person who is named in an appearance notice or promise to appear, or in a recognizance entered into before an officer in charge or another peace officer, that has been confirmed by a justice under section 508 and who fails, without lawful excuse, the proof of which lies on the person, to appear at the time and place stated therein, if any, for the purposes of the *Identification of Criminals Act* or to attend court in accordance therewith, is guilty of

(*a*) an indictable offence and liable to imprisonment for a term not exceeding two years; or

(*b*) an offence punishable on summary conviction.

(6) For the purposes of subsection (5), it is not a lawful excuse that an appearance notice, promise to appear or recognizance states defectively the substance of the alleged offence."

Section 502 of the *Criminal Code* states as follows:

"**502.** Where an accused who is required by an appearance notice or promise to appear or by a recognizance entered into before an officer in charge or another peace officer to appear at a time and place stated therein for the purposes of the *Identification of Criminals Act* does not appear at that time and place, a justice may, where the appearance notice, promise to appear or recognizance has been confirmed by a justice under section 508, issue a warrant for the arrest of the accused for the offence with which the accused is charged."

Dated this _____ day of _____ A.D., at _____ .

_____
(Signature of accused)

R.S., 1985, c. C-46, Form 11; 1992, c. 1, s. 58; 1994, c. 44, s. 84; 1997, c. 18, s. 115.

FORM 11.1

(Sections 493, 499 and 503)

UNDERTAKING GIVEN TO A PEACE OFFICER OR AN OFFICER IN CHARGE

Canada, Province of _____ , (*territorial division*).

I, A.B., of _____ , (*occupation*), understand that it is alleged that I have committed (*set out substance of the offence*).

In order that I may be released from custody by way of (a promise to appear *or* a recognizance), I undertake to (*insert any conditions that are directed*):

(*a*) remain within (*designated territorial jurisdiction*);

(*b*) notify (*name of peace officer or other person designated*) of any change in my address, employment or occupation;

(*c*) abstain from communicating, directly or indirectly, with (*identification of victim, witness or other person*) or from going to (*name or description of place*) except in accordance with the following conditions: (*as the peace officer or other person designated specifies*);

(*d*) deposit my passport with (*name of peace officer or other person designated*);

(*e*) to abstain from possessing a firearm and to surrender to (*name of peace officer or other person designated*) any firearm in my possession and any authorization, license or registration certificate or other document enabling the acquisition or possession of a firearm;

(*f*) report at (*state times*) to (*name of peace officer or other person designated*);

(*g*) to abstain from

(i) the consumption of alcohol or other intoxicating substances, or

(ii) the consumption of drugs except in accordance with a medical prescription; and

(*h*) comply with any other conditions that the peace officer or officer in charge considers necessary to ensure the safety and security of any victim of or witness to the offence.

I understand that I am not required to give an undertaking to abide by the conditions specified above, but that if I do not, I may be kept in custody and brought before a justice so that the prosecutor may be given a reasonable opportunity to show cause why I should not be released on giving an undertaking without conditions.

I understand that if I give an undertaking to abide by the conditions specified above, then I may apply, at any time before I appear, or when I appear, before a justice pursuant to (a promise to appear *or* a recognizance entered into before an officer in charge or another peace officer), to have this undertaking vacated or varied and that my application will be considered as if I were before a justice pursuant to section 515 of the *Criminal Code*.

I also understand that this undertaking remains in effect until it is vacated or varied.

I also understand that failure without lawful excuse to abide by any of the conditions specified above is an offence under subsection 145(5.1) of the *Criminal Code*.

Subsection 145(5.1) of the *Criminal Code* states as follows:

"(5.1) Every person who, without lawful excuse, the proof of which lies on the person, fails to comply with any condition of an undertaking entered into pursuant to subsection 499(2) or 503(2.1)

(*a*) is guilty of an indictable offence and is liable to imprisonment for a term not exceeding two years; or

(*b*) is guilty of an offence punishable on summary conviction."

Dated this _____ day of _____ A.D., at _____.

_____

(*Signature of accused*)

1994, c. 44, s. 84; 1997, c. 18, s. 115; 1999, c. 25, s. 24; 2002, c. 13, s. 86(F).

FORM 12
(Sections 493 and 679)
UNDERTAKING GIVEN TO A JUSTICE OR A JUDGE

Canada, Province of _____ , (*territorial division*).

I, A.B., of _____ , (*occupation*), understand that I have been charged that (*set out briefly the offence in respect of which accused is charged*).

In order that I may be released from custody, I undertake to attend court on _____ day, the _____ day of _____ A.D. _____ , and to attend after that as required by the court in order to be dealt with according to law (*or, where date and place of appearance before court are not known at the time undertaking is given*, to attend at the time and place fixed by the court and after that as required by the court in order to be dealt with according to law).

(*and, where applicable*)

I also undertake to (*insert any conditions that are directed*)

(*a*) report at (*state times*) to (*name of peace officer or other person designated*);

(*b*) remain within (*designated territorial jurisdiction*);

(*c*) notify (*name of peace officer or other person designated*) of any change in my address, employment or occupation;

(*d*) abstain from communicating, directly or indirectly, with (*identification of victim, witness or other person*) except in accordance with the following conditions: (*as the justice or judge specifies*);

(*e*) deposit my passport (*as the justice or judge directs*); and

(*f*) (*any other reasonable conditions*).

I understand that failure without lawful excuse to attend court in accordance with this undertaking is an offence under subsection 145(2) of the *Criminal Code*.

Subsections 145(2) and (3) of the *Criminal Code* state as follows:

"(2) Every one who,

(*a*) being at large on his undertaking or recognizance given to or entered into before a justice or judge, fails, without lawful excuse, the proof of which lies on him, to attend court in accordance with the undertaking or recognizance, or

(*b*) having appeared before a court, justice or judge, fails, without lawful excuse, the proof of which lies on him, to attend court as thereafter required by the court, justice or judge,

or to surrender himself in accordance with an order of the court, justice or judge, as the case may be, is guilty of an indictable offence and liable to imprisonment for a term not exceeding two years or is guilty of an offence punishable on summary conviction.

(3) Every person who is at large on an undertaking or recognizance given to or entered into before a justice or judge and is bound to comply with a condition of that undertaking or recognizance, and every person who is bound to comply with a direction under subsection 515(12) or 522(2.1) or an order under subsection 516(2), and who fails, without lawful excuse, the proof of which lies on them, to comply with the condition, direction or order is guilty of

(*a*) an indictable offence and liable to imprisonment for a term not exceeding two years; or

(*b*) an offence punishable on summary conviction."

Dated this _____ day of _____ A.D., at _____ .

_____
(*Signature of accused*)

R.S., 1985, c. C-46, Form 12; R.S., 1985, c. 27 (1st Supp.), s. 184; 1994, c. 44, s. 84; 1999, c. 25, s. 25; 2008, c. 18, s. 45.1.

FORM 32
(Sections 493, 550, 679, 706, 707, 810, 810.1 and 817)
RECOGNIZANCE

Canada, Province of _____ , (*territorial division*).

Be it remembered that on this day the persons named in the following schedule personally came before me and severally acknowledged themselves to owe to Her Majesty the Queen the several amounts set opposite their respective names, namely,

Name	Address	Occupation	Amount
A.B.			
C.D.			
E.F.			

to be made and levied of their several goods and chattels, lands and tenements, respectively, to the use of Her Majesty the Queen, if the said A.B. fails in any of the conditions hereunder written.

Taken and acknowledged before me on the _____ day of _____ A.D. _____ , at _____ .

_____
Judge, Clerk of the Court, Provincial Court Judge *or* Justice

1. Whereas the said _____ , hereinafter called the accused, has been charged that (*set out the offence in respect of which the accused has been charged*);

Now, therefore, the condition of this recognizance is that if the accused attends court on day, the _____ day of _____ A.D. _____ , at _____ o'clock in the _____ noon and attends thereafter as required by the court in order to be dealt with according to law (*or, where date and place of appearance before court are not known at the time recognizance is entered into if the accused attends at the time and place fixed by the court and attends thereafter as required by the court in order to be dealt with according to law*) [515, 520, 521, 522, 523, 524, 525, 680];

And further, if the accused (*insert in Schedule of Conditions any additional conditions that are directed*),

the said recognizance is void, otherwise it stands in full force and effect.

2. Whereas the said _____ , hereinafter called the appellant, is an appellant against his conviction (*or* against his sentence) in respect of the following charge (*set out the offence for which the appellant was convicted*) [679, 680];

Now, therefore, the condition of this recognizance is that if the appellant attends as required by the court in order to be dealt with according to law;

And further, if the appellant (*insert in Schedule of Conditions any additional conditions that are directed*),

the said recognizance is void, otherwise it stands in full force and effect.

3. Whereas the said _____ , hereinafter called the appellant, is an appellant against his conviction (*or* against his sentence *or* against an order *or* by way of stated case) in respect of the following matter (*set out offence, subject-matter of order or question of law*) [816, 831, 832, 834];

Now, therefore, the condition of this recognizance is that if the appellant appears personally at the sittings of the appeal court at which the appeal is to be heard;

And further, if the appellant (*insert in Schedule of Conditions any additional conditions that are directed*),

the said recognizance is void, otherwise it stands in full force and effect.

4. Whereas the said _____ , hereinafter called the appellant, is an appellant against an order of dismissal (*or* against sentence) in respect of the following charge (*set out the name of the defendant and the offence, subject-matter of order or question of law*) [817, 831, 832, 834];

Now, therefore, the condition of this recognizance is that if the appellant appears personally or by counsel at the sittings of the appeal court at which the appeal is to be heard the said recognizance is void, otherwise it stands in full force and effect.

5. Whereas the said _____ , hereinafter called the accused, was ordered to stand trial on a charge that (*set out the offence in respect of which the accused has been charged*);

And whereas A.B. appeared as a witness on the preliminary inquiry into the said charge [550, 706, 707];

Now, therefore, the condition of this recognizance is that if the said A.B. appears at the time and place fixed for the trial of the accused to give evidence on the indictment that is found against the accused, the said recognizance is void, otherwise it stands in full force and effect.

6. The condition of the above written recognizance is that if A.B. keeps the peace and is of good behaviour for the term of _____ commencing on _____ , the said recognizance is void, otherwise it stands in full force and effect [810 and 810.1].

7. Whereas a warrant was issued under section 462.32 or a restraint order was made under subsection 462.33(3) of the *Criminal Code* in relation to any property (*set out a description of the property and its location*);

Now, therefore, the condition of this recognizance is that A.B. shall not do or cause anything to be done that would result, directly or indirectly, in the disappearance, dissipation or reduction in value of the property or otherwise affect the property so that all or a part thereof could not be subject to an order of forfeiture under section 462.37 or 462.38 of the *Criminal Code* or any other provision of the *Criminal Code* or any other Act of Parliament [462.34].

Schedule of Conditions

(*a*) reports at (*state times*) to (*name of peace officer or other person designated*);

(*b*) remains within (*designated territorial jurisdiction*);

(*c*) notifies (*name of peace officer or other person designated*) of any change in his address, employment or occupation;

(*d*) abstains from communicating, directly or indirectly, with (*identification of victim, witness or other person*) except in accordance with the following conditions: (*as the justice or judge specifies*);

(*e*) deposits his passport (*as the justice or judge directs*); and

(*f*) (*any other reasonable conditions*).

Note: Section 763 and subsections 764(1) to (3) of the *Criminal Code* state as follows:

"**763.** Where a person is bound by recognizance to appear before a court, justice or provincial court judge for any purpose and the session or sittings of that court or the proceedings are adjourned or an order is made changing the place of trial, that person and his sureties continue to be bound by the recognizance in like manner as if it had been entered into with relation to the resumed proceedings or the trial at the time and place at which the proceedings are ordered to be resumed or the trial is ordered to be held.

764.(1) Where an accused is bound by recognizance to appear for trial, his arraignment or conviction does not discharge the recognizance, but it continues to bind him and his sureties, if any, for his appearance until he is discharged or sentenced, as the case may be.

(2) Notwithstanding subsection (1), the court, justice or provincial court judge may commit an accused to prison or may require him to furnish new or additional sureties for his appearance until he is discharged or sentenced, as the case may be.

(3) The sureties of an accused who is bound by recognizance to appear for trial are discharged if he is committed to prison pursuant to subsection (2)."

R.S., 1985, c. C-46, Form 32; R.S., 1985, c. 27 (1st Supp.), ss. 101, 184, 203; c. 42 (4th Supp.), s. 7; 1993, c. 45, ss. 13, 14; 1999, c. 25, s. 27.

Police Discretion

7

LEARNING OUTCOMES

After completing this chapter, you should be able to:

- Define the term *discretion*.
- Explain the role of discretion in policing and explain why discretion requires a balancing act.
- Identify and explain factors that influence police discretion.
- Describe some of the benefits of police discretion.
- Describe some of the challenges posed by police discretion.
- Explain how the challenges posed by police discretion may be addressed—for example, by controlling and limiting discretion through legislation and regulation.
- Explain the range of factors considered by police when using discretion.

It's Tuesday, 11:30 p.m. A police officer and her partner enter a downtown laneway and see a person spray-painting the back of a store. As they approach the building, they see that it's a young woman in her late teens. She is in the process of finishing off a mural of a lake with geese flying overhead.

"Did you get permission to do this?" the officer asks, pointing at the mural. The teenager shakes her head. "No, I didn't know I had to. I'm really sorry. I didn't know I was doing anything wrong. I just thought I'd try to make this neighbourhood look a little nicer. You know … beautify it, like some cities are doing. Look at all the trash around here … and the gang graffiti."

The officer looks at her partner and guesses that he's thinking the same thing she is. Just the night before, they charged a young man at this location for tagging the building with gang symbols; he was marking the gang's turf. That perpetrator, when confronted by the officers, was disrespectful, dismissive of their authority, and even a bit menacing. The two cases of spray-painting are quite different, but they represent the same criminal offence: spray-painting a building without permission is "mischief to property."

What do you think the officers should do in this situation? Should they respond the same way to the two spray-painting offences, regardless of the circumstances, since both constitute the criminal act of mischief to property? Do they have a duty to do so? Or should officers be authorized to take different approaches depending on the situation—in other words, to use discretion?

Introduction

discretion
the freedom or authority to make judgments and to act as one sees fit

What is discretion? The meaning of the word *discretion* varies according to context. For the purposes of this chapter, **discretion** may be defined as the freedom or authority to make judgments and to act as one sees fit. In terms of policing, Kenneth Culp Davis (1971, p. 4) has described police discretion as follows: "A public officer has discretion wherever the objective limits on his power leave him (or her) free to make a choice among possible courses of action or inaction."

In this chapter, we will explore police discretion. You will learn what it is and what are some of the factors shaping when and how it is used, such as the "objective limits" to which Davis refers. You will be introduced to the benefits of using discretionary powers. You will also consider the challenges of using discretion and explore how these challenges may be addressed. How police use their discretionary powers determines the choices they make and the outcomes that result from these choices. Making the correct choice in the midst of an interaction can be difficult. However, understanding the limits and challenges of discretion can help a police officer make the best decision possible under the circumstances.

The Role of Discretion in Policing

Considering discretion's importance in policing, you would think that a definition of it would be readily available. You would certainly expect to find a definition in, say, *Martin's Annual Criminal Code*, in a law textbook, or in a legal journal. Yet if you turn to these sources, you find that they provide no clear or explicit definition of police discretion or of its use. Evidently the concept is not easily defined.

Discretion and a Police Officer's Job

Section 42 of the *Police Services Act* (1990) says that the main duties of police include

- preserving the peace,
- preventing crimes and other offences,
- assisting victims of crime,
- apprehending criminals and other offenders, and
- laying charges and participating in prosecutions.

Viewed in these terms—that is, as a list of responsibilities—the job of a police officer seems straightforward. However, it is far from being so. Officers are called on to make crucial decisions in a wide variety of situations, often unique in their particular circumstances. Their decisions often need to balance the needs of the community, the needs of their own policing organization, and their own needs as individuals. Captain Tag Gleason of the Seattle Police Department (2006) has described this balancing act as follows:

> Every day, police professionals decide and act while balancing competing and conflicting values and interests, frequently with incomplete or inaccurate information, often in highly emotional and dynamic circumstances, and typically under pressure.
>
> Police officers are held to a higher standard of behaviour by society, because they are stewards of the public trust and are empowered to apply force and remove constitutional privileges when lawfully justified. They take an oath of office, are expected to comply with professional codes of ethics, and are subject to various laws, rules, and regulations.
>
> An officer develops his or her moral compass, character, or ethical base, from interacting with other individuals and studying ethics.

Because they need to balance different, often conflicting demands, officers cannot be bound by a rigid set of regulations. They must have both the scope and the ability to make decisions based on their assessment of a given situation. In other words, officers need the freedom and authority to make decisions that suit the circumstances: discretionary decisions.

In *R v. Beaudry* (2007, para. 37), the SCC reflected on the importance of giving officers the discretion to make policing choices:

> Applying the letter of the law to the practical, real-life situations faced by police officers in performing their everyday duties requires that certain adjustments be made. Although these adjustments may sometimes appear to deviate from the letter of the law, they are crucial and are part of the very essence of the proper administration of the criminal justice system, or to use the words of s. 139(2), are perfectly consistent with the "course of justice." The ability—indeed the duty—to use one's judgment to adapt the process of law enforcement to individual circumstances and to the real-life demands of justice is in fact the basis of police discretion. What La Forest J. said in *R. v. Beare* ... is directly on point here: "Discretion is an essential feature of the criminal justice system. A system that attempted to eliminate discretion would be unworkably complex and rigid."

For police officers, discretionary decisions often involve choosing from a number of possible courses of action, which may include taking no action at all. For example, one approach to a traffic infraction might be to issue a ticket in strict accordance with the *Highway Traffic Act*, regardless of the particular situation. Another approach might be to educate the motorist on what he or she did wrong, then issue a verbal caution. Or the circumstances of the infraction may be such that no action is required. The decision will be based on individual circumstances, among other factors.

IT'S YOUR MOVE, OFFICER!

Scenario 7.1

You are responding to an emergency call. You arrive at a busy downtown intersection. Here, you need to make a left turn if you're taking the quickest route to the emergency. You see that a group of young children are crossing the intersection. Which of the following choices should you make?

- Make the left turn, potentially putting the children in danger.
- Proceed straight through the intersection, thus keeping the children safe but delaying your arrival on scene and thereby potentially jeopardizing the health and safety of those at the scene of the emergency.

Explain how you ought to proceed and give reasons for your choice.

Three Influences on Police Discretion

Let's take a look at three of the factors that affect how and when police discretion is exercised: environmental factors; administrative factors; and individual and situational factors.

Environmental Factors

It has been noted (Department of Justice, 2013) that the environment in which police operate has a tremendous influence on how they use discretion. Environmental factors include, for example, the social, economic, and demographic makeup of the local community. The policing circumstances in a large urban centre are quite different from those in a small rural town. One of these variable circumstances is the officer's own place in the community and his or her relationship with community members. These considerations will often affect how an officer chooses to respond to certain situations. In the graffiti scenario at the start of the chapter, for instance, an officer has to consider the community's view of graffiti. Does the community view it as artistic expression, or does it view it in terms of a gang tag that puts fear and intimidation in the neighbourhood?

When it comes to discretion in policing, another important environmental factor is the availability of alternatives to charging individuals. Is there an alternative? Is there a program, treatment centre, or individual, offering a suitable and productive intervention, that could be an alternative to charging the offender and processing him or her in the court system?

Another environmental factor, with respect to police discretion, is how much support officers receive in their job. In most cities and provinces in Canada, front-line police officers work either alone or with a partner and have little direct supervision. Officers must depend on their own discretion to make decisions, often in volatile or violent situations. Their ability and willingness to make these important decisions can be influenced by their relationship with, and how much direction they receive from, the community, their superiors, their police organization, and Crown prosecutors.

Source: Deborah Baic/The Globe and Mail/CP Images.   Source: Stan Behal/Toronto Sun/QMI Agency.

The environment influences how police interact with their community. In some environments, police may be distanced from the public. In others, they may have close and consistent interaction with the community.

Administrative Factors

Administrative direction is closely related to a police officer's environment and could be seen as part of it. The administration shapes the environment in which officers make decisions. As Davis has said (1971, p. 4), there are "objective limits" to a police officer's discretionary decisions. The law is an obvious element in these limits. Another element is the policies and procedures of the officer's own policing organization.

A departmental policy of zero tolerance respecting certain offences restricts an officer's decision-making latitude. For example, consider a situation where a police organization is concerned by the high number of head injuries among cyclists. The cyclists are not wearing bicycle helmets, despite the fact that there is a municipal bylaw mandating their use. The police organization decides to implement a zero-tolerance policy regarding the helmet law. This curtails the officers' discretionary power with respect to the helmet law; they must take a strict enforcement approach. Failing to do so would be a breach of organization policy and might result in discipline actions against the officer.

The police officers faced with spray-painters, in this chapter's opening scenario, would need to consider their own police service's policies toward graffiti. Is the offence taking place within a community that is experiencing a great deal of gang activity? If so, the officers' police service may have a zero-tolerance policy toward such activities. This would take away the discretionary powers of the officers at the scene, compelling them to charge the young muralist with mischief to property.

Individual and Situational Factors

Individuality plays a big part in police discretion. Police officers are human, after all. Like anyone else, their decisions are influenced by personal thoughts, beliefs, values, and personal traits. A police officer's discretionary decision-making is also affected by his or her level of experience. Consider, for example, a situation where police observe a jaywalking infraction. When confronted, the person is courteous and apologizes for his or her lack of judgment. A 25-year veteran and a rookie just out of police college might view this situation quite differently. The rookie officer would probably be looking to enforce the law strictly, whereas the veteran officer would see that there is room for discretion.

Source: Monika Schurmann. Used with permission.

Police may use discretion when dealing with situations such as spray-painting a building without permission.

Other factors in discretion are the gender, age, and demeanour of the suspect. Police officers will also consider whether the suspect is a first-time or a repeat offender. In our graffiti scenario, for example, both suspects have committed a criminal offence by defacing a building without permission. However, the officers may respond to the two situations differently on the basis of the individual and situational factors involved in each.

CHECK YOUR UNDERSTANDING

1. How would you describe police discretion?
2. Explain why discretionary decision-making requires a balancing act from police.
3. Identify and explain three influences on police discretion.

Some Benefits of Police Discretion

The Ontario *Police Services Act* (PSA) says that police officers should apprehend criminals, lay charges, and participate in prosecutions. It also says that the goal of policing is to preserve the peace and prevent crime. But are these goals always complementary? That is, does the laying of charges and the prosecution of offenders necessarily lead to greater peace or a reduction in crime? Or are there times when alternative approaches, such as giving a caution or educating the offender, lead to more productive and longer-lasting outcomes?

The SCC observed in *R v. Beaudry* (2007, para. 25) that "police discretion exists in matters of criminal justice and is a response to, among other things, the community's wish that not all those who commit minor offences should be arrested by the police or prosecuted." Why don't communities want all offences to be prosecuted? Let's consider a few examples.

Compassion in Policing

Canada is not a police state that operates like a machine, devoid of humanity. We pride ourselves on being a fair and compassionate society. Our communities expect police to enforce laws, but they also expect them to respect community members and to work with the community. A policy of strict enforcement prevents police from meeting all of our expectations of them. Compassion in policing requires discretionary power.

IT'S YOUR MOVE, OFFICER!

Scenario 7.2

You are a uniform officer on patrol when you observe a vehicle go through a red light. Pedestrians have to jump back onto the sidewalk to avoid being struck by this vehicle. You activate your emergency roof lights and pull the vehicle over.

You speak to the female driver. She is upset and says she didn't realize she had gone through the red light. She also tells you that she was hurrying to her eight-year-old son's school, having just learned that he has fallen off a swing and might have a broken arm.

What are you going to do and why?

Working with the Community

Police services are part of the communities they serve, and communities play an important role in police discretion. Discretionary power enables police to cooperate with community members in deciding how laws will be enforced. A community may want zero tolerance toward some laws or offences, but more lenience toward others. With community-based policing, the community members have a voice in how they are policed and how problems in the community are addressed.

For example, a community that often experiences gridlock might want police to take a zero-tolerance approach to infractions that contribute to the problem. The same community may want police to be lenient about cycling on sidewalks. Though cycling on sidewalks is a nuisance and constitutes an offence, community members may believe that police should stop and educate the cyclists involved rather than charging them. Though the police do not necessarily have to carry out the community's wishes, it is often in their best interest to do so.

Addressing Economic Realities

The cost of policing and putting offenders through the criminal justice system is enormous. Most police agencies are being forced to cut spending. Staffing levels are one of the areas affected by this shortage. The reduction of police resources can put communities at risk. Imagine the effect on these already limited resources—and on communities—if police were expected to pursue and lay charges for every last infraction, with no exercise of discretionary power.

Discretionary power enables officers to decide whether it is worthwhile to put someone through the criminal justice process. For some infractions, letting someone off with a simple caution may offer an economic benefit in terms of dollars spent, and it may free up officers' time, so that they can pursue other policing activities that will have a greater impact. The end result is a more efficient and effective policing system.

Protecting the Safety of Police Officers

The role of a police officer is to ensure that laws are not being broken and to arrest those who break them. When an officer's personal safety becomes an issue, should the officer have the discretionary right to avoid his or her sworn duties and choose not to immediately engage? Is a police officer's personal safety a justifiable reason for making a discretionary decision not to act? Under what circumstances is a police officer's decision not to engage deemed acceptable?

There are no clear guidelines for these types of discretionary decisions. Some members of the public believe that officers are trained and armed to deal with any situation and that they should immediately engage lawbreakers and protect bystanders. On the other hand, most people understand that policing can be a dangerous profession and that officers can't always be expected to put themselves into situations of extreme jeopardy. After all, police officers are not just individuals doing a job. They are also fathers, mothers, sons, and daughters. They need to be able to assess a situation and make a judgment about the risks involved, and consider their own safety.

IT'S YOUR MOVE, OFFICER!

Scenario 7.3

Consider the following situations:

- You are responding to a call about a large brawl inside a bar. When you arrive at the scene, the bar manager tells you that ten men or so are fighting inside the bar and that the bartender and a bouncer are trapped inside and are in immediate danger. Your dispatcher informs you that backup officers are five to ten minutes away.

- You are a uniform police officer walking a downtown beat alone late at night. As you enter the rear parking lot of a strip plaza, you hear the sound of breaking glass. You watch three men hurriedly enter and then leave an appliance store through a smashed glass door. They carry televisions toward a van.

What would you do in each of these two situations? Why? Compare your approaches to these two situations, and compare the thought processes underlying the approaches.

Enhancing Policing Effectiveness

Police work in a dynamic environment and are continually having to make snap discretionary decisions. The power to make discretionary decisions is particularly beneficial in the following areas of policing:

- *Arrests and enforcement.* In some areas of the law, police officers have discretion when it comes to enforcement. They also have discretion in the area of enforcement *strategies*—over whether to issue tickets, for example, and over when and where arrests may be made.

    The benefit of their having discretion in these areas is not merely economic. Consider speeding tickets, for example. By not ticketing everyone who is driving above the speed limit, police officers gain the time and the resources to target aggressive or dangerous driving. Similarly, officers' discretionary power in the area of arrests enables them to make arrests only in the most clearcut cases and in the cases where there is the greatest risk of recurrence.

- *Crime prevention.* Police are not meant to blindly follow rules. Their decision-making ability and ability to improvise lead to effective crime-prevention strategies. For example, if front-line officers followed the same pattern each time they patrolled, their movements would become predictable, and sophisticated criminals would begin to map them. That is why these officers use their discretion in varying how, when, and where they patrol.

- *Use of force.* The use of force is part of a police officer's job. He or she must be able to judge what level of force—from active communication to lethal force—is appropriate for the situation. Discretionary powers allow officers to do this.

CHECK YOUR UNDERSTANDING

1. What aspect of policing does a policy of strict enforcement fail to take into account?

2. Identify three areas of policing where discretionary power is particularly beneficial, and explain why.

3. How does working with the community enable police to make discretionary decisions?

Some Challenges for Police Discretion

Not everyone believes that police should have the authority to make discretionary decisions. Some argue that these types of decisions undermine the *Criminal Code*. They say that the Code is there to create order and to keep people safe, and ought to be strictly followed by police. And they claim that allowing police to make discretionary decisions can create inconsistencies and uncertainty in the legal system. A further concern is that discretionary power could be driven either by favouritism or by discrimination against certain people or groups. People who have these concerns sometimes argue that strict adherence to the Code and a policy of zero tolerance would prevent these pitfalls of discretionary power.

Inconsistencies in Enforcement

One of the strongest arguments against giving police discretionary powers is that it opens the way to uneven or inconsistent enforcement of laws. Not every officer will interpret or enforce the law in the same way. These differences derive from individual personalities, department policies, and environmental factors.

Dealing with the problem of inconsistency is largely a matter of managing public expectations and understanding of police work. The public and the police may be disconnected in this regard. What the police see as fairness and efficiency may seem the opposite from the public's perspective. Distrust, and even tension and confrontation, can arise when a community feels that laws are being applied unevenly.

Police discretionary powers do, strictly speaking, lead to inconsistent application of the law on a case-by-case basis. So do discretionary decisions that are influenced by community standards. As we mentioned above, giving the community a voice in policing decisions is only possible because of police discretionary power; it is one of the benefits of this power.

Communities can be very different, and may have very different views on the kinds of behaviour they are willing to tolerate. Using their discretionary powers, police are able to tailor their law enforcement policies to the communities they serve.

However, police face challenges in this regard. It is sometimes difficult for police to determine what the public really wants them to enforce. Who within the community determines what the policing priorities are? Is it the person or group that makes the loudest noise, such as organized protesters? Or are these decisions made by the community at large? How does *that* work? And how should police proceed when there are divergent views within a single community about a particular enforcement matter, with strong support on both sides? Such circumstances create difficulties for the police.

Uncertainty Caused by Changing Norms

Changes in social norms contribute to inconsistent community standards and thereby compound the problem of inconsistent enforcement. A society decides over time what is and isn't sanctioned behaviour. Through the political process of electing officials, new laws get made and out-of-date ones get dropped. Actions once considered illegal become tolerated over time. How does this affect police?

Take, for example, the changing social attitudes about marijuana use. In some US states, such as Colorado, personal use is now legal. In other states and in the Canadian provinces, there is some degree of tolerance, even though laws against the possession and use of marijuana are still in effect. As these social attitudes change, it is often left to the front-line officers to decide how to respond. In some cases, they find themselves in the position of enforcing changes that the public may not understand or be aware of. This can cause conflict between the police and members of the community.

Discrimination: Direct, Indirect, and Systemic

The decisions police officers make, like all human decisions, are influenced by personal thoughts, beliefs, values, and traits. These influences can include prejudices, which can produce implicit or even explicit **discrimination** toward certain people or groups. The concern is that a police officer's prejudices can lead to unfair discretionary decisions.

Discrimination can be direct, indirect, or systemic (see Figure 7.1).

Direct Discrimination

Direct discrimination is the most common type. It is discrimination directed toward characteristics such as age, gender, culture, and sexual orientation. In recent years, the problem of direct discrimination has been highlighted in public concerns about **racial profiling**. What is racial profiling? It is the practice of targeting people of a particular race based on stereotypes. The Ontario Human Rights Commission (OHRC, n.d.) defines racial profiling as "any action undertaken for reasons of safety, security or public protection, that relies on stereotypes about race, colour, ethnicity, ancestry, religion, or place of origin, or a combination of these, rather than on a reasonable suspicion, to single out an individual for greater scrutiny or different treatment." Age and gender are also factors in racial profiling.

For example, a police officer may decide to pull over a young black male driver not because he has committed a driving infraction, but on the basis of his race and age.

Another type of prejudice that can be a problem in policing is preferential treatment—in other words, treating a person favourably because of who they are. For example, an officer who chooses not to lay charges against a friend or a colleague may be making a

discrimination
treating people differently as a result of prejudice

direct discrimination
discrimination directed toward characteristics such as age, gender, culture, and sexual orientation

racial profiling
practice that targets for police investigation people of a particular race, based on stereotypes

FIGURE 7.1 Three Types of Discrimination

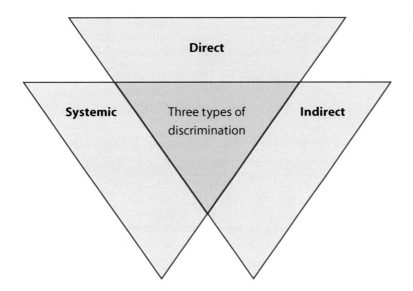

prejudiced decision and misusing his or her discretionary powers. One strong argument against giving police discretionary powers is that it enables them to operate above the law. It gives them the power to exempt whomever they want—friends, family, or fellow police officers—from the consequences of criminal wrongdoing. Under the PSA code of conduct (see Chapter 2), officers who give preferential treatment to someone are no less guilty of "discreditable conduct" than if they had committed an act of prejudice against someone.

Indirect Discrimination

Indirect discrimination is more difficult to identify than direct discrimination because it is often seen as justified; there tends to be an arguable rationale for it. For example, there used to be a height requirement for police officers. It was based on the idea that tall officers would have a more imposing physical presence than short ones and would convey a stronger sense of authority. This practice indirectly discriminated against women and against certain short-statured ethnic groups, though such discrimination wasn't the direct intention. The height requirement also failed to take into account the many traits apart from height that are important to effective policing.

Here is another example of indirect discrimination. Some communities have bylaws imposing an 11 p.m. curfew in city parks. These bylaws were intended to prevent loitering and all-night parties, but they have indirectly discriminated against the homeless, who often sleep in parks at night.

indirect discrimination
discrimination, generally unintentional, that results from a policy or practice that on the face of it seems reasonable, such as a height requirement for police

Systemic Discrimination

Systemic discrimination is a more problematic type of discrimination. With this type, certain attitudes or values become the accepted standard in an organization or a community. People who hold these beliefs or values fit in with the organizational culture and are more apt to be recruited, promoted, or assigned to specialized jobs. Other qualified candidates who do not share exactly the same beliefs or values are discriminated against and passed over. This perpetuates the values and attitudes that underlie the organization's systemic discrimination.

systemic discrimination
discrimination in which certain attitudes or values become the accepted standard in an organization or even a community

Systemic discrimination can adversely affect the internal operations of a police department, shaping policies and procedures and creeping into actual practices. Front-line officers who believe they are simply carrying out the lawful procedures of their police service may be practising discriminatory policing.

Mistakes and Misjudgment

Police officers are human and they make mistakes. In many police organizations, front-line officers are usually the youngest members of the organization. This means that they have limited experience to consult in their decision-making. Proper training offsets this scant experience to some extent. Nonetheless, these inexperienced officers often have to make split-second decisions without the benefit of a partner's advice and with very little supervision. For a young officer, what appears the right choice in a situation may turn out to be a breach of duty. Even worse, because of the nature of a police officer's job—because so much is sometimes at stake in his or her decisions—a mistake or lapse in judgment can have long-lasting effects. It can mean the difference between freedom and detention for someone, or even between life and death.

CHECK YOUR UNDERSTANDING

1. What is the difference between direct and indirect discrimination?
2. What is meant by "racial profiling"? What role, if any, should it play in the exercise of police powers?
3. What is systemic discrimination?

Addressing Challenges: Controlling Police Discretion

Police must respect the members of the communities they serve. The public bestows considerable discretionary powers on police (as on other public officials), and the public needs assurances that these powers won't be abused.

Eliminating every pitfall of police discretion is not possible, and aiming to do so is not realistic. However, certain steps can be taken to improve how the public perceives it. As the SCC (2007, para. 25) stated in *R v. Beaudry*, "the police may exercise this discretion in respect of anyone ... as long as they do so honestly, transparently, and on valid and reasonable grounds."

One thing that police may do to reduce the public's negative perception of police discretion is to ensure, through public relations and public education, that the policing environment is properly understood, particularly in light of rapidly changing norms. In the end, police discretion can best be controlled and made effective through legislation and internal regulation, and through effective hiring and training practices.

Legislation and Regulation

At the beginning of this chapter, we considered Kenneth Culp Davis's account of police discretion. An important part of his definition is the term *objective limits*. This phrase reflects the fact that officers' freedom and authority to make discretionary decisions are limited by outside forces. These objective limits include the following: the extensive legislation that governs a police officer's actions; the police organization's internal policies and procedures; and the oversight of multiple layers of watchdogs.

Internal Policies, Procedures, and Regulations, and Oversight Bodies

Policing is managed and made effective through legislation and through the rules, policies, and procedures prescribed by policing organizations. In Ontario, as we have seen, the statute governing police is the *Police Services Act*. The PSA is very explicit about the duties and behaviours expected of sworn police officers and the consequences of police misconduct. Beyond this legislation, direction for police comes from the numerous levels of supervision that exist within the ranks of the police service, as well as from oversight bodies. The latter include the police organization's internal professional standards units, the external Office of the Independent Police Review Director (OIPRD), and (in Ontario) the Special Investigations Unit (SIU).

The Charter of Rights and Freedoms and Human Rights Statutes

Police are expected to understand and respect the human rights of others. Their discretionary powers make this all the more crucial.

The need to treat individuals fairly and equitably is enshrined in Canadian law, particularly in the *Charter of Rights and Freedoms* (1982) and the *Canadian Human Rights Act*, assented to in 1977. This legislation aims to ensure that officers always behave and treat people in a fair, professional manner. The Charter outlines the rights and freedoms guaranteed to everyone in Canada. These rights and freedoms are inviolable, proof against the discretionary power of police. The Charter also seeks to ensure that all Canadians are treated equally. Section 15(1) states the following: "Every individual is equal before and under the law and has the right to the equal protection and equal benefit of the law without discrimination and, in particular, without discrimination based on race, national or ethnic origin, colour, religion, sex, age or mental or physical disability."

Police abuse of any of these laws leaves officers and their organizations open to criticism and even prosecution.

The Ontario Human Rights Code

As we have noted, systemic discrimination can be the most difficult type of discrimination to root out and eliminate. It involves the culture of an organization and tends to be protected by policies, rules, and procedures. To prevent this type of discrimination, the rules and procedures in a police organization need to send a strong signal that discrimination of any kind will not be tolerated. This signal also needs to come from legislation.

In Ontario, the *Human Rights Code* meets this need. It says that it is contrary to law to treat people unequally based on any of the following grounds: race, ancestry, place of origin, colour, ethnic origin, citizenship, creed, sex/pregnancy, sexual orientation, age, marital status, family status, disability, receipt of public assistance, record of offences, gender identity, and gender expression.

To ensure that police in Ontario are bias-free in their dealing with the public, the police code of conduct set out in O. Reg. 268/10, under the PSA, has directly incorporated the principles of the *Human Rights Code*. Here are some examples of misconduct involving human rights violations, as set out in the code of conduct:

2(1) Any chief of police or other police officer commits misconduct if he or she engages in,

(a) Discreditable Conduct, in that he or she,

(i) fails to treat or protect persons equally without discrimination with respect to police services because of race, ancestry, place of origin, colour, ethnic origin, citizenship, creed, sex, sexual orientation, age, marital status, family status or disability,

(ii) uses profane, abusive or insulting language that relates to a person's race, ancestry, place of origin, colour, ethnic origin, citizenship, creed, sex, sexual orientation, age, marital status, family status or disability.

For more on the Ontario police code of conduct, see Chapter 2.

Hiring and Training

The recruitment and training of officers is an important tool when it comes to guiding police in the effective use of discretion. Certain qualities in a recruit promise some facility with discretionary power: good character, integrity, honesty, compassion, professionalism, and cultural sensitivity.

Character

An individual's moral values and ethical sense have generally been formed long before he or she joins a police organization. The term *ethics* refers to our understanding of right and wrong, legal and illegal, good and bad. Our ethics come to us, generally speaking, at a very early age, from the environment in which we are raised. But they are also shaped by the organizational environment in which we work.

A police officer on the job sometimes has to take a course of action that conflicts with his or her own values but is in the best interest of the public. For example, in the early 1980s, a police officer was asked to protect an abortion clinic in downtown Toronto, the courts having recently ruled that abortions were legal. He refused to do so because of his religious belief that abortion is wrong. This officer's refusal put him in direct conflict with his own organization's rules.

Ethics play a key role in a police officer's proper use of discretionary powers. When police are called on to make split-second decisions, they often rely on their ethical judgments, which are a by-product of their values.

IT'S YOUR MOVE, OFFICER!

Scenario 7.4

You are a front-line uniform officer. You work in a mid-sized Ontario town that has its own police service. Although the town is growing, it is still the type of community where everybody seems to know each other.

On a quiet Friday night, you and your partner respond to a call regarding a domestic incident involving a husband and wife. Upon arrival at the home, you and your partner listen outside the door. You both hear a woman crying inside. Then a male voice says, "The cops in this town will do nothing, because my dad is the mayor."

You knock on the door and announce your presence, and are allowed to enter the house. Inside, you observe that the female is still crying, and you notice redness on her right cheek. She tells you that her husband slapped her across the face during an argument over their personal finances.

You take the husband aside to question him privately. He claims that he did not hit his wife; he says she slapped herself to incriminate him, then called the police. He says she told him that she would have him locked up. He then advises you that his father is the mayor and is also very good friends with the chief of police. He implies that it would not be in your best interest to charge him, especially since he did not touch or hit his wife.

Subsequently your partner, having spoken to the wife, tells you that she insists her husband slapped her face. She wants him charged. You keep the husband and wife apart while you and your partner discuss your options.

What would your ethical judgment tell you to do in this situation?

When recruiting potential officers, organizations look for particular character traits and core values in the candidates. These traits and values can influence a police officer's performance and the decisions they make.

Integrity

Integrity is a key part of discretionary decisions. Police officers can't simply be taught integrity. It is a character trait that is developed through life and should be part of a person's makeup before he or she becomes a police officer. That said, police organizations can offer specialized training in this area. Such training helps officers better understand the dynamics of integrity and how integrity affects the decisions they make. This training can include situational learning methods—for example, case studies that analyze ethical dilemmas officers may face. Organizations can also ensure that there is close supervision always available to working officers, to help them navigate their ethical dilemmas.

integrity
soundness of moral character

Honesty

Honesty is considered a core value in many Canadian police organizations, including the Toronto Police Service, whose mission statement (2014) says the following : "We are truthful and open in our interactions with each other and members of our communities." Police officers must be open and transparent in their decision-making and about their reasons for taking a particular course of action. Any form of deceit or deception by officers will cause them and their organization to be seen in a negative light; it will diminish the public's esteem for them.

Compassion

Police officers are continually called upon to exercise discretion effectively and to make good decisions. Compassionate regard for others can help with this challenge. It is a reliable guide when, as they often do, police have to deal with horrific events and with people in great physical and emotional pain.

Professionalism

Front-line police officers engage with members of the public every day. In doing so, they represent law and order as well as the police service that employs them. The Canadian public has high expectations of its police officers; we expect professionalism and high levels of competency.

Professionalism has a couple of facets. Officers in public must be professional in their dress and demeanour and must, when making decisions, be able to communicate openly, honestly, and consistently with the public. A professional appearance and manner help give the public confidence that police are accountable for their actions and transparent in all their dealings.

Consider, for example, a front-line officer who stops a motorist for speeding and decides to issue him a ticket. If the officer is sloppy in his or her appearance and is rude to the driver—in short, if he or she lacks professionalism—the driver will be left with a deeply negative impression of the officer and of policing in general. This impression will be quite different if the officer appears professional and is respectful to the driver, taking the time to explain why the ticket is being issued.

Multiculturalism and Cultural-Sensitivity Training

Multiculturalism in Canada poses unique challenges to police officers. In their daily activities, officers must deal with many different cultures, languages, morals, and values. To deal with these challenges, they receive special training. They learn, for example, that they need to be sensitive to individuals whose understanding of Canada's laws may be unclear or unusual owing to their cultural background. A zero-tolerance approach does not serve police officers well in these situations. Their discretionary powers, on the other hand, are very useful.

CHECK YOUR UNDERSTANDING

1. How does legislation, such as the Charter and the Ontario *Humans Rights Code*, affect police discretion?

2. Identify two important traits of a police candidate.

3. Why is cultural-sensitivity training so important for police officers in Canada?

Providing a Framework for Discretionary Decisions

Training is perhaps the key tool in ensuring that police officers exercise discretion lawfully and effectively. This training includes an established process for making discretionary decisions—a framework that takes certain factors into account.

Four Factors

The following are four factors that police consider when making discretionary decisions:

1. the offence that has been committed,
2. the person(s) involved,
3. any applicable organizational policies and procedures, and
4. potential alternative outcomes (see Figure 7.2).

To illustrate how these factors may affect discretionary decisions, let's consider the following scenario.

A 15-year-old girl enters the local drugstore. The store security officer observes her removing two packages of makeup from the shelf and placing them in her coat pocket. She leaves the store without paying for them. The security officer follows her outside and places her under arrest and seizes the stolen merchandise. They return to the store and go to its

FIGURE 7.2 Four Factors for Discretionary Decisions

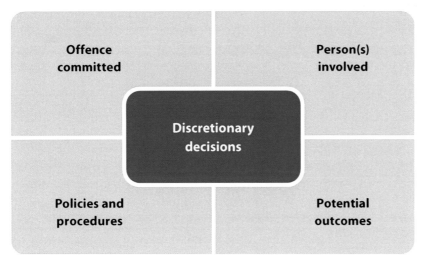

office, and the officer calls the police. When the attending officer arrives, she speaks to the security officer and confirms what took place and determines the value of the stolen property to be $10. The girl tells the officer she is in grade nine and states that she has no money to pay for the makeup. She is very sorry for having stolen the property and pleads with the officer not to charge her. The officer determines that the girl has never been in trouble with the police, that she comes from a good home, and that she does well in school. The police officer contacts her parents, who are very concerned about what their daughter has done and are coming to the store.

The Offence That Has Been Committed

The officer has to decide whether the girl's breach of the law is minor or major. One measure of this is whether the infractions relate to property damage, which constitutes a minor breach, or to a personal attack, assault, or threat against another person.

Our shoplifting scenario involves theft under $5,000—in other words, a minor property infraction. In fact, the stolen merchandise, valued at $10, has been fully recovered, so there is no monetary loss by the victim.

The Person(s) Involved

This factor takes into account the offender, the victim or complainant, and any witnesses. The officer would consider whether any extenuating circumstances exist with respect to either the offender or the victim. These circumstances may be related to the following factors, among others:

- age,
- physical size,
- mental stability, and
- motive.

In our scenario, the offender is a 15-year-old grade-nine student who comes from a good home, has never been in trouble with the police, and is remorseful. Another consideration is that her parents are concerned about what has happened and are involved in their daughter's life.

Applicable Organizational Policies and Procedures

The officer attending the scene would consider whether any policies and procedures are in place, including any laws, that would direct an officer in the laying of charges. In Ontario, for example, the Ministry of the Attorney General expects police to lay charges in incidents of domestic violence when there is sufficient evidence to do so. This expectation affects police discretion.

In the case of this shoplifting scenario, officers have to consider their police organization's policies and procedures regarding theft under $5,000 (shoplifting in particular), and they have to consider store policies. The officer in our shoplifting scenario might ask herself the following questions:

- Does the police service I work for have a zero-tolerance policy regarding this kind of crime?
- Does the drugstore (which is the victim, in this case) have a zero-tolerance policy toward shoplifting, regardless of the circumstances?

If either the store or the police service has such a policy, then the attending front-line officer has no discretionary powers.

Alternative Outcomes

Once the first three factors have been considered, the officer may consider alternatives to laying charges. In the process, the officer must consider not only the offender but the victim, too. The victim is sometimes left out of the police decision-making process, but the victim may have needs that must be met. For example, a young person joyriding in his or her parents' car may be accused of stealing the car by the police who stop him. The parents, who are the victims in this case, may want the police to deal with the matter in a way that does not involve the full weight of the justice system. Accordingly, when considering alternative outcomes, officers should ask the following questions:

- Is there sufficient evidence to arrest and charge the offender?
- Does charging the person meet the public interest?
- What are the victim's preferences in the matter?

In our shoplifting scenario, the offence of the girl's theft has been clearly established. This fact supports the laying of the charge. However, is laying a charge in the best interest of the girl, the drug store, or the public? Answering these questions is far more problematic.

Evaluating Public Interest

The consideration of what is in the public interest is central to any exercise of police discretion. Decisions resulting from police discretion must be based on each individual situation and on the officer's careful consideration of the circumstances. In the *Beaudry* decision, the SCC (2007, p. 191) stated the following:

> In determining whether a decision resulting from an exercise of police discretion is proper, it is therefore important to consider the material circumstances in which the discretion was exercised. The justification offered must be proportionate to the seriousness of the conduct and it must be clear that the discretion was exercised in the public interest.

As this quotation indicates, the highest court in Canada, while recognizing the need for police discretion, has stipulated that it must serve the public interest.

Officers must consider, then, whether the laying of the charge and the subsequent prosecution of the case is in the best interest of all those involved, including the larger community. Would a charge provide the best overall deterrent factor? Would it best serve the larger public interest? Here are a few factors that the officer may consider when evaluating what is in the public's best interest.

Nature of the Offence

- Has the offender injured the victim?
- Does the offender still pose a substantial threat to the victim, and does the victim fear the offender?
- Has the offender caused a significant monetary loss through theft or damage?

If violence is involved, or if the victim fears the perpetrator, the officer is likely to arrest and charge the suspect. And if the crime involves significant amounts of money, it is in the public interest to pursue charges rather than to issue a warning. These police decisions send a clear message to the suspect and to the public that actions threatening others' well-being and material security will not be tolerated.

Mitigating Factors

Officers often need to consider any mitigating factors relating to the following persons:

1. Victim
   - Is the victim a young person or a senior who may be vulnerable because of his or her age?
   - What was his or her physical condition at the time of the offence?
   - Was the victim able to defend himself or herself, based on the above two factors?
2. Witness(es)
3. Other members of the public negatively affected by the offence
4. Offender
   - What is the offender's age? Is the offender a young person or a senior?
   - What was the offender's physical condition at the time the offence was committed?
   - What was the offender's state of mind at the time the offence was committed? Was the offender under any influence, such as alcohol or drugs, that may have impaired his or her thinking at the time?
   - What is the offender's level of intelligence? Is the offender sufficiently intelligent to appreciate the offence he or she has committed?
   - Is the offender of sound mind? Is he or she mentally disabled in some way, or suffering from a mental condition that impairs his or her understanding?

Relationship Between Offender and Victim (or Witness)

Is there a relationship between the offender and the victim (or the witness) that may be an important factor in why the offence occurred and whether it is likely to recur? This is often a significant factor in discretionary decisions. A person charged with an assault against a total stranger will likely be released on the condition that he or she has no further communication or contact with the victim. A person charged with an assault against a spouse or a family member potentially poses a greater risk, and this will affect the decision to release and the conditions of release.

Costs of Arresting, Charging, and Prosecuting the Offender

Although an officer's discretionary decisions should not really be influenced by cost considerations, the expense of prosecution qualifies as a public interest factor and must be taken into account.

The officer in our shoplifting scenario, for example, has to decide whether it is in the public interest to prosecute a first-time 15-year-old offender for stealing ten dollars' worth of makeup. The nature of the offence (shoplifting) hardly warrants a charge. Her age also argues against a charge. Under these circumstances, the cost of prosecuting the offender also becomes a factor and argues for an alternative (that is, a discretionary) course of action.

In our shoplifting scenario, the argument for a discretionary decision on the officer's part and an alternative to laying charges may seem straightforward, but it isn't. The officer has to consider what she is hoping to achieve by her decision. What response will best deter the young girl from reoffending? What message will her decision send out to other young people and to the community as a whole? The appropriate decision is the one that confirms the public's confidence that the police and the justice system may be trusted to do the right thing for the right reasons.

CHECK YOUR UNDERSTANDING

1. What are the four main factors that police must consider in discretionary decisions?

2. In domestic violence situations, how does police organizational policy affect an officer's discretionary decisions?

3. Describe one or two ways that public interest influences police decisions.

CHAPTER SUMMARY

You cannot, as a police officer, foresee every situation in which you'll find yourself. What is certain is that you'll be required to make discretionary decisions very often and sometimes in a split second. Discretionary power enables you to respond fluidly to unforeseen and unprecedented situations. But, as this chapter has shown, making discretionary decisions is a balancing act influenced by many factors—your community's needs (environment); the mandates of legislation and of your police organization (administration); and your own experience and needs (that is, individual and situational factors).

The benefits of discretionary decision-making by police must be weighed against the challenges it poses. On the one hand, discretionary power is crucial to a policing system that is compassionate and that reflects community needs. Discretionary power enables police forces to use their resources judiciously and to stay within their operating budgets. On the other hand, as critics allege, the discretionary powers conferred on police can create a policing system that is uneven and inconsistent. It can also create uncertainty for officers as they try to adapt to changing laws and morals within communities that are themselves divided over these changes. Discretionary powers can also lead to discriminatory practices insofar as they authorize individual police officers to make decisions based on their personal values and beliefs.

The problems posed by police discretion admit of no perfect solutions. Lawmakers can help by passing legislation that realistically acknowledges the purposes and challenges of policing. The policies of police services, including thoughtful hiring and training practices, can fortify these legislative efforts. In the end, a police officer strives to make decisions that balance the various imperatives involved in any policing situation—public interest, departmental policy, and official legislation, as well as his or her own perceptions and ethical sense.

KEY TERMS

direct discrimination, 152
discretion, 144
discrimination, 152
indirect discrimination, 153
integrity, 157
racial profiling, 152
systemic discrimination, 153

REFERENCES

Beaudry, R v. (2007). 2007 SCC 5, [2007] 1 SCR 190.

Canadian Charter of Rights and Freedoms. (1982). Part I of the *Constitution Act, 1982*, RSC 1985, app. II, no. 44.

Canadian Human Rights Act. (1985). RSC 1985, c. H-6.

Davis, K.C. (1971). *Discretionary justice: A preliminary inquiry.* Baton Rouge, LA: Louisiana State University Press.

Department of Justice. (2013). Police discretion with young offenders. Retrieved from http://www.justice.gc.ca/eng/rp-pr/cj-jp/yj-jj/discre/rep-rap.html.

Gleason, T. (2006, November). Ethics training for police. *The Police Chief, 73*(11). Retrieved from http://www.policechiefmagazine.org/magazine/index.cfm?fuseaction=display_arch &article_id=1054&issue_id=112006.

Greenspan, E.L., & Rosenberg, M. (2014). *Martin's Annual Criminal Code: Incorporating RSC 1985.* Aurora, Ont.: Canada Law Book.

Human Rights Code. (1990). RSO 1990, c. H.19.

Ontario Human Rights Commission (OHRC). (n.d.). What is racial profiling? (fact sheet). Queen's Printer for Ontario. retrieved from http://www.ohrc.on.ca/en/what-racial-profiling-fact-sheet.

Police Services Act. (1990). RSO 1990, c. P.15.

Police Services Act, O. Reg. 268/10. (2010). General.

Quickfall, R c. (1993). 78 CCC (3d) 563, [1993] RJQ 468 (CA).

Toronto Police Service. (2014). Mission statement. Retrieved from http://www.torontopolice.on.ca/mission-values.php.

FURTHER READING

Civilian Review and Complaints Commission for the Royal Canadian Mounted Police. (2014). Features and highlights. Retrieved from http://www.crcc-ccetp.gc.ca/.

Department of Justice. (2013). Police discretion with young offenders. Retrieved from http://www.justice.gc.ca/eng/rp-pr/cj-jp/yj-jj/discre/rep-rap.html.

Lewis, C.D. (2011). Policing Aboriginal critical incidents. *The Police Chief*, *78*(6), 60-65. Retrieved from http://www.policechiefmagazine.org/magazine/index.cfm?fuseaction=display &article_id=2400&issue_id=62011.

REVIEW QUESTIONS

Multiple Choice

1. An officer's use of discretion is *not* affected by
   a. regulations found within provincial offences
   b. the officer's mental state
   c. a quota for arrests imposed by the officer's own police organization
   d. how the media reports the story

2. Section 42 of the *Police Services Act* states that the main duties of the police include
   a. preventing crimes and other offences
   b. preserving the peace
   c. apprehending criminals and other offenders
   d. all of the above

3. Environmental factors have a tremendous influence on how police officers use discretion. Which of the following is *not* considered an environmental factor?
   a. the social makeup of the community
   b. the economic makeup of the community
   c. the personal thoughts of the officer
   d. the demographic makeup of the community

4. Direct discrimination is based on different characteristics, such as
   a. age
   b. gender
   c. culture
   d. all of the above

5. When police organizations recruit potential officers, they look for particular traits and core values in the candidate. Which of the following is *not* considered an essential trait in a candidate?

   a. honesty

   b. assertiveness

   c. integrity

   d. compassion

True or False

_____ **1.** Police officers exercise their discretion every day in performing their duties.

_____ **2.** Racial profiling is an effective and valuable police tool.

_____ **3.** It is easy to establish guidelines for the use of discretion.

_____ **4.** Discretion and the ability to exercise it are what make law enforcement work.

_____ **5.** Discretion involves considering not only what to do in a given situation, but also how to do it.

_____ **6.** Every exercise of discretion may be questioned by the public.

_____ **7.** Exercising discretion can require a police officer to choose which of two incompatible duties he or she will perform in a given situation.

_____ **8.** A police officer should make an arrest for every offence he or she witnesses, even when the arrest may result in a riot.

_____ **9.** Every exercise of discretion can be an opening through which the police officer's personal biases may surface.

_____**10.** When making a discretionary decision, police officers must take into consideration how the public would perceive their decision.

Short Answer

1. Explain why police need to have the power to make discretionary decisions. Should there be limits on this power?

2. How might an officer's individual character and level of experience affect his or her discretionary decision-making abilities? Explain, providing examples.

3. How do environmental factors affect the discretionary decision-making of police?

4. What role does compassion have in discretionary decision-making?

5. Police often look for alternatives to charging young offenders. Do you believe young offenders should be treated differently from adult offenders? Explain.

It's Your Move, Officer!

A. Nineteen-year-old Boris is an avid hockey fan. He hears from a buddy that the sporting goods store in his neighbourhood has a new line of hockey caps, so he decides to drop by to browse. At the store, he tries on several caps. They are $30 each and he can't afford one. He doesn't have a job. When he thinks no one is looking, he puts a hat on and pulls up the hood of his sweatshirt to hide it and heads for the door. As he steps outside the store, he is stopped by the store security and taken back to the store's security office. The police are called.

You are the responding officer. The store security advises you that the store has no specific policy for laying charges and leaves the decision to you. Meanwhile, Boris is very remorseful and tells you that he has never before been in trouble with the law. You confirm this to be true.

As the responding officer, you have the discretion to charge or not to charge. Assess the situation and try to make the decision that is right for all the parties involved. State the reasons for your decision.

B. At around 1:00 a.m., while on foot patrol in the club district in downtown Toronto, you and your partner hear a loud argument. Turning toward the noise, you see two young women arguing as they stand in line outside a club. You and your partner decide to intervene.

You learn that Tia is the first name of one of these women and that she is only 18 years old. You become concerned—the licensed nightclub should be restricted to patrons 19 years of age and older. While discussing this with Tia, you notice that she is upset and starts to cry. She blurts out that she is scared because she has a small amount of marijuana in her coat pocket. She pulls out the plastic bag containing it. You have not placed Tia under arrest up to this point and therefore, prior to this admission of hers, have had no authority to search her. Simple possession of marijuana is a summary conviction offence under the authority of the *Controlled Drugs and Substances Act*, and it is, in this instance, a found committing offence. Since Tia has admitted to possessing the drug and has turned it over to you, you have a number of options available to you.

As the investigating officer, how would you proceed in this situation? Provide reasons for your decision.

C. You are a front-line uniform officer in Ontario who witnesses two similar events, both involving a young man kicking in the basement window of an abandoned building. In the first case, the young man is wearing a suit and tie. In the second case, the young man is wearing the colours of a local gang. Both men explain to you that they have just lost their jobs and are looking for a place to shelter for the night.

You can either warn the offender not to do it again and let him go, or arrest and charge him for mischief under $5,000. What would you do in each case? Why?

Warrantless Search and Seizure

8

LEARNING OUTCOMES

After completing this chapter, you should be able to:

- Explain the relationship between police search authority and the Charter.

- Compare *search incident to arrest* with *search incident to investigative detention*.

- Describe the situations where a police officer can search without a warrant.

- Describe the police authority to search outside of an arrest.

- Describe warrantless search authority under special circumstances, including school searches.

- Describe search powers under the plain-view doctrine.

- Explain what the term *continuity* means in relation to seized property.

ON SCENE

It's late on a snowy December night.* Officer Chu and Officer Lancing are responding to a noise complaint at an apartment building in Peterborough. One of the tenants, Frank Harkin, has been drinking with friends much of the evening. Harkin's friends have left, but he refused to turn down his music when the building's manager asked him to. The exasperated manager called in the complaint, hoping that police officers might be able to force Harkin to cooperate. When the officers arrive and Harkin finally answers his door, he is abusive and refuses to turn the music down.

As the conversation progresses, Officer Chu observes that Harkin appears to have an object in his right hand, hidden behind the top of his right leg. She asks him what's in his hand, but he doesn't respond. She repeats her question, and again Harkin ignores her. Instead, he continues to be rude and makes no move to turn down the music. Officer Chu continues to monitor Harkin's right hand, and she gently pushes the door open a few inches more so that she can see inside his apartment and perhaps get a better look at what he is hiding behind his leg. All at once her deepest fear is confirmed: she recognizes the butt of a handgun.

"Gun!" she calls out, alerting her partner. At the same time, she reaches forward to take control of Harkin's right hand and arm, and the two officers push through the door, subduing the struggling man. After a short struggle, the officers successfully disarm Harkin, seizing a loaded 9 mm Beretta. He is placed in handcuffs and arrested on several charges. One of them relates to s. 86(1) of the *Criminal Code*—handling a firearm in a careless manner or without reasonable precautions for the safety of other persons.

Do you think the officers acted appropriately? Will the arrest stand up in court? Or was this an unlawful search and seizure that violated Harkin's Charter rights?

Introduction

warrantless search
a search conducted without a warrant; presumed to be unreasonable unless the Crown demonstrates, on a balance of probabilities, that it is reasonable

Police powers of search and seizure are extremely important. **Warrantless searches** are a routine part of an officer's job, conducted every day by police across Canada. At the same time, s. 8 of the Charter guarantees that every person in Canada "has the right to be secure against unreasonable search or seizure." This right is founded on an individual's reasonable expectation of privacy. The consequence of this tension between a police officer's duty and a citizen's Charter right to privacy has been far-reaching; in almost every criminal trial in Canada, trial judges must deal with the question of whether a search and seizure was "reasonable."

What are "search and seizure" powers? Definitions of them are fairly general. The Law Reform Commission of Canada (1983, p. 10) has defined them as "powers to perform intrusions for the purpose of obtaining things, funds or pre-existing information." These powers include the right to search a person, place, or vehicle, and they now include indirect searches in the form of wiretap and video surveillance. The term *seizure* has been

---

*   This scenario is based on *R v. MacDonald* (2014).

defined in case law. The Supreme Court of Canada (SCC) ruled in *R v. Dyment* (1988, para. 26) that "the essence of a seizure under s. 8 is the taking of a *thing* from a person by a public authority without that person's consent [emphasis added]." The significance of this wording is that it restricts *seizure*, under s. 8 of the Charter, to "tangible things" only. This interpretation was affirmed in the trial matter of *Thomson Newspapers Ltd. v. Canada (Director of Investigation and Research, Restrictive Trade Practices Commission)* (1990). As for a definition of *search*, there is no explicit definition of this term in case law, even though the SCC ruling in *R v. Evans* (1996, para. 41) suggests that search involves some form of examination or scrutiny by officials representing the government.

It is important that police officers understand the nature and limits of their search and seizure powers. If a trial judge finds that any evidence was obtained in a manner that infringed on or denied a person's s. 8 Charter right, the evidence collected *may* be ruled inadmissible in court. This is called a **Charter remedy**. Any person accused of a crime who believes their Charter rights were infringed upon can apply for a Charter remedy. When police officers can show that the arrest and search were lawful, the search and seizure of property will generally survive any s. 8 Charter challenge. In this chapter, we will explore the conditions under which warrantless searches can be conducted, and you will learn about the limits on these searches.

Charter remedies
remedies that the courts provide to ensure that any information or evidence gathered by police was obtained in accordance with the accused's Charter rights; may include the exclusion of items from evidence at trial

Search Authority

The police authority to conduct warrantless searches of a person, of the person's immediate surroundings, and, in some cases, even of the person's home flows from a basic necessity of policing. Police need to be able to gain control of a situation and to obtain information and evidence. The authority given to police in this regard does not presume any reduced right to privacy for the arrested person. The accused's s. 8 Charter right must be respected. This means that a search must be deemed to be "reasonable."

In 1984, the SCC made its first ruling with respect to reasonable search under the newly instituted Charter. In *Hunter v. Southam Inc.*, the court (1984, pp. 2-3) stated the following:

> Section 8 of the Charter guarantees a broad and general right to be secure from unreasonable searches and seizures which extends at least so far as to protect the right of privacy from unjustified state intrusion. Its purpose requires that unjustified searches be prevented. It is not enough that a determination be made, after the fact, that the search should not have been conducted. This can only be accomplished by a requirement of prior authorization. Accordingly, prior authorization, where feasible, is a precondition for a valid search and seizure. It follows that warrantless searches are *prima facie* unreasonable under s. 8. The party seeking to justify a warrantless search bears the onus of rebutting the presumption of unreasonableness.

This statement makes two important points about warrantless searches:

1. *Prior authorization is the preferred precondition for a valid search and seizure.* This reflects the recommendations made by the Law Reform Commission of Canada (1983). The commission concluded that search *with* a warrant should be the rule, and search without a warrant the exception.

2. *Warrantless searches are considered **prima facie** to be unreasonable.* Any search that is conducted without a warrant is presumed to be unreasonable until proven otherwise. The onus rests with the Crown, then, to demonstrate, on a balance of probabilities, that a warrantless search was reasonable.

prima facie
Latin for "at first look"; evident from the facts; evidence that, if not contradicted, will be sufficient to prove a particular proposition or fact

However, as you will learn in this chapter, police do have the authority to conduct warrantless searches under certain circumstances. This authority has been set out in various case law decisions, the following two in particular:

- *Cloutier v. Langlois* (1990), and
- *R v. Caslake* (1998).

Warrantless searches conducted under circumstances deemed acceptable in these case law decisions will usually survive a Charter challenge in court, as long as the police can clearly articulate why they believed the search was necessary.

CHECK YOUR UNDERSTANDING

1. What is a Charter remedy?
2. Identify two important aspects of the SCC ruling in *Hunter v. Southam Inc.*
3. Explain what is meant by *"prima facie* unreasonable" with respect to warrantless searches.

Search Power Incident to Arrest and Incident to Detention

Until recently, the search powers of police were similar for arrest and for investigative detention. In either case, suspects could be searched to ensure the officers' safety. This situation changed in 2014, with the SCC ruling in *R v. MacDonald* (2014). Let's take a look at police searches under these two circumstances—arrest, on the one hand, and investigative detention on the other—and explore how the recent ruling has changed them.

Search Incident to Arrest

Search incident to arrest is the type of search that an officer most routinely performs. In the case of lawful arrest, the various courts throughout Canada have stated that police may search a person to ensure the officer's safety and to secure evidence related to the offence.

The test for a legitimate search, whether the search is incident to arrest or to a lawful detention, is the following: *Was it reasonably necessary in the circumstances?* In conducting a search incident to a lawful arrest, police officers are looking for weapons, for evidence directly related to the offence, for tools of escape, and for evidence that will establish and confirm the arrested person's identity. Police searches, in other words, must be performed to one of the following three ends:

1. to ensure the safety of the police and the public by removing any weapons or tools of escape that are in the possession of the arrested person;
2. to protect evidence from destruction at the hands of the arrested person or others; or
3. to effect the prompt and effective discovery of evidence relevant to the commission of an offence, which can be used at the trial of the accused.

The authority to search without a warrant a person who has been arrested is derived from English common law. The SCC confirmed in *R v. Golden* (2001, para. 84) that such a search is "an established exception to the general rule that warrantless searches are *prima facie* unreasonable." Any question regarding the lawfulness of such a search will depend on the lawfulness of the original detention and arrest. In other words, the police officer does not need to establish an independent set of reasonable grounds in order to conduct the search.

There are time limits on search incident to arrest. As a general rule, searches that are truly incidental to arrest will occur within a reasonable period of time after the arrest. That said, a delayed search may qualify as being incidental to arrest.

Police officers must understand that if their initial detention and arrest of a person were lawful and their subsequent search was reasonable, then they'll be able to rebut any presumption of unreasonableness related to the search. This point is crucial for both the police and the arrested person. A search incident to arrest may support charges against a guilty party, but it may also uncover information or evidence that exonerates an innocent party and enables officers to make the quick decision to set the person free.

Search Incident to Investigative Detention

The police power to search incident to investigative detention is quite different from the police power to search incident to arrest. Police authority in this area is in flux; police organizations and their officers must stay abreast of these changing circumstances. Until recently, police officers had the authority to do a safety search on a detained individual if the officer(s) had reasonable grounds to *believe* that the individual might have a weapon or any other item that threatened the safety of the officer(s), of the suspect, or of the general public. In *R v. Mann* (2004), the courts clearly distinguished between the circumstances authorizing an officer to detain an individual and the circumstances authorizing an officer to search an individual:

1. To *detain* an individual, police need reasonable grounds to *suspect* that an individual may be connected to a particular crime.

2. To *search* an individual, police need reasonable grounds to *believe* that the officers' safety or the safety of others is at risk.

In 2014, as a result of the SCC's ruling in *R v. MacDonald*, the conditions justifying a police search incident to investigative detention became more stringent. The scenario at the opening of this chapter is based on the *MacDonald* case. In 2009, two Halifax police officers, Constable Pierce and Sergeant Boyd, were attending the apartment of Erin MacDonald after he refused to turn down his music. As in the vignette, MacDonald refused to divulge to police what he was hiding behind his leg and he had to be subdued when they realized it was a handgun. As in the opening vignette, Sergeant Boyd had pushed the apartment door open slightly to get a better look at what MacDonald was hiding.

MacDonald challenged the arrest in court, saying that Sergeant Boyd's act of pushing the door open constituted a search, which violated his right to a reasonable expectation of privacy and his s. 8 Charter right. The trial judge agreed that the officer's action did, in fact, constitute a search because it surpassed an officer's "implied licence to approach the door of a residence and knock," as described in *R v. Evans* (1996, paras. 15, 21). The trial judge also ruled, as did the SCC (2014, para. 27) when it heard the case, that Sergeant Boyd's action "constituted an intrusion upon Mr. MacDonald's reasonable privacy interest in his dwelling." However, the judge also stated that the officers' search was reasonable because it met the three conditions under which, according to the SCC decision in *R v. Collins* (1987), a warrantless search is deemed to be reasonable: (1) it is authorized by law; (2) the law itself is reasonable; and (3) the manner in which the search is carried out is also reasonable. The officer's actions were aimed at eliminating what the SCC later described, in considering the same case (2014, para. 32), as "threats to the safety of the public or the police."

MacDonald challenged this decision, but it was upheld by the SCC. The court stated that the officers' actions were necessary to protect their safety. As to the question whether their actions constituted a Charter violation, the court ruled that these actions did not so qualify; the officers had not gone far enough in violating MacDonald's reasonable expectation of privacy.

The wording of the SCC's ruling in *MacDonald* is crucial to our understanding of the law concerning searches incident to investigative detention. The SCC emphasized—by referring several times to the fact—that the officers' actions were *only* justifiable because the officers had reasonable grounds to believe that MacDonald was *armed and dangerous*. Having reasonable grounds to *believe* that a person is armed with an **offensive weapon** is a more stringent standard than having reasonable grounds to *believe* that the officers' safety or the safety of others is at risk.

After the SCC ruling in *MacDonald*, police officers, in order to conduct a pat-down search of a person being detained, have to have reasonable grounds to believe that the detained person *is in possession of an offensive weapon*. In other words, officers are not authorized to conduct a search incident to investigative detention unless they have reasonable grounds to believe the detained person is armed and dangerous. They cannot be merely searching for evidence.

The law concerning search incident to investigative detention is evolving, and police must follow this evolution closely. The SCC's ruling in *MacDonald* was not unanimous; the dissenting justices expressed a belief that this new standard puts police in jeopardy. Many people in the legal community believe that this search authority will be further refined in future decisions.

offensive weapon
an object designed to be used or intended to be used to cause injury, death, threat, or intimidation

IT'S YOUR MOVE, OFFICER!

Scenario 8.1

You are a uniform police officer out on general patrol. You receive a radio call telling you that a street robbery just occurred in a park near where you are. You're told that, during the robbery, the victim was threatened with a knife. A very generic description of the suspect is provided.

You head toward the park to look for the suspect. When you are about two blocks away from the park, you see a male who bears some resemblance to the generic description you were given. You approach him for questioning. While talking to him, you notice a bulge in the inner right pocket of his jeans. You believe it may be the handle of a knife.

What will you do now?

CHECK YOUR UNDERSTANDING

1. Identify four things that police are looking for when conducting a search incident to arrest.

2. What is the difference between search incident to arrest and search incident to investigative detention?

3. What is the only thing an officer can search for when conducting a search incident to investigative detention?

Where Can Officers Search?

Once an arrest has been made, officers have the lawful right to search the person's clothes along with anything the person has in his or her possession, such as a knapsack or a purse. The scope of authorized search extends to the immediate surroundings of the arrest—for example, to the arrested person's motor vehicle (if that is the place where he or she was placed under arrest).

The Search of a Person

When searching a person, police have four levels of search power (see Table 8.1). These categories are based on common law and must be incident to the person's lawful arrest. In addition to this search power incident to arrest, police have a search power incident to investigative detention (as discussed above).

TABLE 8.1 Four Levels of Search Power

LEVEL 1 Field Search	This level of search involves a search on the street or out in the field. It usually consists of a pat-down search (a frisk) after a person has been arrested. However, it may also be conducted incident to investigative detention if the officer has reasonable grounds to believe that the person being investigated is armed. Officers will generally inspect the pockets of the clothing worn by the arrested person. The search will not generally involve the removal of any clothing other than outerwear, such as a jacket, headwear, and gloves/mitts.
LEVEL 2 Thorough Search	This level of search is generally conducted at a police facility or at least in private, away from public view. It involves the removal of some clothing, but none that would expose a person's undergarments. Unless exigent circumstances exist at the time of the arrest, a police officer will not conduct a thorough search of an arrested person in the public view.
LEVEL 3 Complete or "Strip" Search	This level of search is conducted at a police facility and involves the removal of all the clothing. Because this is a very intrusive search, the police officer requesting to do the search must have strong grounds to believe the person may be concealing evidence, weapons, or a tool of escape. It's not lawful for a police organization to have a general policy of strip-searching prisoners entering a police facility or detention area. The onus of proving the necessity of this kind of search is on the officer who is making the request, not on the supervisor at the police facility who is booking the prisoner into the police facility.
LEVEL 4 Body Search	This level of search involves a body search, and must be conducted at a hospital by a medical doctor. It involves a situation where the arresting officer believes the arrested person has concealed drugs within his or her body (e.g., in the anus or vagina). Because this is such an intrusive search, it has to be conducted with the consent of the arrested party. If the person will not consent to a body search, the police must obtain a search warrant to allow the medical doctor to conduct the search. In the absence of consent or a warrant, the medical doctor would actually be committing an assault on the person. In most instances, simply stating that the police need to obtain the drugs for evidence does not justify such a search. Justification generally requires an explanation that the drugs need to be removed to protect the health of the person concealing the drugs within his or her body.

A TURNING POINT IN STRIP SEARCHES

The fact that strip searches today need both to be justified and to be done in private is owing to the SCC decision in *R v. Golden* (2001). In that case, police had a suspected drug trafficker under observation at a downtown sandwich shop in Toronto, a place where trafficking was known to occur. Officers decided to arrest the suspect after observing him participate in what they believed to be several drug-related transactions.

After the arrest, police found what appeared to be crack cocaine under the table where the suspect was sitting at the time of his arrest. One officer also saw the suspect crushing between his fingers what the officer believed to be crack cocaine. A pat-down search failed to produce any weapons or narcotics, so the officers took the suspect to a stairwell for a further search. They undid his pants and pulled the waistband of his pants and of his underwear back from his skin. This police action revealed, protruding from between the suspect's buttocks, a plastic bag containing a white substance. A brief altercation ensued in which an officer was hip-checked and scratched. Then the officers took the suspect to a booth inside the shop where they bent him over a bench, pulled his pants and underwear down to his knees, and attempted to remove the plastic bag from between his buttocks. This proved astonishingly difficult. After some considerable effort, a package containing 10.1 grams of cocaine was obtained. The man was placed under arrest for possession of a narcotic for the purpose of trafficking and for police assault. He was strip-searched again at the police station before being fingerprinted and detained.

The defence counsel argued that the case should be dismissed because the strip search, and the way that it was conducted, violated the suspect's rights under ss. 8 and 24 of the Charter. The court disagreed, and the suspect was convicted. However, in 2001, the SCC overturned the lower court's ruling, allowing the appeal, overturning the conviction, and entering an acquittal. In its ruling, the court (2001, para. 90) said that strip searches are "inherently humiliating and degrading for detainees regardless of the manner in which they are carried out." In light of that fact, the court emphasized the importance of preventing unjustified searches, and it stressed that police should not routinely perform strip searches of the sort undergone by Golden.

The SCC ruling in *R v. Golden* went further in defining police authority with respect to strip searches. The court specified, for example, when and where such searches

Source: Mike Drew/Calgary Sun/QMI Agency.

Officers in Calgary conduct a pat-down search of a suspect after arresting him in a parking lot.

should be conducted, and it stated that the reasonable grounds justifying an arrest did not include the right to carry out a strip search. Police must provide—in addition to the reasonable grounds that justify the arrest—reasonable grounds for the strip search. Reasonable grounds for the strip search would be the need to discover weapons in the detainee's possession or to discover evidence that he or she might otherwise dispose of or destroy. The court also stressed the importance of conducting a strip search in such a way that it does not infringe the detainee's s. 8 Charter rights.

The decision in *R v. Golden* is an important one for all police officers in Canada. Police must find the justification for a strip search in the circumstances of each particular incident. Strip-searching cannot be a standard procedure based on a police organization's blanket policy. Also, unless exigent circumstances exist, police must conduct the strip search at a police facility in a professional manner, and not in a manner that humiliates or embarrasses the arrested person.

The Search of a Vehicle Incident to Arrest

As we noted above, the common law authority to search incident to an arrest extends to an accused's immediate surroundings—his or her car, for example, if that is where the arrest occurred. This applies regardless of whether the accused is actually the owner of the vehicle. However, the police authority to search a vehicle incident to an arrest, as well as the scope of the authorized search, is not absolute. It depends on a number of factors, including the following:

- the basis for the arrest and whether the search is for a valid purpose related to the offence;
- the location of the motor vehicle in relation to the place of arrest; and
- other relevant circumstances.

The arrested person has no heightened expectations of privacy relating to a motor vehicle. The usual common law principles regarding search incident to arrest apply to a motor vehicle. This common law authority was affirmed in *R v. Mohamad* (2004). In that case, police arrested an individual while he was in possession of a stolen motor vehicle. The police proceeded to conduct a search of the vehicle incident to the arrest. During the search, officers found a briefcase, which they opened and searched. In the trial that followed, the defendant asked that the evidence in the briefcase be dismissed because the search violated his Charter right under s. 8. The court dismissed the request on the grounds that the arresting officer had the authority, incident to the arrest, to discover and to preserve evidence, as well as the duty to search the vehicle and its contents for that purpose.

As with any form of warrantless search, the warrantless search of a motor vehicle incident to arrest will be justified so long as it can be proven that the arrest was both lawful and reasonable. Such proof rebuts the presumption that a warrantless search is unreasonable.

CHECK YOUR UNDERSTANDING

1. Identify four levels of searches that police may conduct.
2. Describe what is involved in a police strip search, also known as a complete search.
3. List two factors determining whether police have the right to search a vehicle incident to arrest.

Search Outside of Arrest

The Law Reform Commission of Canada (1983) has acknowledged that there are circumstances outside of arrest in which police officers may need search and seizure powers. Let's take a look at some of these circumstances.

Consent Searches

The police authority to search incident to arrest, as we have discussed, is derived from common law. The Law Reform Commission of Canada (1983, para. 116) has identified *search on consent* as one of the two "major crime-related categories of searches or seizures" that are "still recognized at common law." The commission (1983, para. 81) has stated the following:

concurrence
agreement that negates
the intrusive potential
of a search-and-seizure
activity; principle whereby
a search consented to by
the person being searched
requires no authorizing
document from police

In the case of "consent" searches, the distinct underlying premise has been that since the intrusive potential of a search and seizure activity is negated by the **concurrence** of the individual affected, no document need authorize the peace officer's actions. [emphasis added]

The commission's fifth recommendation (1983, p. 157) with respect to consent searches is as follows:

A peace officer should be authorized to search without a warrant:
    (a) any person who consents to a search of his person; and
    (b) any place or vehicle, with the consent of a person present and ostensibly competent to consent to such a search.
    A peace officer should be empowered to seize any "objects of seizure" found in the course of a consent search.

The law concerning consent search is among the most confusing areas of criminal law in Canada. In many trial proceedings, lawyers and judges often disagree in their interpretations of it.

Let's start by considering the question most often asked by people who have been stopped by the police: *Do I have to consent to a police request to search?* The simple answer is *no*. But it's never really that simple when it comes to interactions with the police. A person stopped by the police needs to keep in mind that, as we have seen, the circumstances in which police are authorized to search a person and his or her immediate surroundings without consent are very numerous. So the police can't always be refused, even if they seem to be asking for consent. In situations where police actually do require consent, the consent must be voluntary and informed, and the person being searched must have given it without any form of coercion.

Third-Party Consent

third-party consent
search consent given
by someone other
than the accused

An individual can consent to a warrantless search by police, but can a person do this if it would implicate another person? This kind of consent is referred to as **third-party consent**.

As you would expect, the owner of a home or the authorized occupant can give the police consent to search the residence. However, this is not always straightforward. For example, can a husband give consent to a search that might turn up evidence of an offence committed by his wife? Can a parent consent to a search of a child's bedroom if the parent believes that the child is involved in illegal activity? Can a landlord consent to a search of an apartment in a building he or she owns?

In each of these cases, the answer is *no*. In the case of the husband and wife, both jointly own or lease the property, and police need *both* rightful owners' consent in order to search it. In the case of children living at home, the law has determined that they have a reasonable expectation of privacy in the space they occupy in the home, even if they don't have title to the property. Any search of this area without a warrant or without their consent would be considered a breach of their Charter rights.

Similarly, as established in *R v. Mercer* (1992), a landlord, even though he or she holds title to a property, does not qualify as an *authorized occupant* of the residence and cannot give consent to search it when it is leased to another individual. The same is true for hotel owners and management, with respect to guest rooms. A guest at a hotel can expect reasonable privacy within his or her room, and the hotel owner or management cannot authorize entry into that room (or open a hotel safe for police) without a warrant.

One final question to consider is whether a *guest* at a home or residence can give police consent to conduct a warrantless search of the residence. The answer is *yes*. However, such

FIGURE 8.1 Consent Conditions

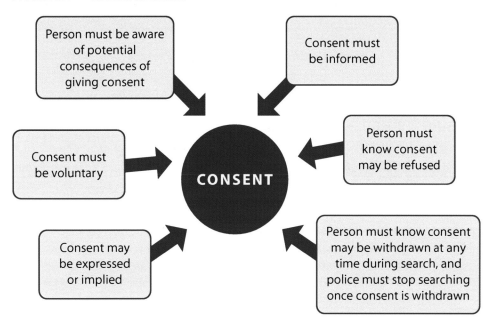

consent can be immediately revoked by the homeowner. This limitation was established in *R v. Thomas* (1991). In this case, police officers in St. John's, Newfoundland, responding to a noise complaint, entered a premises at the invitation of an individual who was hosting a party in his friend Mrs. Thomas's home. When the police confronted Mrs. Thomas, she demanded that they leave immediately. Before officers could comply with her request, an altercation broke out between police officers, a person attending the party, and Mrs. Thomas. Charges were laid but later dismissed because the court ruled that the officers were no longer rightfully on the premises. The court (1991, para. 46) stated the following: "Unless authorized by statute or the common law, a police officer may not enter the premises of another without that other's permission and must leave if and when that permission is revoked."

For all consent searches involving third-party consent, the police must have a subjective belief that they have consent to conduct the search, and it must be an objectively reasonable belief in the circumstances. Where the police wrongly rely upon the consent of a third party, the reasonableness of their belief will likely face a strong Charter challenge.

Exigent Circumstances and Search Authority

What about the factor of exigent circumstances, including hot pursuit, in relation to warrantless search and seizure powers?

Police powers with respect to exigent circumstances are clearly laid out in s. 529.3(1) of the Code and have been tested and reinforced in case law. For example, *R v. Godoy* (1999) supported police authority to enter a premises in response to a 911 call even when the resident attempts to deny them access. Police are clearly authorized to enter a premises and make an arrest under these circumstances. But what about their search and seizure authority?

Generally speaking, officers in these situations—that is, entering a residence to make a warrantless arrest on the grounds of exigent circumstances—have the same search and seizure authority they would have if the arrest had taken place anywhere else. In other words, by the common law authority of search incident to arrest, they are authorized to search the accused for any weapons, evidence, or instruments of escape. They are authorized to search the immediate surroundings of the arrest site for evidence (for example, the room in which the arrest takes place), but this is as far as their search of the premises is permitted to go. They cannot, for example, search other rooms of the house; this extended search would require a search warrant.

Searching for and Seizing Firearms

Closely related to searches under exigent circumstances are searches involving firearms. The Law Reform Commission of Canada (1983) has acknowledged that situations involving firearms are the ones where police most often need search powers outside arrest. Police powers in these situations are set out in s. 117.02(1) of the Code:

> 117.02(1) Where a peace officer believes on reasonable grounds
>
> (a) that a weapon, an imitation firearm, a prohibited device, any ammunition, any prohibited ammunition or an explosive substance was used in the commission of an offence, or
>
> (b) that an offence is being committed, or has been committed, under any provision of this Act that involves, or the subject-matter of which is, a firearm, an imitation firearm, a cross-bow, a prohibited weapon, a restricted weapon, a prohibited device, ammunition, prohibited ammunition or an explosive substance,
>
> and evidence of the offence is likely to be found on a person, in a vehicle or in any place or premises other than a dwelling-house, the peace officer may, where the conditions for obtaining a warrant exist but, by reason of exigent circumstances, it would not be practicable to obtain a warrant, search, without warrant, the person, vehicle, place or premises, and seize anything by means of or in relation to which that peace officer believes on reasonable grounds the offence is being committed or has been committed.

According to the court decision in *R v. T.A.V.* (2001), a warrantless search for firearms is justified so long as the following conditions exist: (1) the police have reasonable grounds to believe that evidence of the offence is likely to be found within one of the locations listed in s. 117.02(1); and (2) exigent circumstances make obtaining a search warrant impracticable. It is important to note that the authority established by the decision in *R v. T.A.V.* does not require the police to have reasonable grounds to make the arrest, but merely requires that the police have the *reasonable belief* that an offence has been committed and that evidence is likely to be found during the search.

An even more specialized seizure power for police authorizes them to protect society from those who should not be in possession of prohibited weapons or firearms. This authority is set out in s. 117.04(2) of the Code:

> (2) Where, with respect to any person, a peace officer is satisfied that there are reasonable grounds to believe that it is not desirable, in the interests of the safety of the person or any other person, for the person to possess any weapon, prohibited device, ammunition, prohibited ammunition or explosive substance, the peace officer may, where the grounds for obtaining a warrant under subsection (1) exist but, by reason of a possible danger to the safety of that person or any other person, it would not be practicable to obtain a warrant, search for and seize any such thing, and any authorization, licence or registration certificate relating to any such thing, that is held by or in the possession of the person.

This provision gives police officers the authority to act in circumstances where the grounds for obtaining a warrant exist but where immediate action is required for the safety of the public, of the officers, or of the person who is in possession of the weapon. Within 30 days of the event, police can, under s. 117.05(4), apply to have the items seized and "forfeited to Her Majesty or be otherwise disposed of." For such an application to succeed, police must establish that such forfeiture is in the interests of the safety of the person from whom the items have been seized.

CHECK YOUR UNDERSTANDING

1. What is consent search?
2. State six conditions that are imposed on police when they conduct consent searches.
3. Describe a circumstance in which s. 117.02 of the Code would apply.

Search Using Police Dogs

Most large police organizations around the world, including Canada, use police dogs for search purposes. Dogs are used to search for missing people and criminal suspects, as well as for illegal substances, such as drugs and explosives. But the use of police dogs in substance searches comes with legal challenges.

Warrantless search authority is limited, as we have seen. For example, police have limited authority to search a person who has not been placed under arrest, and they have limited authority to search a location where consent for the search has not been given by the resident. But when does a search become a *search*? As we saw in *R v. MacDonald*, a police officer's pushing a door open a mere few inches constitutes a search in the eyes of the law. What about detection of hidden items by the sensitive nose of a police dog? Is that considered a search? Can a dog's sense of smell violate an individual's expectation of privacy?

These legal questions surrounding sniffer dogs are interesting, and they are questions that the courts have struggled to answer. It is an evolving area of law. Let's consider a few important cases in order to see how the courts' views in this area have changed.

2008: Reasonable Grounds Are Needed

In 2008, the SCC ruled on two cases involving sniffer dogs and the question whether sniffer-dog searches violate an individual's Charter rights. The court's ruling limited the admissibility of evidence collected by police sniffer dogs.

The first case was *R v. Kang-Brown* (2008). It involved a man whom the police approached at the main Calgary bus depot. Police monitored this depot and buses travelling through it because they knew drugs were being transported by these routes. When Gurmakh Kang-Brown disembarked from a bus, he made eye contact with an undercover police officer. The officer approached Kang-Brown and identified himself as a police officer. During the ensuing discussion, Kang-Brown became increasingly nervous. When the officer asked to look in his bag, Kang-Brown initially opened the bag, but then yanked it away when the officer began looking through it. The officer then signalled for a K-9 unit to approach the man. When the dog reached Kang-Brown's bag, it sniffed the bag and then sat down, indicating the presence of drugs. A subsequent search of the bag turned up a large quantity of narcotics, and Kang-Brown was charged with possession of cocaine for the purpose of trafficking, as well as with possession of heroin.

The defence challenged the lawfulness of the sniffer dog's search, claiming that it was a violation of Kang-Brown's expectation of privacy and that the search was unreasonable because there was no reasonable grounds for it. The lower courts, including the Alberta Court of Appeal, disagreed. They said that the search was reasonable because the odours from the bag were emitted into a public space. However, the SCC overturned this ruling, stating that the sniffer dog's search violated Kang-Brown's Charter rights. The SCC also dismissed the prosecution's claim that the officers had *reasonable suspicion* that Kang-Brown was involved in criminal activity. The court stated that the threshold for conducting a search is higher than mere suspicion. In a split decision, the court ruled that, for the sniffer dog's search to be deemed reasonable, the officers would need to have *reasonable grounds* to believe that the man was in possession of the drugs. Kang-Brown was acquitted of the charges.

In the second case concerning sniffer dogs, *R v. A.M.* (2008), the principal of St. Patrick's High School in Sarnia, Ontario invited police to bring a sniffer dog into the school to search for drugs. In accepting this invitation, the police had no prior knowledge that there would be drugs at the school and therefore could not have gotten a search warrant to search the school in this way. All students were confined to their classrooms while the sniffer dog searched the school. The dog "indicated to" a knapsack that was lined up with others along the wall of the gym. The police handler opened the knapsack, without a search warrant, and found marijuana and "magic mushrooms" inside the bag. This led to the arrest and charging of A.M., a student at the school.

A.M.'s defence counsel, like Kang-Brown's, argued that the use of the sniffer dog to search the knapsack was a breach of the accused's rights under s. 8 of the Charter. The Youth Court trial judge agreed: the drugs were excluded as evidence, and A.M. was acquitted. In the subsequent appeals by the Crown, the SCC declined to overturn the lower courts' decisions, ruling that the subject matter of the dog's sniffing was not public air space but the concealed contents of the knapsack. The SCC (2008, pp. 571-572) also stated that there was no authority at common law for a sniffer dog search and that teenagers "expect the contents of their knapsacks not to be open to the random and speculative scrutiny of the police."

2013: Reasonable Suspicion Is Enough

Five years after its rulings in *R v. Kang-Brown* and *R v. A.M.*, the SCC took a rather sharp turn in its position on sniffer dogs. The vehicle for this change was two cases the court ruled on in 2013.

The first case was similar in many respects to *R v. Kang-Brown*. In 2005, the RCMP decided to use a sniffer dog to investigate the luggage of Mandeep Singh Chehil, who had arrived at a Halifax airport from Vancouver. Chehil was travelling alone, had only a single checked bag, and had bought his ticket at the last minute, using cash. This way of travelling is often associated with drug couriers. When the officers had the sniffer dog approach Chehil's luggage, the dog indicated the presence of drugs, which led to a further search of Chehil's luggage. When a large amount of cocaine was found, Chehil was placed under arrest and charged with the possession of narcotics.

The trial judge in *R v. Chehil* ruled that the sniffer dog's being led to the luggage constituted a search and that the police did not have sufficient grounds to conduct such a search. On this basis, the judge ruled that the drugs were inadmissible as evidence under s. 24(2) of the Charter. In 2009, however, the Nova Scotia Court of Appeal disagreed with the lower court's ruling and admitted the evidence. The case subsequently made its way to the SCC.

The SCC ruled that the standard of reasonable suspicion *had* been met in the *Chehil* case, so the sniffer dog's being led to the luggage—in other words, the search—*was* justified.

This was a reversal of the court's earlier position. The court (2013, p. 221), in this case, stated the following:

> The deployment of a dog trained to detect illegal drugs using its sense of smell is a search that may be carried out without prior judicial authorization where the police have a reasonable suspicion based on objective, ascertainable facts that evidence of an offence will be discovered.

The court also considered whether the search represented a breach of Chehil's expectation of privacy. The prosecution had argued that a person had no expectation of privacy in a public place, such as an airport. The court did not accept this argument, but it did rule that the expectation of privacy is lowered in public places. This is particularly true in places, such as airports, where security is a pressing concern and where searches of people and luggage are relatively common. It has been noted (Bowal & Knight, 2014) that, as a result of this SCC ruling, sniffer-dog searches carried out on the basis of officers' reasonable suspicion are now legal in public places across Canada.

The ruling in *R v. Chehil* was reinforced in another SCC ruling later in 2013. In *R v. MacKenzie*, the court was considering the justification for a sniffer dog's search of a vehicle pulled over on an Ontario highway. Police claimed that the accused, Benjamin MacKenzie, was driving erratically, was nervous in discussions with police, had bloodshot eyes, and gave contradictory information about where he was travelling and the timeline of his travels. Officers believed this gave them reasonable grounds to suspect that MacKenzie was involved with transporting drugs. The sniffer dog's search returned a positive result, leading to MacKenzie's arrest. The lawfulness of the search was subsequently challenged.

Again, the SCC upheld the search. The court stated that, while the power of police to search individuals has to be balanced against a person's Charter rights, the person's reasonable expectation of privacy is lowered on a public highway. In delivering its ruling in *R v. MacKenzie*, the court did little to clarify the circumstances in which these types of searches were justified; it ruled that such searches need to be considered on a case-by-case basis. The court (2013, p. 251) stated that police

> may use sniffer dogs for routine crime prevention in contexts where individuals have a reasonable, but lesser expectation of privacy and the police have reasonable grounds to suspect that a search will reveal evidence of a criminal offence. The use of sniffer dogs as a police investigative technique should be approached one case at a time, in each instance having regard to the context of the situation, balancing the extent of any privacy interest and the state's countervailing interest in law enforcement.

As you can see, trained police dogs are extremely useful for police investigations that involve a search component. But the police handlers deploying these dogs must ensure that they are not breaching an individual's Charter rights. Civil liberty groups and the courts will continue to challenge the use of police dogs by police services.

CHECK YOUR UNDERSTANDING

1. Explain the basis on which defence teams have challenged searches by sniffer dogs.
2. Explain how the SCC's position on sniffer dogs changed between 2008 and 2013.
3. Explain why the courts disallowed the evidence obtained in the use of a sniffer dog on school premises in the case of *R v. A.M.*

School Searches

Our communities expect that our children will have a safe and secure environment at school. For that reason, school authorities in Ontario have special search powers in the school context, under s. 265(1)(a) of the province's *Education Act*. Section 265(1)(a) requires school authorities to "maintain proper order and discipline in the school." This gives them the power to search a student or his or her locker if they have reasonable grounds to believe that the student has violated either the law or the rules of the school. This is, in effect, a warrantless search.

The Authority of School Officials on School Property

A landmark case in this area of law is *R v. M. (M.R.)* (1998). In this case, a junior high school vice-principal searched and seized some marijuana that students had brought to school to sell. He conducted the search after being tipped off by another student, and he called the police to have an officer present when the search was done. After the marijuana was found, the accused was placed under arrest and read his rights, and the officer conducted a further search of the accused's locker. Defence counsel launched a s. 8 Charter challenge and won in a lower court.

The Crown appealed this ruling, and the case was eventually heard by the SCC. The SCC ruled that the Charter applies to both police officers and school officials when they are conducting a school search. However, the court (1998, para. 33) also said the following: "It would not be reasonable for a student to expect to be free from such searches. A student's reasonable expectation of privacy in the school environment is therefore significantly diminished." The SCC ruling in this case proceeded to present a modified standard for what constitutes reasonable search in a school setting. The court (1998, para. 54) summarized as follows the factors to be considered in determining whether a search conducted by a teacher or principal in the school environment is reasonable:

1. The first step is to determine whether it can be inferred from the provisions of the relevant *Education Act* that teachers and principals are authorized to conduct searches of their students in appropriate circumstances. In the school environment, such a statutory authorization would be reasonable.
2. The search itself must be carried out in a reasonable manner. It should be conducted in a sensitive manner and be minimally intrusive.
3. In order to determine whether a search was reasonable, all the surrounding circumstances will have to be considered.

The SCC then posed the question, *When and to whom does this standard apply?* The court's answer (1998) was as follows:

> This modified standard for reasonable searches should apply to searches of students on school property conducted by teachers or school officials within the scope of their responsibility and authority to maintain order, discipline and safety within the school. This standard will not apply to any actions taken which are beyond the scope of the authority of teachers or principals. Further, a different situation arises if the school authorities are acting as agents of the police where the normal standards will apply.

The court's ruling noted that this modified standard for school searches is limited in its application. It applies to teachers and principals in their efforts to keep order and discipline within the school and thereby ensure the safety of students and staff. It does not apply to them except when they are engaged in meeting these requirements. Nor does it apply if school authorities are acting under the direction of the police and are thereby police agents. In these circumstances, normal standards for warrantless searches apply.

Even under the modified standards, the scope of a school search must be reasonable. Reasonableness will be determined according to the objective of the search and to its intrusiveness in light of the alleged infraction and of the student's age and sex. For example, it is reasonable for a teacher to take immediate action and to undertake whatever search is required where he or she has reasonable grounds to believe that a student is carrying a gun or some other dangerous weapon. The same search would not be justified where there is no dangerous weapon involved—where, for example, a teacher, aiming to enforce a school's no-cellphones policy, decides to search a student's pocket because he believes there may be a cellphone there. Also, the age and gender of the student are a factor. As with police searches, a male teacher's intrusive search of a female student may be considered inappropriate and unreasonable.

Police Search Authority on School Property

Where does this leave a police officer who has been called to support the investigation of a crime on school property? The school authorities' special search powers do not extend to the police; police officers have no special search powers in the school context. To search a person or a locker in a school, police officers must have the same reasonable grounds that they must have to search a person outside of a school—although the courts may give them extra leeway, in the school context, as to what constitutes reasonable grounds for the search. In most investigations and in most circumstances, police officers should obtain a warrant to search a locker unless there is some type of emergency, such as a bomb threat, that would justify a warrantless search.

When it comes to school searches and the relation between school authorities' power and police power, police officers and school officials need to keep in mind the statement we quoted above, from the SCC ruling in *R v. M. (M.R.)*:

> This standard will not apply to any actions taken which are beyond the scope of the authority of teachers or principals. Further, a different situation arises if the school authorities are acting as agents of the police where the normal standards will apply.

This means that school officials forfeit their special search authorities as soon as they assume an agency relationship with police. School officials can call in the police to provide support for safety reasons, but the police cannot influence the nature of a search. As soon as they do, the search becomes subject to the same legal standards as a police-conducted search.

Consider a situation where a school principal observes a student on school property rolling what the principal believes to be a marijuana cigarette. He calls the police, but searches the student for drugs before the police arrive, on his own initiative. When the police arrive, the officer suggests that the principal search the student's locker, since more marijuana is likely to be found there. This would be considered an agency relationship if it can be proven that the principal would not have searched the student's locker without the directive from the attending officer. A search conducted by a school official who has an agency relationship with the police would be unlawful without a search warrant.

To avoid this problem, the police officer could explain to the school authority that he or she (the school authority) has search powers under s. 265(1)(a) of Ontario's *Education Act*, but that this authority does not extend to the police. The police officer could then—for safety reasons—proceed to stand by the location where the school official is conducting the search, but not actually assist in the search. The officer *is* authorized to seize any contraband or other evidence related to a criminal offence that the school authority finds in the course of his or her search.

IT'S YOUR MOVE, OFFICER!

Scenario 8.2

You have been sent to a local high school after the dispatcher received a call from the school principal. When you arrive, the principal tells you she has learned that a student has a freezer bag of marijuana in his school locker. The student is currently in his English class.

1. What course of action should you take? Are you going to arrest the student in his class? Are you going to search his locker without a warrant or suggest that the principal do so? Or will you secure his locker and apply for a search warrant? Explain your answer.

2. How would your decision about how to proceed vary depending on where the principal got her information about the marijuana in the locker? For example, what if she got her information about the marijuana in the locker from only one student, albeit a student whom she considers credible? What if she got the information from several students? What if she got it from a teacher who observed the student placing the bag in his locker?

CHECK YOUR UNDERSTANDING

1. Under what circumstances can a school principal search a student's locker?
2. What grounds do the police require to search a student or the student's locker while on school property?
3. Can a police officer direct a school official to conduct a warrantless search of a student's locker? Explain your answer.

Search and Seizure of Unexpected Items

There are times when evidence presents itself unexpectedly. This can occur during a search incident to arrest or during a search that has been consented to, or it may be the lucky result of interactions between police and the public.

Additional Items Found During a Search

Keep in mind that once you, as a police officer, have established a lawful basis for a search—be it incident to arrest or incident to consent—you may use against the person anything illegal that you find during the search. This is true even if the item is unrelated to the offence for which the search is being conducted.

Consider, for example, a situation where a detained person has given police consent to search him or her. During the ensuing search, the officer finds a quantity of marijuana in the suspect's pocket. An officer in this situation is bound by law to arrest the individual for possessing the drugs. The officer must then inform the person that he or she is under arrest, and explain why, and provide him or her with the Charter right to counsel. (Failure with respect to this Charter right would likely result in the charge being dismissed.) The officer can then continue to search the person for further evidence, under the common law authority of search incident to arrest. If the subsequent search turns up a stolen cellphone, the police can charge the person both with the drug offence and with possession of the stolen property. Both the search and seizure would survive any Charter challenge, as long as the police officer properly articulated the grounds for both the search and the seizure.

The Plain-View Doctrine

The courts have to make rulings not only on police search powers but also on their seizure powers with respect to any property they take from a person during a warrantless search. According to s. 489(2) of the Code, any police officer who is lawfully in a place pursuant to a warrant or otherwise in the execution of their duties may seize anything that the officer believes on reasonable grounds

- has been obtained by the commission of an offence,
- has been used in the commission of an offence, or
- will afford evidence in respect of an offence.

The courts have stated that there needs to be a reasonable connection between the property being taken from the person and the alleged crime for which the person is being arrested. It does sometimes happen that officers will inadvertently encounter items (narcotics, for example) that, though not related to the crime being investigated, are criminal in themselves. Under the authority known as the **plain-view doctrine**, police officers can seize these items and lay charges on their basis.

There exists a three-part test for deciding whether the plain-view doctrine applies to items seized during a search. The three criteria, presented in Figure 8.2, have been articulated in case law. One contributing case was *R v. Belliveau*, whose ruling stated (1986, p. 16) the following:

> First, the police officer must lawfully make an "initial intrusion" or otherwise properly be in a position from which he can view a particular area. Second, the officer must discover incriminating evidence "inadvertently," which is to say he may not "know in advance the location of [certain] evidence and intend to seize," relying on the plain view doctrine only as a pretext. Finally, it must be "immediately apparent" to the police that the items they observe may be evidence of a crime, contraband, or otherwise subject to seizure. These requirements having been met, when police officers lawfully engaged in an activity in a particular area perceive a suspicious object, they may seize it immediately.

Police power of seizure under the plain-view doctrine originated in US law and was incorporated into Canadian law through the following cases:

- *R v. Shea* (1982)
- *R v. Longtin* (1983)
- *R v. Belliveau* (1986)
- *R v. Nielsen* (1988)

The Saskatchewan Court of Appeal recognized, in the case of *R v. Spindloe* (2001, para. 50), that the plain-view doctrine "confers a seizure power not a search power." This is an important point. It means that the plain-view doctrine does not confer on the police officer the authority to expand an exploratory search in order to find further evidence of a crime.

Consider, for example, an officer who is lawfully carrying out his or her duties in relation to a motorist. During the encounter, the officer sees evidence of a crime in the passenger-side glove compartment of the vehicle, which happens to be open. The officer may seize the

plain-view doctrine
a doctrine according to which a police officer who is lawfully in a place can seize items that are in plain view and that are, on their face, illegal; requires that the initial intrusion by police be lawful and that the evidence be discovered inadvertently

FIGURE 8.2   Plain-View Doctrine Three-Part Test

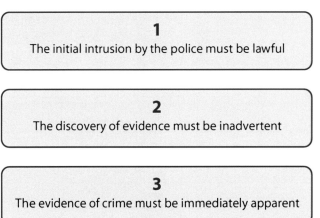

1
The initial intrusion by the police must be lawful

2
The discovery of evidence must be inadvertent

3
The evidence of crime must be immediately apparent

item(s) without obtaining a warrant. However, while the plain-view doctrine allows the officer to seize evidence that is in plain view, it does not permit him or her to search *enclosed* places, such as a closed glove compartment or a closed trunk. But if the officer has a lawful reason to search the glove compartment or trunk, and while doing so discovers evidence in plain view, the plain-view doctrine would permit seizure of that evidence.

Consider another example. An officer is called by the superintendent of an apartment building because water is seeping from an upstairs apartment unit into the unit below it. The superintendent asks the police to assist him when he enters the apartment. According to the contract signed by the tenant, the landlord (or a deputized superintendent) has the right to enter the apartment for emergency repairs. Upon entry, the officer follows the superintendent to the bathroom from which the water is issuing. Here, in the bathtub, they discover five pots of marijuana being watered by the tub faucet. The drain has plugged, causing the water to overflow the tub and leak into the apartment below. Because the officer is legally authorized to be in the apartment, he or she may seize the marijuana under the plain-view doctrine; the plants are clearly illegal *on their face* (in other words, readily observable as illegal). But the officer cannot now continue to walk through the apartment or start opening cupboards and drawers, looking for further incriminating evidence.

The courts have made the following points very clear regarding the plain-view doctrine:

- the items seized under its authority must be clearly illegal on their face;
- the officer who seizes the item must not have been "snooping" to find the item or any other supporting evidence; and
- the officer is not authorized, having seized an item under the plain-view doctrine, to expand his search and look for further incriminating evidence.

That said, an officer who finds illegal objects under the plain-view doctrine may seize them and then seal the location for continuity purposes. He or she can then apply for a search warrant, which can be exercised to obtain further evidence that may support the initial findings.

IT'S YOUR MOVE, OFFICER!

Scenario 8.3

You and your partner attend a radio call regarding a domestic situation at an apartment. The female complainant comes to the door, and you see she has a bruise under her eye. She tells you that she and her husband got into an argument over finances. During the argument, he struck her with an open hand.

The complainant asks you to come in, and when you look in the kitchen you observe the husband seated there, wearing only his boxers and an undershirt. He readily admits to hitting his wife, so you place him under arrest for assault. You inform him that you need to provide him with proper clothing, and you need to retrieve his identification. He directs you to the bedroom that he shares with his wife, telling you that his wallet is in the top drawer of his bedroom dresser.

When you open the drawer to retrieve the wallet, you observe what appears to be a .38 calibre handgun in the corner of the drawer.

What is your next move? Can you seize the handgun? Can you look around the room for ammunition? What if the wife gives you permission to do so? Can you make the search then?

1. Name the three-part test that courts apply to seizures made under the plain-view doctrine.

2. What are the two reasons that police may enter a dwelling?

3. Does the plain-view doctrine allow police officers to carry out an exploratory search? Explain your answer.

Continuity of Seized Property

As we have seen, police officers must be able to clearly articulate their search-and-seizure authority if they are to withstand a Charter challenge. This ability is very important. It is no less important that they gather, process, and manage seized material properly. Officers *must* carefully observe and take thorough notes concerning the details of what they have seized from a person, from a vehicle, or even from a crime scene. This is an area where officers often fall down and where defence lawyers often cross-examine officers. From the moment an officer has seized an item from its initial search location, the **continuity break** begins. The continuity break is the transfer of any property or evidence from one location to another, or from one person to another.

Table 8.2 shows some legal points that officers must deal with when they seize any items.

continuity break
the transfer of any property or evidence from one location to another, or from one person to another

TABLE 8.2   Legal Considerations for Search and Seizure

1. From where were the items seized?	Officers must describe the location in detail.
2. What else was with or near the seized items?	For example, if an officer had the opportunity to seize illegal drugs, it would be important to note if he or she also seized cash, paraphernalia, debt lists, and other items.
3. What is a non-technical description of the items?	When seizing anything that may be very technical to police investigations or forensic evidence, the police should try their best to describe the items seized in a way they believe the average citizen could understand. Going back to the drug example above, the police should avoid simply stating "seized marijuana." Instead, they should describe in detail the colours of the drug, the shape and size, the texture, the packaging—for example, plastic baggies or paper bags or tin foil.
4. How were the seized items protected?	Police officers must also make clear notes regarding what they did with the seized items to protect them as evidence and to prevent any cross-contamination.
5. What were the items placed in?	The officer would need to describe what they placed the seized item in. For example, if the seized item was small, did the officer put it in his or her own clothing?
6. Were any items seized from the accused at the scene?	If the officer arrests a person for an offence and takes him or her to a police station, the officer must note whether he or she seized any items from the prisoner prior to transporting him or her.

Identifying Seized Property

To guard against continuity problems and court challenges to seized property, police officers must be able to clearly identify this property. Officers may be called on to make this identification months or even years after they seize the property. Officers' notes in this regard must be very detailed.

Officers must clearly identify seized property with labels or markings. It is usually best not to place such markings directly on the items seized; this may destroy forensic evidence. Officers will often package the seized item in a paper or plastic bag, or in a cardboard box that can be sealed shut, and then mark the package with some identifying details. These details should include the following:

- the date and time of the seizure, and
- the seizing officer's initials and badge number.

Seizing Items at a Crime Scene

evidential chain
the chain of evidence establishing the events that, seen in sequence, account for the actions of the suspect, the victim, and even the witnesses in an incident; can also account for different forms of evidence found within the time frame in which the crime may have occurred

Following the correct procedure for the seizure, packaging, and presentation of exhibits ensures the protection and the preservation of the evidence and maintains the integrity of the **evidential chain**. The evidential chain will typically establish a series of events that, seen in sequence, can usually account for the actions of the suspect, the victim, and even the witnesses in an incident. The evidential chain can also account for different forms of evidence found within the time frame in which the crime may have occurred. Generally, police need to protect and preserve any exhibit at a crime scene for forensic examination and for the photographic record. Reducing the number of people handling the item is a way of safeguarding against the loss of evidence and its contamination by (for example) fingermarks.

Exigent circumstances sometimes require that evidence be handled—sheltered or taken to the police station, for example. This should only be done where there is some risk of its being removed, destroyed, or tampered with. In the event of such a risk, the articles should be handled with care, by edges or surfaces not normally handled, and then placed in a protective covering as soon as possible.

Detention of Seized Property

Anything the officer seizes is subject to seizure law, regardless of what search authority he or she uses—whether search incident to arrest or the plain-view doctrine.

Under the authority of s. 489.1(1) of the Code, a peace officer who has seized anything under a warrant or during the execution of his or her lawful duties must return the property to the rightful owner, including an owner who is charged with a criminal offence. The only exception to this is a case where police require the item seized for further investigation or as evidence for trial purposes. In this case, a police officer must do the following:

report to justice
a legal document, commonly referred to as a "5.2," that police use when asking a justice of the peace or judge for lawful permission to hold seized property for further investigation or until the completion of the trial

1. Bring the seized item before the justice of the peace (JP) or judge.
2. Complete a **report to justice** asking the JP or judge for lawful permission to hold the seized property for further investigation or until the completion of the trial.

Police must complete this legal document, commonly referred to as a "5.2," because the person from whom the item was seized may apply for its return. If this occurs, and the item is an essential piece of evidence, the Crown may not be able to prove its case against the charged person.

If the police complete a 5.2 report so that they can further investigate the seized item, but have not arrested anyone in relation to the seized property, they will have 90 days to continue the investigation. If charges relating to the seized property have not been laid after 90 days, police must return the property to the person they seized it from. Police may apply for an extension if they can convince the justice they need time to investigate beyond the 90-day period. The justice may grant an extension of up to one year. Police must always provide a property receipt to an individual from whom they have seized property.

When police decide to return seized property, they must first prove

- that there is no dispute as to who is lawfully entitled to the property that was seized; and
- that the property seized is not required for further detention.

IT'S YOUR MOVE, OFFICER!

Scenario 8.4

While on patrol in downtown Sudbury, you stop and investigate a crack cocaine addict named Alex, well known to police. You have dealt with him many times yourself. You know that he steals property to support his drug addiction. On this occasion, Alex is in possession of an expensive mountain bike. He says that he found the bike abandoned by a park bench and that he is trying to locate the rightful owner so that he can return the bike to him. So far, he says, he has been unable to find anyone claiming to be the owner.

You check the serial number of the bike against police records and confirm that the bike has not been reported stolen. You cannot locate a registered owner for the bike. You are very suspicious about how Alex came to possess this bike, but you do not have sufficient grounds to charge him with stolen property. You seize the bike and provide him with a property receipt.

Now that you have seized the bicycle, explain what investigative steps you would take and what timelines you are facing.

CHECK YOUR UNDERSTANDING

1. When does a break in continuity of evidence occur?
2. What is the evidential chain, and why is it important?
3. If the police wish to hold on to seized property for further investigation or for trial, what must they do?

CHAPTER SUMMARY

As this chapter has shown you, the law surrounding search and seizure can be very involved and quite confusing. In Canada, the police have common law and statutory powers to conduct searches of people, dwellings, and vehicles, among other places and things. This police power must be kept in balance with individuals' s. 8 Charter rights. Section 8 provides that everyone has the right to be secure against unreasonable search and seizure, and that everyone can expect a reasonable degree of privacy.

Canada's courts are very aware of the tension between police search powers, on the one hand, and the rights of individuals on the other hand. They carefully review the "reasonableness" of searches conducted by police. Police officers in Canada should always remember that, in this country, warrantless searches are presumed to be unreasonable. Whether a search is reasonable can affect the outcome of a trial: an unreasonable search may render the seized items inadmissible as evidence. Police must ensure that searches and seizures are conducted in a professional manner and that the officers involved in them can articulate the grounds for their search. After a search and seizure, officers must also ensure—and be able to show—that the continuity of evidence was protected, that details concerning the seized items were recorded properly and accurately, and that the integrity of the evidence was preserved at all times. If the officers meet these requirements, their search and seizure will usually withstand any Charter challenge.

KEY TERMS

Charter remedies, 169
concurrence, 176
continuity break, 187
evidential chain, 188

offensive weapon, 172
plain-view doctrine, 185
prima facie, 169
report to justice, 188

third-party consent, 176
warrantless search, 168

REFERENCES

A.M., R v. (2008). 2008 SCC 19, [2008] 1 SCR 569.

Belliveau, R v. (1986). 75 NBR (2d) 18 (CA).

Bowal, P., & Knight, E. (2014, March 6). What ever happened to … the law of sniffer dog searches: Part 2. *Law Now*. http://www.lawnow.org/whatever-happened-law-sniffer-dog-searches-2/.

Canadian Charter of Rights and Freedoms. (1982). Part I of the *Constitution Act, 1982*, RSC 1985, app. II, no. 84.

Caslake, R v. (1998). [1998] 1 SCR 51.

Chehil, R v. (2013). 2013 SCC 49, [2013] 3 SCR 220.

Cloutier v. Langlois. (1990). [1990] 1 SCR 158.

Collins, R v. (1987). [1987] 1 SCR 265.

Criminal Code. (1985). RSC 1985, c. C-46.

Dyment, R v. (1988). [1988] 2 SCR 417.

Education Act. (1990). RSO 1990, c. E.2.

Evans, R v. (1996). [1996] 1 SCR 8.

Godoy, R v. (1999). [1999] 1 SCR 311.

Golden, R v. (2001). 2001 SCC 83, [2001] 3 SCR 679.

Hunter v. Southam Inc. (1984). [1984] 2 SCR 145.

Kang-Brown, R v. (2008). 2008 SCC 18, [2008] 1 SCR 456.

Law Reform Commission of Canada. (1983). Police powers—search and seizure in criminal law enforcement. *Working Paper, 30*. Minister of Supply and Services. Retrieved from https://archive.org/stream/policepowerssear00lawr/policepowerssear00lawr_djvu.txt.

Longtin, R v. (1983). 41 OR (2d) 545 (CA).

M. (M.R.), R v. (1998). [1998] 3 SCR 393.

MacDonald, R v. (2014). 2014 SCC 3, [2014] 1 SCR 37.

MacKenzie, R v. (2013). 2013 SCC 50, [2013] 3 SCR 250.

Mann, R v. (2004). 2004 SCC 52, [2004] 3 SCR 59.

Mercer, R v. (1992). 70 CCC (3d) 180 (Ont. CA).

Mohamad, R v. (2004). 69 OR (3d) 481 (CA).

Nielsen, R v. (1988). [1988] 6 WWR 1 (Sask. CA).

Schreiber v. Canada (Attorney General). (2002). 2002 SCC 62, [2002] 3 SCR 269.

Shea, R v. (1982). 38 OR (2d) 582 (SC).

Spindloe, R v. (2001). 2001 SKCA 58, [2002] 5 WWR 239.

T.A.V., R v. (2001). 2001 ABCA 316, [2002] 4 WWR 633.

Thomas, R v. (1991). 67 CCC (3d) 81 (NLCA).

Thomson Newspapers Ltd. v. Canada (Director of Investigation and Research, Restrictive Trade Practices Commission). (1990). [1990] 1 SCR 425.

FURTHER READING

A.M., R v. (2008). 2008 SCC 19, [2008] 1 SCR 569.

Belliveau, R v. (1986). 75 NBR (2d) 18, 1986 CanLII 88 (CA).

Buhay, R v. (2003). 2003 SCC 30, [2003] 1 SCR 631.

Caslake, R v. (1998). [1998] 1 SCR 51.

Chehil, R v. (2013). 2013 SCC 49, [2013] 3 SCR 220.

Cloutier v. Langlois. (1990). [1990] 1 SCR 158.

Collins, R v. (1987). [1987] 1 SCR 265.

Dyment, R v. (1988). [1988] 2 SCR 417.

Evans, R v. (1996). [1996] 1 SCR 8.

Godoy, R v. (1999). [1999] 1 SCR 311.

Golden, R v. (2001). 2001 SCC 83, [2001] 3 SCR 679.

Hunter v. Southam Inc. (1984). [1984] 2 SCR 145.

Kang-Brown, R v. (2008). 2008 SCC 18, [2008] 1 SCR 456.

Klimchuk, R v. (1991). 67 CCC (3d) 385 (BCCA).

Longtin, R v. (1983). 41 OR (2d) 545 (CA).

M. (M.R.), R v. (1998). [1998] 3 SCR 393.

MacDonald, R v. (2014). 2014 SCC 3, [2014] 1 SCR 37.

MacKenzie, R v. (2013). 2013 SCC 50, [2013] 3 SCR 250.

Mann, R v. (2004). 2004 SCC 52, [2004] 3 SCR 59.

Mercer, R v. (1992). 70 CCC (3d) 180 (Ont. CA).

Mohamad, R v. (2004). 69 OR (3d) 481 (CA).

Nielsen, R v. (1988). [1988] 6 WWR 1 (Sask. CA).

Polashek, R v. (1999). 45 OR (3d) 434, 172 DLR (4th) 350 (CA).

Shea, R v. (1982). 38 OR (2d) 582 (SC).

T.A.V., R v. (2001). 2001 ABCA 316, [2002] 4 WWR 633.

Thomas, R v. (1991). 67 CCC (3d) 81 (NLCA).

Thomson Newspapers Ltd. v. Canada (Director of Investigation and Research, Restrictive Trade Practices Commission). (1990). [1990] 1 SCR 425.

REVIEW QUESTIONS

Multiple Choice

1. A warrantless search is considered reasonable if it meets three criteria. Which of the following is not one of these criteria?

   a. The search is authorized by law.

   b. The search is carried out in the daytime hours.

   c. The law itself is reasonable.

   d. The search is conducted in a reasonable manner.

2. If the police complete a 5.2 report so that they can further investigate a seized item, but they have not arrested anyone in relation to the seized property, how many days will they have in which to continue the investigation?

   a. 30 days

   b. 60 days

   c. 90 days

   d. 120 days

3. Police performing a consent search must meet various conditions. Which one of the following is not one of them?

   a. The consent must be informed.

   b. The consent is incident to the lawful arrest.

   c. The consent is implied.

   d. The consent must be voluntary.

4. According to s. 117.02(1) of the *Criminal Code*, the police do not need a warrant to search for which of the following?

   a. a prohibited weapon

   b. an imitation firearm

   c. a prohibited device

   d. all of the above

5. If police believe that an item they have seized is required for further investigation or as evidence for trial purposes, they must do which of the following?

   a. Bring the seized item before a justice of the peace.

   b. Photograph the seized item and return it to the accused.

   c. Notify the Crown attorney of the seizure.

   d. none of the above

True or False

_____ 1. A Level 1 field search consists of the removal of some of an arrested person's clothing, but not all the clothing or the undergarments.

_____ 2. A Level 3 complete (or strip) search must be conducted at a hospital by a medical doctor.

_____ 3. The common law police authority to conduct a search incident to an arrest extends to an accused's vehicle, since it is part of his or her immediate surroundings.

_____ 4. Under the plain-view doctrine, police officers may only seize weapons or things that they believe may harm them.

_____ 5. If the police, though they have neither arrested the person nor obtained a search warrant to search the person, have stopped the person on the street and are investigating the person, they have the authority to search the person.

_____ **6.** If the police search an individual subsequent to his or her lawful arrest and find something related to another offence, they can charge the person with the second offence.

_____ **7.** When officers are in hot pursuit of a person wanted for a criminal offence, they may enter the person's home without consent and without a search or arrest warrant in order to capture and arrest the fleeing suspect.

_____ **8.** If police can establish that the forfeiture of items seized under the authority of s. 117.05(4) of the Code is in the safety interest of the person from whom they seized the items, they can apply for this forfeiture for up to 90 days after the incident in which the items were seized.

_____ **9.** The SCC has held that the Charter applies to both police officers and school officials when they are conducting a school search.

_____**10.** A police officer who has arrested a person and is taking him or her to a police station needs to note, prior to transporting the person, whether the officer has seized any items from the person.

Short Answer

1. Why is s. 8 of the Charter important? In other words, why is it important to guarantee all individuals the right to be secure against unreasonable search and seizure?

2. Do the police have the authority to search a person who is being held under investigative detention? Explain your answer.

3. Once a person has been arrested, the police can search the person, their clothing, and their immediate surroundings. Why do the police require such a broad power of search?

4. Why is it important that an individual who consents to be searched by the police also have the right to refuse or stop the search at any time?

5. Why, in your view, do school officials have more power to search on school property than the police do?

It's Your Move, Officer!

A. You and your partner are on general patrol late at night in a residential area. You see a young male pushing a motorcycle along the sidewalk. You stop the car so that you and your partner can ask the young man some questions. He tells you that he owns the motorcycle and that it has run out of gas.

You check the vehicle identification number of the motorcycle on your police computer. The computer check reveals that the motorcycle in question is on file as being stolen two days ago from a house in the area where you are now. On the basis of this information, you and your partner arrest the male.

Upon his arrest, the young man orally identifies himself to you. He points to a house across the street and says that he lives there and that his wallet with his driver's licence is there. Your partner advises the young man that he is going to be escorted into his house so that he can obtain his wallet and identification. The young man states several times that he does not want you to go into his house.

You and your partner search him and discover what appears to be a house key in his pants pocket. Your partner advises you to stay with the young man while he goes into the house to get the wallet. You watch as your partner uses the key obtained from the suspect to enter the house by the front door. He returns a short time later to where you are standing with the suspect.

Your partner advises you that he obtained the young man's wallet and identification, and he tells you that when he was in the house he observed a large quantity of marijuana packaged in bags on the kitchen table.

1. Was your original search of the male lawful? Explain.

2. Was your partner's entry into the house—against the arrested male's objection—lawful? Explain.

3. Could your partner have seized the marijuana, under the plain-view doctrine? Explain.

4. Could you now obtain a search warrant for the marijuana? Explain.

B. You and your partner are in uniform and are on general patrol when you receive a priority radio call asking you to attend a residence for an "unknown trouble" call. You are told that a female called 911 and screamed, "Hurry! He's going to kill me!" That was the last thing heard before the line went dead.

The police dispatcher advises you that they have called the number back several times, but there is no answer. The dispatcher gives you the address of the house the call came from and tells you that the police have attended this address on two previous occasions for domestic abuse.

You and your partner arrive at the house. There are lights on. As you approach the front door, you hear a female screaming inside. You and your partner bang on the door several times and announce, "Police officers. *Open the door!*" But nobody answers, and the screaming suddenly stops.

This scenario appears to involve a life-threatening situation, and your decision must be quick; somehow, you need to get into the house. What is your legal authority for entering the house?

Search with a Warrant 9

LEARNING OBJECTIVES

After reading this chapter, you should be able to:

- Explain the purpose of a search warrant.
- Describe the general requirements for obtaining a search warrant.
- Explain what an information to obtain (ITO) is.
- Explain the Three Fs—full, fair, and frank.
- Describe what personal sourced information is.
- Explain the sealing and unsealing of search warrants.
- Describe how search warrant applications are submitted.
- Explain the process of executing a search warrant and any special circumstances involved in this process.
- Describe guidelines for drafting a search warrant.

ON SCENE

Officer Kim is the affiant (writer) of a search warrant to enter someone's home to search for stolen property. She briefs the officers on her team before proceeding to the address named in the search warrant. Arriving there, she suggests that the team members kick in the front door and enter the home as rapidly as possible, to prevent anyone from escaping the building or from destroying evidence, such as the stolen property that is inside the house.

As the affiant of the search warrant, it is Officer Kim's responsibility to ensure that the search warrant is executed professionally and lawfully.

Do you think Officer Kim should allow the team to kick in the door, or are there other options and legal requirements to consider?

Introduction

The *Canadian Charter of Rights and Freedoms* clearly states in s. 8 that everyone in Canada "has the right to be secure against unreasonable search or seizure." In doing so, the Charter guarantees that every person has a reasonable expectation of privacy. At the same time, searches are an important part of a police officer's job; they are conducted thousands of times a day across Canada, both with and without warrants. How does our legal system balance individuals' Charter rights to privacy against officers' needs to conduct searches?

In *R v. Collins* (1987), the Supreme Court of Canada (SCC) stated that, although the police are empowered and mandated to search for evidence, their search must be lawful and proper. In its ruling, the SCC established a three-pronged test for determining whether any search—warrantless or otherwise—is lawful and proper:

1. The search must be authorized in law.
2. The search must be reasonable. Police must have reasonable grounds to believe the items they are searching for will be found in the location they want to search.
3. The manner in which the police conduct their search must be reasonable and not cruel.

In the course of their daily activities, police officers often conduct warrantless searches. These types of searches are considered *prima facie* (on first impression) unreasonable, and officers must always be able to justify them. The Crown will need to present the officer's justification in any subsequent legal proceeding.

Warrantless searches are not ideal. Preferably, a police officer, before conducting a search, will have prepared and applied for a warrant and had it signed by a justice of the peace (JP) or judge. In this chapter, we will learn about searches with warrants. By the end of it, you will understand the purpose of a search warrant, what a search warrant application needs to include, how the search warrant application is prepared and submitted, and how the search warrant is executed. Police officers must have a thorough knowledge of the law relating to search warrant applications and to the actual execution of a search warrant. A further challenge for officers is that this area of law is constantly changing.

Search with a Warrant

A search warrant has been defined, in *A.G. (Nova Scotia) v. MacIntyre* (1982, p. 179), as "an order issued by a justice under statutory powers, authorizing a named person to enter a specified place to search for and seize specified property which will afford evidence of the actual or intended commission of a crime." The primary rule for searches is that, whenever practicable, police should obtain a search warrant. Another important rule is that the officer conducting the investigation must write and apply for the warrant. The officer who writes the warrant application is called the **affiant**.

You may think of the warrant as a substitute for consent, which officers would otherwise require in order to enter a home or any other location where a person would have a reasonable expectation of privacy. Again, the lawfulness of any search, with or without a warrant, is measured against the three criteria listed above. The difference between a warrantless search and a search with a warrant is that, in the case of the latter, the investigating officer is presenting the justification for the search *prior* to the search taking place. Getting this justification approved ahead of time ensures that the judge or JP believes that the search is authorized by law and that the grounds for the search are reasonable.

A search warrant permits investigators (in most instances, police officers) to perform three important law enforcement functions, outlined in Table 9.1.

affiant
the police officer who writes the warrant application

TABLE 9.1   Objectives of Search Warrants

Objective	Description
Locate	Locate items named in the warrant, which can then be used as evidence in a future criminal proceeding.
Examine	Not only do items have to be seized to link a person to a crime, but in many cases these items need to be examined as well. This may include taking fingerprints and DNA samples, or doing ballistics testing relating to firearms. It also includes examining other items of investigative value, such as pry marks for a break-and-enter, fibres taken from the scene of a sexual assault or homicide, or electronic data from computers.
Preserve	Seizing evidence from the crime scene or other location through the execution of a search warrant ensures that evidence is not lost, removed, or destroyed.

A search warrant not only enables police to collect evidence of a crime that has actually taken place. It can also serve as an investigative tool, enabling police to collect evidence about an ongoing activity they believe to be criminal. For example, if police believe they need to intercept the communications between individuals they suspect are colluding in some form of criminal activity, they may apply for a wiretap warrant to intercept telephone calls for a certain period of time. Such an application would be made to a judge, in writing, before any steps were taken to intercept the communications.

General Requirements for a Search Warrant

The requirements for obtaining a search warrant are rigorous. In *R v. Turcotte* (1987), the Saskatchewan Court of Appeal stated (1987, p. 14) that, before granting the warrant, the justice must be satisfied

1. that an offence has been committed or is suspected of being committed;
2. that the location of the search is a building, receptacle or place;
3. that the item sought will provide evidence of the commission of the offence or that the possession thereof is an offence of itself;
4. that the grounds stated are current so as to lend credence to the reasonable and probable grounds;
5. that there is a nexus between the various considerations set out.

nexus of search
a direct relationship, or nexus, between the offence that has been committed, the evidence that the police need to secure in their investigation, and the location where the police believe the evidence will be located

The last item in this list is known as the **nexus of search** (see Figure 9.1). (The word *nexus* means a connection or series of connections that link several items, concepts, or ideas.)

Before officers apply for a search warrant, then, they must complete a thorough investigation, ensuring that there is a direct connection, or nexus, between

- the offence that has been committed, or an ongoing criminal investigation;
- the evidence being sought in relation to that offence; and
- the place that investigators want to search.

Officers cannot simply provide information based on the belief that the item(s) *could* be in the place they wish to search; rather, they must believe on reasonable grounds that the items *will* be there.

The courts have deemed that police descriptions should not be overly broad. Investigators seeking warrants must meet rigorous requirements when it comes to providing specifics about the items they expect the search to yield. Section 487 of the Code sets out the information that a justice requires before he or she will endorse a search warrant:

487(1) A justice who is satisfied by information on oath in Form 1 that there are reasonable grounds to believe that there is in a building, receptacle or place

(a) anything on or in respect of which any offence against this Act or any other Act of Parliament has been or is suspected to have been committed,

(b) anything that there are reasonable grounds to believe will afford evidence with respect to the commission of an offence, or will reveal the whereabouts of a person who is believed to have committed an offence, against this Act or any other Act of Parliament,

(c) anything that there are reasonable grounds to believe is intended to be used for the purpose of committing any offence against the person for which a person may be arrested without warrant, or

(c.1) any offence-related property,

may at any time issue a warrant authorizing a peace officer or a public officer who has been appointed or designated to administer or enforce a federal or provincial

FIGURE 9.1   Nexus of Search

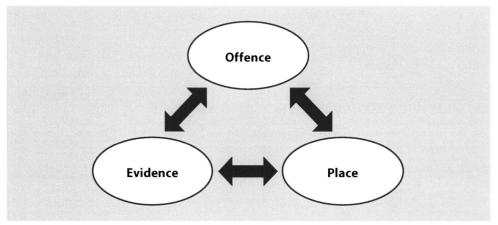

law and whose duties include the enforcement of this Act or any other Act of Parliament and who is named in the warrant

    (d) to search the building, receptacle or place for any such thing and to seize it, and

    (e) subject to any other Act of Parliament, to, as soon as practicable, bring the thing seized before, or make a report in respect thereof to, the justice or some other justice for the same territorial division.

Let's illustrate how much detail is expected in a search warrant application. Consider a situation where police are investigating a break-and-enter into a computer shop and the theft of ten laptop computers. In applying for a warrant to search the place where they believe the stolen laptops are stashed, investigators cannot simply state that they are looking for "stolen laptops." Rather, they have to draw a strong "nexus" to the offence that has been committed; they are required to state the date, time, and location of the break-in; the number of laptops believed to be at the location; and a full description of the stolen laptops, including manufacturer, model, and serial number. Then, to continue to draw the nexus of the offence to the evidence, investigators have to explain in detail why they believe the ten stolen laptops are associated with the named suspect(s) and why they believe these ten laptops are within the location where they wish to search.

Different Types of Search Warrants

Different types of search warrants are required for different types of offences. The majority of search warrants are issued under the authority of s. 487(1) of the Code. This section of the Code says that police have the authority to enter and search a building, receptacle, or place to obtain evidence relating to criminal activity, but only if the justice is satisfied that there are reasonable grounds to believe that items related to criminality will be found in the location.

Most search warrants are required for the investigation of criminal offences defined in the Code. Different sections of the Code cover different kinds of warrants. A Feeney warrant, for example, would be sought under s. 529. Different sections of the Code would apply when police seek warrants for seizing intangible items, such as data from computers or cellphones. (Table 9.2 presents some of the most common search warrants used by police officers in Canada, and the sections of the Code under which they are sought.) However, police sometimes investigate offences not covered in the Code, in which case they go to other statutes for their warrant authority. For example, a warrant for a drug investigation would be sought under s. 11 of the *Controlled Drugs and Substances Act*.

TABLE 9.2   Common Search Warrants in Canada

Type of Warrant	Criminal Code Section Number(s)
Firearms warrant	117.04
Obscene materials	164
Interception with consent wiretap	184.2
Wiretap	186
Impaired driving—blood samples	256

(Table 9.2 is concluded on the next page.)

TABLE 9.2   (Concluded)

Type of Warrant	Criminal Code Section Number(s)
Proceeds of crime	462.32
General search warrant	487
Production order	487.011-013
DNA sample	487.05
Bodily impressions	487.092
Telewarrants	487.1
Explosive warrants	492
Tracking warrants	492.1
Number recorders	492.2
Telephone records	492.2(2)
Entry for arrest	529, 529.1

CHECK YOUR UNDERSTANDING

1. Explain the term *nexus of search*.

2. What is the primary rule for police officers involving searches?

3. Identify four common search warrants.

Information to Obtain (ITO)

information to obtain (ITO)
a statement of facts concerning the investigation, the place to be searched, the items being sought, and the reason for their being sought

The police (or other investigators) must make an application in writing to obtain a search warrant. This requires completing a s. 487 Form 1 **information to obtain (ITO)**, as well as a s. 487 Form 5 warrant to search. The ITO is a statement of facts concerning the investigation, the place to be searched, the items being looked for, and why the police believe these items are in the place they wish to search.

The ITO is the most crucial document in many criminal investigations. It must cover many aspects of the police investigation, and it includes whatever knowledge the affiant possesses at the time the ITO is being drafted. An ITO can be relatively short or it can be very long and detailed, depending on the complexity of the investigation. Some ITOs are five pages long; others are 500 pages. When presenting the ITO, the affiant must swear an oath or affirmation to a justice of the peace or a judge. The information provided by the affiant has to convince the JP or the judge to grant the warrant, and it will be further scrutinized by lawyers and the courts throughout the judicial process.

FORM 1   Information to Obtain

INFORMATION TO OBTAIN SEARCH WARRANT
DÉNONCIATION EN VUE D'OBTENIR UN MANDAT DE PERQUISITION   Form / *Formule* **1**   Section / *(Article)* **487**

INFORMATION of
Les présentes constituent
LA DÉNONOCIATION de

CANADA
PROVINCE OF ONTARIO
PROVINCE DE L'ONTARIO

of
de

hereinafter called the informant, taken.   *(Occupation)/(Profession)*
ci-après appelé le dénonciateur, portée devant moi.

The informant says that he/she has reasonable and probable grounds to believe and does believe that there is(are) in a certain building, receptacle or place, namely, the
Le dénonciateur déclare qu'il(qu'elle) a des motifs raisonnables de croire qu'il y a dans un certain bâtiment, contenant ou lieu, savoir :

(Dwelling-House, Building, Receptacle, or Place)
(habitation, bâtiment, contenant ou lieu)

of
de
(Owner or Occupant of Dwelling-House, Building, etc.)
(propriétaire ou occupant de l'habitation, bâtiment, etc.)

at
à/au
(Address or Location of Dwelling-House, Building, etc.)   in the said region,
(adresse ou emplacement de l'habitation, du bâtiment, etc.)   *dans ladite région*

(Describe things to be searched for)
(décrire les choses à rechercher)

which there are reasonable grounds to believe *will afford evidence with respect to*
*dont on a des motifs raisonnable de croire *qu'elles fourniront une preuve touchant la perpétration**

○ the commission,   ○ suspected commission, or   ○ intended commission
d'une infraction,   *présumée, ou*   *en voie d'être perpétrée*

of an offence against the Criminal Code, namely, the offence of:
au Code criminel, savoir:

(Describe offence in respect to which search is to be made)
(décrire l'infraction à l'égard de laquelle la perquisition doit être effectuée)

State grounds of belief *(énoncer les motifs)*

and that his/her grounds for so believing are that
et que ses soupçons reposent sur les motifs suivants:

WHEREFORE the informant prays that a search warrant may be granted to search the said
EN CONSÉQUENCE, le dénonciateur demande qu'un mandat de perquisition soit accordé pour perquisitionner dans ledit/ladite

for the said thing(s).
(Dwelling-House, Building, etc.)   *en vue de trouver lesdites choses.*
(habitation, bâtiment, etc.)

Sworn before me at the City of Toronto in the said Toronto Region, this
Déclaré sou serment devant moi dans la ville de Toronto, dans la région de Toronto, ce

day of
jour de

*or *is(are) intended to be used for the purpose of committing an offence against the person for which a person may be arrested without warrant, namely, the offence of
* ou *sont destinées à servir aux fins de la perpétration d'une infraction contre une personne, pour laquelle un individu peut être arrêté sans mandat, savoir:*

A Commissioner of Oaths/Justice of the Peace/Judge of   Informant
the Ontario Court of Justice   *Dénonciateur*

YC 0918 (rev. 07/2012)

Form/*Formule* 5
(Section/*Article* 487)

WARRANT TO SEARCH
MANDAT DE PERQUISITION

CANADA
PROVINCE OF ONTARIO
PROVINCE DE L'ONTARIO
} To the Peace Officers in the Toronto Region and the Province of Ontario
Aux agents de la paix dans la région de Toronto et dans la province de l'Ontario

WHEREAS it appears upon the information of
ATTENDU QU'il appert de la dénonciation de _____

that there are reasonable grounds to believe that there are in
qu'il existe des motifs raisonnables de croire qu'il y a dans _____

_____ at/*à/au* _____

_____ , herein called
ci-après appelés

the premises, certain things namely:
les lieux, certaines choses, savior :

that are being sought as evidence in respect to
qui sont recherchées comme preuve

○ the commission,   ○ suspected commission, or   ○ intended commission
   d'une infraction,   *présumée, ou*   *en voie d'être perpétrée*

of an offence against the Criminal Code, namely:
au Code criminel, savoir:

THEREFORE, this is to authorize and require you, between the hours of _____ to enter into
A CES CAUSES, les présentes ont pour objet de vous autoriser et obliger à entrer, entre   *dans*

the premises and to search for the above things, and to bring them before me or some other justice to be dealt with according to law.
les lieux et de rechercher lesdites choses et de les apporter devant moi ou devant tout autre juge de paix afin quil en soit disposé selon la loi.

DATED _____ this day of _____ , _____ , at the City of Toronto, in the Toronto Region
FAIT le   *jour de*   , *dans la ville de Toronto, dans la région*

_____
Judge or Justice of the Peace in and for the Province of Ontario
Juge ou juge de paix dans et pour la province de l'Ontario

OFFICE FOR DISABILITY ISSUES   OFFICE DES AFFAIRES DES PERSONNES HANDICAPÉES
INFORMATION SERVICE FOR BARRIER FREE COURTS   SERVICE D'INFORMATION SUR LES TRIBUNAUX À ACCÈS FACILE
1-800-387-4456   **1-800-387-4456**
TORONTO AREA 326-0111   **RÉGION DE TORONTO 326-0111**

FORM 5   Warrant to Search

Executed on the _____ day of _____ , _____
Exécuté le *jour de*

by _____ , P.C. _____ , Division _____
par *C.P.* *Division*

Seizure under: ☐ section 487;   ☐ section 489;   ☐ no seizure
Saisie aux termes de: *art. 487;* *art. 489;* *aucune saisie*

Return made before _____ , on the
retour effectué devant *le*

_____ day of _____ , _____ at _____
jour de *à/au*

The Three Fs: Full, Fair, and Frank

***ex parte* motion**
a legal term referring to a proceeding or application where one of the parties has not received notice and, therefore, is neither present nor represented

Three Fs
describes the criteria for search warrant applications—full, fair, and frank

A search warrant is an ***ex parte* motion**—a legal term meaning that one of the parties related to a particular proceeding or application has not been made aware of the motion, so he or she is not present or represented. For obvious reasons, this is the case with a search warrant application—the suspect is not made aware of the motion. It is crucial, then, that the affiant of the warrant provide the JP or judge with *all* material facts that investigators possess, both the strong and the weak information, and not simply "cherry-pick" the best material.

Warrants must meet strict disclosure requirements, often referred to as the **Three Fs**: full, fair, and frank. The information provided needs to be reliable, balanced, and material. It does not have to include every minute detail of the investigation, but it does need to be clear and concise, as well as legally and factually sufficient. A *legally sufficient* ITO is one that meets the requirements set out in the Code and other federal statutes. A *factually sufficient* ITO shows the grounds on which the informant (that is, the police officer) believes the offence has occurred, and it states that the things they are looking for will provide evidence in relation to the offence. An ITO cannot be based on mere suspicions or allegations.

To meet the requirements of the Three Fs, the affiant needs to provide in the warrant application

- specific details,
- full disclosure, and
- any embarrassments in the investigation.

Providing Specifics

The ITO should answer the following questions:

1. *Why does the affiant believe the offence has occurred?* The affiant must ensure that the ITO contains detailed information supporting his or her belief.

2. *What items is the affiant looking for?* The items listed in the search warrant must be related to the crime and must be items that will assist the investigator(s) in building a case to implicate their suspect. They should afford evidence of the actual or intended commission of a crime, linking the suspect to the crime scene. If a firearm has been used in the commission of an offence, the affiant must provide in the ITO as much detail as possible about the firearm.

3. *Where does the affiant want to search for these items?* The affiant must describe in detail where an identified item is located. For example, if the affiant believes that a firearm being searched for is hidden in a CEO's office in a large building, he or she would need to identify this office specifically in the ITO. The affiant could not simply list the entire building. The JP or judge in this case would likely authorize a search warrant for the CEO's office *only*, not for the entire building.

4. *Why does the affiant expect to find the items in the specified location?* The affiant must provide sourced or well-documented material stating why he or she believes the items are in the specified location. This material may include information from a reliable and trusted source.

5. *Why will the items being searched for provide evidence about the offence being investigated?* The affiant needs to explain in the ITO the relationship between the items he or she is proposing to search for and the crime he or she is investigating.

     Consider a case where the police are investigating a sexual assault offence that the affiant believes took place in the suspect's bed. The affiant's request may be to search the location and seize any bedding, which may contain DNA or hair samples from either the suspect or the victim. The DNA and hair samples may not prove the sexual assault, but they could be crucial evidence linking the suspect and victim to the bed and bedroom—preventing the suspect from denying that the victim was ever in the house. Once police have these samples, they would obtain a DNA sample from the suspect to implicate him conclusively in the offence. If the suspect refused to provide such a sample voluntarily, a subsequent search warrant would be required. The police would also obtain a DNA sample from the victim for comparison to any DNA found within the bedroom.

Providing Full Disclosure

The affiant must include in the ITO not only the information or facts that support the application, but *all* information the affiant has received relating to the investigation. This includes information that seems to contradict the affiant's belief about the offence. Such information, which may jeopardize the application, includes the following:

- *Information suggesting that the offence did not occur.* Although the affiant may have overwhelming evidence that the offence did in fact occur and that evidence of this exists at a certain location, he or she may also have contradictory evidence, and this too must go into the ITO.

- *Information suggesting that the items being sought may not be at the location named in the warrant.* The affiant may have strong evidence that the items he or she wishes to search for are at the identified location, but he or she may also have information to the contrary.

    Consider, for example, a case where a reliable informant has told the affiant that a known person is selling crack cocaine out of his house and that she (the informant) saw the cocaine on the kitchen table the last time she was there. It so happens, however, that when an undercover officer went to the address in question and tried to buy crack cocaine, the suspected dealer said that he had no crack cocaine left to sell. The undercover officer's experience with the suspected dealer must be included in the affiant's ITO, even though this information does not support the application.

    Note that, despite the undercover officer's experience, the suspected dealer may in fact have crack cocaine in the house; he may simply not have wanted to sell to the undercover officer. On the other hand, he may be telling the truth and may, in fact, have run out of the drugs that he possessed when the informant was at his house. In this case, the affiant would be expected to conduct surveillance on the suspect's home to determine whether the suspected drug activity is continuing at the address. If the affiant determines that the suspect is actually sold out, he should probably abandon the application for a search warrant and continue with the investigation.

Disclosing Embarrassments in the Investigation

There are times when the details of a police investigation may reflect negatively on it and may reflect negatively, by extension, on the search warrant application. Nonetheless, these details must be disclosed. Following are some questions that may disclose "embarrassments" in the investigation.

1. *Has the affiant previously applied for a warrant for the same location and been turned down?* If the affiant applies for a search warrant and is turned down by a JP or judge, he may apply again. Reapplication often means that the ITO is read by a

different JP or judge. An affiant who is reapplying for a search warrant must disclose the following in the ITO: (1) that he or she has previously been turned down; (2) the name of the JP or justice who turned down the application; (3) when the application was turned down (if known); and (4) the reasons why the application was denied.

An affiant who is reapplying for a search warrant may seek to remedy the problems that the JP or judge cited in denying the earlier application. If, for example, the affiant's earlier application was turned down for lack of supporting information or evidence, he or she can include in the reapplication whatever new information has been acquired in the meantime, clearly specifying it in the new application. In some cases, a JP or judge may have turned down the previous application owing to a procedural issue. The officer, in this case, may simply ensure that his or her reapplication involves no procedural problems.

2. *Did the police (or others) obtain evidence unconstitutionally?* If, during the investigation, the police or anyone violated someone's Charter rights in obtaining evidence, the affiant must reveal this in the ITO. Perhaps a statement was obtained from an arrested person without a proper caution. Or perhaps the police entered the location in question without a warrant and observed, in the process, something of evidentiary value. The affiant would do well to disclose these Charter violations in the ITO, rather than have them come out at trial.

CHECK YOUR UNDERSTANDING

1. Define what an information to obtain (ITO) is.
2. List five questions that an ITO must answer.
3. Give an example of an "embarrassment" that must be disclosed in an ITO.

Personal Sourced Information

As discussed above, the affiant must provide very specific information when applying for a search warrant. This information must constitute more than a basis for suspicion; it must support the affiant's reasonable grounds for belief regarding the person or the search location. Such information often comes from someone, such as a confidential informant or police agent, who has first-hand knowledge of the circumstances.

Confidential Informants

confidential informants
informers who provide valuable information to the police and whose identity cannot be revealed by the Crown or the police unless the informant agrees to it

Confidential informants provide valuable information to the police. Their information can provide the primary basis for a search warrant application. Informants put themselves in danger by providing this information. For many years, the courts have recognized the important role that confidential police informants play and the need to protect their identities. As a result, police informants are granted absolute privilege. Absolute privilege means that the informant's identity must be kept completely confidential. The police and Crown cannot reveal a confidential informant's identity; only the informant can release this information. Everyday citizens will not come forward to report a crime unless they have this level of security and can provide information without fearing the offender's retribution.

The courts take confidential informants' absolute privilege extremely seriously. Not all informants are confidential ones. However, many potential informants will choose to remain silent if not granted absolute privilege. Sometimes, the case for granting an informant absolute privilege is obvious. Once privilege is granted, it must be respected by all involved.

The definition of a confidential informant is outlined in *R v. Brown* (1999, para. 6), in which the Ontario Superior Court stated the following:

> Not everyone who gives information to the police is a confidential informant. It is one thing to be an informant—it is another thing to be a confidential informant. To be a confidential informant an informant must request the privilege, expressly or by necessary implication, and receive an assurance of confidentiality, expressly or by necessary implication, from the officer. Regard must be had for all of the circumstances of the case. A would-be confidential informant does not begin with a right of confidentiality but does have a right to silence. One need not give information to the police. But, if the privilege attaches to the relationship, a right of confidentiality in the confidential informant is created and must be recognized by everyone.

Police Agents

Investigators may also obtain information from a **police agent**. A police agent is not necessarily employed by the police, but he or she acts under the direction of the police. This person goes out into the field with instructions to gather and convey information back to the police. This kind of informant is a police agent and is not protected by informer privilege.

police agent
a person who, acting under the direction of the police, goes out into the field to gather, obtain, and convey to the police the information he or she receives

Distinguishing Between a Confidential Informant and a Police Agent

It is sometimes unclear whether an informant has crossed the line from being a confidential informant to being a police agent. To make this determination, the Crown prosecutor must examine the relationship between the informer and the police. In *R v. Broyles* (1991, p. 596), the SCC clarified the difference by introducing the following test, which is applied to the informant's communications with the accused: "[W]ould the exchange between the accused and informer have taken place, in the form and manner in which it did take place, but for the intervention of the state or its agents?" If the police had a hand in shaping the "form and manner" of the informant's exchange with the accused, the informant may be an agent of the state and is not protected by informer privilege.

To highlight the difference between a confidential informant and a police agent, let's consider two scenarios. Both involve a problem home within a particular neighbourhood. Neighbours have complained numerous times that the home is the site of drug dealing. One day, police receive a call from a man who states that his wife is a drug addict and that he is trying to help her kick her habit.

Scenario 1: The husband tells police that his wife picks up crack cocaine every day from the owner of the home in question. He asks the police to do something about the dealer, and even provides the dealer's name and phone number. He advises the police that he himself would likely be in danger if it were ever revealed that information came from him, so he doesn't want to provide his name and does not want the police to reveal anything about him. He just wants the place shut down. The police proceed to conduct an active investigation, and they use the information the husband has provided, along with other investigative tools, in forming their grounds to obtain a search warrant.

Scenario 2: The husband calls police about the home and his wife, providing his name and other identifiers. He does not provide any information about the drug dealer. Instead, police ask him to go with his wife to buy the crack cocaine, then provide police with a description of what took place. He agrees.

In the first scenario, the husband has volunteered information and has requested anonymity. This makes him a confidential informant whose identity is protected by the absolute privilege granted to him by the legal system. The husband in the second scenario has not requested anonymity, and he has agreed to follow police directions in going to the house with his wife to buy drugs. This would make him a police agent, and he would not qualify for the absolute privilege of a confidential informant. The police would have to advise him of this fact before asking him to go to the address to collect the information.

Sealing Warrants

Once a warrant has been executed by the police, the courts must make the ITO available to the public. The problem is that these documents may contain sensitive information, such as the identity of confidential informants or details about covert investigative methods used by police. The release of these documents would reveal this information to the accused, to other members of the public, and to the media.

sealing order
an order that the details of a warrant and an ITO not be disclosed to the public after the warrant has been executed

To prevent this from happening, the affiant must apply for the courts to place the ITO and warrant under a **sealing order**. A sealing order prohibits the information in the ITO from being released. Under s. 487.3(1) of the Code, a judge, on an application to seal the warrant and the ITO, may make an order prohibiting access to and the disclosure of any of the information they contain. When making such an application, the affiant must provide specific reasons why these documents should be sealed.

Unsealing a Warrant

While the affiant needs to protect the sensitive information within a warrant and an ITO, the accused standing trial needs the case against him or her disclosed, so a proper defence can be prepared. The conflict between these needs is satisfied through a pre-trial vetting process; working together, the affiant and the Crown prosecutor closely examine, or vet, the documents to decide what information must remain protected. Everything except the protected information is unsealed and made available to the accused. The strength of the warrant will then be determined by a judge; he or she will review the edited warrant based on what has been unsealed. The Crown prosecutor must ensure that the edited version of the ITO contains enough information to convince the reviewing judge that the search warrant is valid, and enough information to enable the defence attorney to properly prepare for trial.

The courts have designated the Crown the "caretaker" of confidential information privilege. This means that, though the police help vet and edit the ITO, it is ultimately the Crown prosecutor's responsibility to protect the identity of any confidential informant identified in the ITO. This is true even if criminal charges do not result from the execution of a search warrant.

When unsealing an unvetted ITO, the courts should follow the guidelines set out in the SCC case of *R v. Garofoli*. In that case, the court (1990, p. 1425) stated the following:

> The question of whether the packet should be opened is a matter within the discretion of the judge hearing the application, who must balance the interests of the accused in the protection of privacy and a fair trial, including the right to make full answer and defence, with the public interest in the administration of justice. Given the importance of the accused's right to make full answer and defence, the balance will generally fall in favour of opening the packet, subject to editing and special concerns for the administration of justice which may arise in particular cases.

Once the court opens the package of unvetted information, the Crown prosecutor can object to the disclosure of certain of its contents and request that it be edited. The Crown would have to provide reasons for believing the material should be edited. The judge hearing the application would subsequently order that the edited version provided by the Crown prosecutor be provided to the defence counsel for disclosure.

CHECK YOUR UNDERSTANDING

1. Who is considered a confidential informant?
2. What is the difference between a confidential informant and a police agent?
3. What is a sealing order?

Submitting the Warrant Application

Once the ITO is completed, the affiant presents it and the search warrant to a JP, a provincial court judge, or a superior court justice. This may be done either in person or by telewarrant.

Telewarrant

Normally the affiant of a search warrant will attend the JP or judge in person, with the prepared warrant. However, there are times when this may be impractical—for example, with a middle-of-the-night investigation for which police need a search warrant to obtain or preserve evidence. In such cases, where it is impractical for the affiant to attend in person, the affiant may send the search warrant application by way of a **telewarrant** process.

A telewarrant is a warrant requested by any means of telecommunication, most commonly by fax machine. A telewarrant must meet the same standards as a conventional warrant. Under s. 487.1(1) of the Code, a peace officer may only apply for a telewarrant where he or she believes an indictable offence has been committed and where it would be impracticable to appear personally before a justice.

Under s. 158.1(1) of Ontario's *Provincial Offences Act*, a provincial offences officer (for example, a Ministry of Transportation officer or a Conservation officer) or a peace officer may submit an information on oath, by means of telecommunication, if he or she believes that an offence has been committed under the authority of the *Provincial Offences Act* and that it would be impracticable to appear personally before a justice to make application for a warrant. Many search warrants requested for after-hours investigations are for investigations into *Provincial Offences Act* offences—for example, investigations into after-hours clubs.

The information in the ITO for a telewarrant is very similar to the information in a regular warrant's ITO. The affiant is expected to provide

- a description of the dwelling or other place that he or she wishes to search,
- a description of all items in the place that are evidence related to the indictable offence,
- the affiant's reasonable grounds for believing that the items being searched for are currently in the location the affiant wishes to search, and
- the details of any previous search warrant applications made personally or by a telewarrant in respect to the investigation for which the affiant is currently seeking a telewarrant.

telewarrant
a warrant requested by telephone or other telecommunication means, most often a fax machine; used in circumstances where it is impracticable for the affiant to apply for the search warrant in person

Telewarrant applications are also required to provide extra information—information that a regular warrant application does not have to provide. This extra information includes

- an account of why it is impracticable for the affiant to appear personally in support of their search warrant application, and
- a complete description of the indictable offence that is alleged to have taken place.

Section 487.1(5) of the Code provides the legal authority governing how a justice responds to a telewarrant application:

> A justice ... who is satisfied that an information submitted by telephone or other means of telecommunication
>
> (a) is in respect of an indictable offence and conforms to the requirements of subsection (4),
>
> (b) discloses reasonable grounds for dispensing with an information presented personally and in writing, and
>
> (c) discloses reasonable grounds, in accordance with subsection 256(1) or paragraph 487(1)(a), (b), or (c), as the case may be, for the issuance of a warrant in respect of an indictable offence,
>
> may issue a warrant to a peace officer conferring the same authority respecting search and seizure as may be conferred by a warrant issued by a justice before whom the peace officer appears personally pursuant to subsection 256(1) or 487(1), as the case may be, and may require that the warrant be executed within such time period as the justice may order.

If the justice is satisfied that the grounds exist to issue the telewarrant, he or she will issue it, stating the hours when it is valid. He or she will then return the warrant electronically (in most instances, via fax machine). The affiant will bring the faxed copy of the warrant to the address in question as he or she would any warrant.

Jurisdiction of the Justice

One other consideration when submitting an application for a search warrant is the jurisdiction of the justice. If the JP or judge reading the application is satisfied that a warrant should be issued based on the ITO provided by the affiant, he or she will sign the warrant, thus allowing police officers and anyone lawfully assisting the police to search the building, receptacle, or place listed in the warrant. The place listed must lie *within the territorial division where the justice has jurisdiction*.

Jurisdiction is important. Sometimes, the police will prepare a search warrant in one location, but need to search a location in a different jurisdiction. Section 487(2) of the Code states what must be done if this is the case:

> (2) If the building, receptacle or place is in another territorial division, the justice may issue the warrant with any modifications that the circumstances require, and it may be executed in the other territorial division after it has been endorsed, in Form 28, by a justice who has jurisdiction in that territorial division. The endorsement may be made on the original of the warrant or on a copy of the warrant transmitted by any means of telecommunication.

Let's clarify this protocol with an example. If investigators with the Vancouver Police Department need to search a home in Calgary, Alberta as part of their investigation, they would first need to swear to the ITO before a Vancouver justice. Then a Calgary justice would need to endorse the signed warrant. This would authorize police to search the Calgary location. The Vancouver justice has authority to endorse a warrant for the province in which he or she is a justice. In this example, his or her authority to endorse the warrant is limited to the province of British Columbia.

CHECK YOUR UNDERSTANDING

1. Describe what a telewarrant is.
2. What information must be included in telewarrants that is not required in other warrants?
3. Explain why the justice's jurisdiction is important when police are seeking a search warrant.

Executing a Search Warrant

Once a JP or judge authorizes a search warrant, the police must execute it in accordance with the law.

The General Rules for Executing a Warrant

There is a general rule in law that before entering a premises (for example, a house, an apartment, or a business), police officers who are in possession of a search warrant must

- announce their presence outside the address they want to enter,
- identify themselves to the owner or occupants,
- announce the fact that they have a search warrant for the address, and
- request permission to enter the address in question.

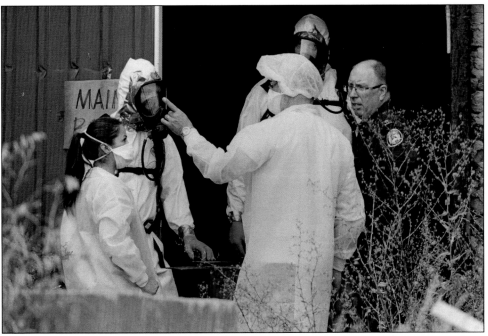

Source: Kevin Van Paassen/The Globe and Mail/CP Images.

Police execute a search warrant at a barn in a rural Ontario farm during a murder and missing person investigation.

This is commonly referred to as the **knock and announce rule**. A further rule is that, once inside the premises, the affiant of the search warrant must show the warrant to the person named on it. If that person is not present at the time the warrant is executed, the affiant should show the warrant to whoever may be in charge of the premises at the time it is being searched.

Special Circumstances

There are rules for executing a search warrant, but sometimes following all of these rules is impractical under the circumstances; doing so may even put people in danger or jeopardize evidence. So, in these cases, the search team may have to take a different approach.

Use of Force

The rules require that police executing a warrant ask for permission to enter a premises. Despite this rule, the person at the residence cannot actually refuse them entry so long as they have a warrant. If he or she does refuse, police are authorized to use as much force as necessary to enter a location. They can also use force if, after allowing occupants reasonable time to answer the door, there is no response from within the premises; or if exigent circumstances exist. The latter include circumstances where evidence could be destroyed or where police believe that there is an immediate threat to themselves or others. Police authority to use force in these situations was confirmed by the SCC's ruling in *R v. Genest* (1989, p. 61), which also established restrictions:

> Fears for the safety of the searchers and the possibility of violence can be reasons for the use of force in the execution of a search warrant. But the consideration of the possibility of violence must be carefully limited. It should not amount to a *carte blanche* for the police to ignore completely all restrictions on police behaviour. The greater the departure from the standards of behaviour required by the common law and the *Charter*, the heavier the onus on the police to show why they thought it was necessary to use force in the process of an arrest or a search. The evidence to justify such behaviour must be apparent in the record, and must have been available to the police at the time they chose their course of conduct.

No-Knock Entry

Another special circumstance is a **no-knock entry**. This means that officers do not announce their presence outside the address before entering. Police take this approach when they believe that it is not in their best interest, or in the best interest of the investigation, to announce their presence. Exigent circumstances may exist; police may believe that if they reveal their presence, lives or evidence may be in jeopardy.

Neither statutory law nor common law prohibits a no-knock entry. However, if the affiant knows that a no-knock entry will be required, he or she will usually note this in the ITO. The justice issuing the warrant does not have the authority to determine whether a no-knock entry will be permitted. The no-knock clause on the search warrant essentially allows police to perform a dynamic entry into the dwelling—in other words, to use as much force as necessary without making their attendance known to the occupiers of the dwelling.

Let's reconsider this chapter's opening scenario. It is clear that Officer Kim's team, though they possess a search warrant, cannot simply force their way into the premises. They would only be authorized to do so if exigent circumstances exist.

Night Searches

Most search warrants are executed during the day. In fact, s. 488 of the Code limits the execution of search warrants by night. It says the following:

> A warrant issued under section 487 or 487.1 shall be executed by day, unless
> (a) the justice is satisfied there are reasonable grounds for it to be executed by night;
> (b) the reasonable grounds are included in the information; and
> (c) the warrant authorizes that it be executed at night.

Section 2 of the Code defines **night** as being from 9:00 p.m. to 6:00 a.m. of the following day. Therefore, an application for a nighttime search warrant would be seeking an authorization for an entry between 9:00 p.m. and 6:00 a.m.

An affiant must include his or her request for a nighttime search in the ITO, and must cite the exceptional circumstances that make a nighttime search necessary.

Consider the following scenario, for example. The police know that a suspect is residing in an apartment with a collection of laptop computers he has stolen. Late one night, police receive reliable information that the suspect plans to move the stolen property sometime the same night. Because the suspect's apartment is in a large building, police cannot watch his apartment door without being detected; they won't be able to determine at what point the stolen property is being removed from the apartment. Because the police in this situation need to act quickly, the affiant would request a nighttime search in the ITO, and he or she would do so by telewarrant.

The affiant in this scenario would need to accurately describe in the ITO the exceptional circumstances requiring a nighttime search, the British Columbia Court of Appeal having found in *R v. Anderson* (2001, para. 17) that evidence seized in an invalid night search is inadmissible. If a nighttime search does not comply with s. 488 of the Code, the search can later be quashed by the courts.

The restrictions on when s. 487 or 487.1 *Criminal Code* search warrants have to be executed are not applicable to s. 11 *Controlled Drugs and Substances Act* (CDSA) search warrants or s. 199 *Criminal Code* search warrants (common bawdy house or common gaming house warrants). These search warrants can be executed at any time, day or night, without seeking special authorization; however, it would be prudent for the search warrant affiant to include the reason for the nighttime entry in his or her ITO. Also, telewarrants for CDSA offences are treated as s. 11 CDSA provisions—that is, there are no nighttime restrictions.

night
defined, in s. 2 of the *Criminal Code*, as the hours between 9:00 p.m. and 6:00 a.m. of the following day

Authority to Search People

A search warrant authorizes police to search an address either (1) to seize items believed to be evidence of an offence that has been committed; or (2) to assist in a current investigation. It does not authorize police to search people inside the place they are searching. There are only three circumstances under which police can search a person while executing a search warrant:

1. If the police locate the suspect(s) wanted for the offence related to the search they are conducting, it is likely that this person(s) would be arrested at the location. Under common law authority, police can search the arrested person for evidence, for anything that may assist the person to escape, or for any item that may be a threat to the safety of the officers, of members of the public, or of the arrested person. This authority to search at the execution of a search warrant is the same search authority police have when making any arrest.

2. Section 11 of the *Controlled Drugs and Substances Act* outlines the conditions under which a justice may issue a search warrant to search for and seize a controlled substance, precursor, or any offence-related property. According to s. 11(5), if an officer believes a person at the site identified in the warrant has any such item on his or her person, the officer has the authority to search the person "for the controlled substance, precursor, property, or thing."

3. If the police have reasonable grounds to believe that any individual at the location of the search represents a safety concern, they have the authority to search that individual. This authority was confirmed by the Ontario Superior Court ruling in *R v. MacIsaac* (2001), though this is a controversial and much challenged search authority. The police need to justify the *type* of search they conduct in these circumstances. In other words, they are authorized to conduct a pat-down search for weapons (to ensure their safety issues are addressed), but they do not have the authority to do a strip search at the location. If something beyond a pat-down search is required, police must be able to justify the further level of search and must conduct it in a lawful manner.

The Time Frame of a Search Warrant

Most search warrants are authorized for a specific date and time period. Depending on the nature of the investigation and the grounds included in the ITO, the JP or judge may also issue a warrant that applies to multiple dates and times. The police may apply for an extension to the dates and hours originally granted as long as they can justify the extension. Another time-related limitation on the warrant is that once the police have searched and then left the location, they are not permitted to return and search it again under the authority of the same search warrant.

CHECK YOUR UNDERSTANDING

1. Identify the general rules for executing a search warrant.
2. Describe the circumstances in which these rules would not have to be followed.
3. In what circumstances may police search a person while executing a search warrant?

Guidelines for Creating a Search Warrant

Let's look now at the elements of a valid search warrant, then consider some guidelines for writing a search warrant, and then explore a sample search warrant.

Mandatory Elements of a Search Warrant

Under the Code, a valid search warrant must meet a number of requirements. These include the following:

1. The ITO must be sworn to under oath.

2. The informant for the search warrant must be a peace officer. In *R v. Semeniuk* (2007, para. 19), the British Columbia Court of Appeal cites the Code in defining a peace officer as "a police officer, police constable, bailiff, constable, or other person employed for preservation and maintenance of the public peace or for the service or execution of civil process." This definition includes all police officers. In some instances, the informant for a search warrant may also be a special constable.

3. The affiant must specify the location that he or she wishes to search.

4. Within the ITO, the affiant must specify the offence(s) the person(s) has committed in relation to the location they wish to search and what items they are searching for.

5. The affiant must describe the items for which he or she wishes to search, based on all of the information the affiant has received when applying for the warrant.

6. The affiant must provide, within the ITO, the reasons for believing that the items will be located in the location named in the warrant.

Drafting a Search Warrant

The following is a guide to drafting a search warrant. It is based on best practices rather than on binding legal requirements, but any affiant of a search warrant would do well to heed its recommendations.

A GUIDE FOR DRAFTING A SEARCH WARRANT AND ITO

1. You must properly identify the type of warrant for which you are applying, including the name of the Act under which the search warrant is being sought and the applicable section numbers in the Act. For example, if the investigation involves stolen property, you would be seeking a *Criminal Code* (CC) search warrant. If the investigation involved drugs, the affiant would be seeking a *Controlled Drugs and Substances Act* (CDSA) search warrant.

2. You must identify the judicial figure to whom you are applying for a warrant—a JP, a provincial court judge, or a superior court justice. Obviously, you need to know which of these three has the judicial authority to grant the type of warrant you are applying for.

3. You must provide pertinent details of your identity, including

   • your name, your current employer (for example, Toronto Police Service), your current rank, and the length of time you have been a police officer

   • the sub-unit in which you are currently working, and that sub-unit's mandate (for example, "the Drug Squad, investigating all aspects of drug investigations" or "a Major Crime Unit, investigating all aspects of property related offences")

   • your role within the investigation for which the search warrant is being sought, and an account of your experience within this investigation

   • an account of your personal and professional experience in criminal investigations that may be relevant to the warrant that is being applied for (for example, a list of previous search warrants that you have been granted, and/or a list of search warrants with which you have been directly involved)

4. It is crucial that you provide all sources of information that you are using in the application for the search warrant, including the following:

   • All databases on which you are relying. For example, the **Canadian Police Information Centre (CPIC)** is a database that you may use to run checks on the suspect(s). It is Canada's central police database, used by all police services across the country to find information about any current charges an individual may be facing or any criminal record he or she may have, any previous interactions he or she may have had with the police, as well as information about his or her address.

   • Any personal sources, such as confidential informants or police agents that may have provided you with information. You must include the informant's name, age, and home address, as well as any criminal record he or she may have. In almost all search warrant applications, the identity of a confidential informant will be included in the warrant application, but you will ask the justice to have the identity sealed so that it is not revealed to anyone outside of yourself and the justice.

Canadian Police Information Centre (CPIC)
the central police database used by all Canadian police services to access information on a number of matters, including the current charges individuals may be facing and any criminal record they may have

5. Any person(s) of interest that you believe, on reasonable grounds, is associated with the investigation. This includes the suspect(s) but may include others, such as family members associated with the suspect(s). For instance, you may be seeking a search warrant related to drugs in a home where the suspect lives. Your investigation may reveal that the suspect lives in the house with family members. In this case, you must include in your warrant application the names of the family members and, if known, any of their personal identifiers, and you must describe any involvement they may have, direct or indirect, with the drugs being searched for. For all persons of interest listed in the search warrant, you should include the following details:

   • their name and age

   • their current home address and any previous addresses (if known)

   • any current charges they may be facing

   • any criminal record they may have

6. You must provide information about the place named in the search warrant, including the address and the location. This should include a description of the address, executed to the best of your ability. Officers performing surveillance on the address may help you with this, as may Internet photos of the address, or information from personal sources who have attended the address and personally been inside the premises. Information about the location should also include

   • the identity of the person who currently owns the property, as well as the identity of whoever is residing at the property. You should be able to use record searches to determine these facts. You should indicate whether any of these individuals are persons of interest to the investigation.

7. You must identify the territorial jurisdiction of the address—in other words, the city, town, or region where it is located (for example, Winnipeg, Manitoba; Edmonton, Alberta; or the Toronto Region). For a search warrant, as for many legal documents, jurisdiction is crucial and must be clearly indicated throughout the document.

8. You must include a detailed summary of the investigation in the ITO. This should include a clear account of the events that have provided you with reasonable grounds to believe the items being sought are actually in the address named on the search warrant. The information needs to satisfy the JP or judge granting the search warrant that you have reasonable grounds.

9. You must provide a record of all previous warrant applications that you or any other police officer has made for this address in connection with the same investigation. If any of these applications failed, you must acknowledge this in the current application, stating the reasons that the request was denied (if known) and identifying the JP or judge who refused the request. At the same time, in the current application, you may remedy the problems that caused the earlier applications to be refused, identify the improvements you have made, and then either reapply in front of another justice or judge or reapply by telewarrant.

10. Identify any special requests you may need to make owing to particular circumstances of the investigation or of the address in question. For instance, you might include a request for a no-knock entry or for a nighttime search.

11. Provide a conclusion for your ITO, reiterating the grounds for the search warrant application. This should be, in essence, a summary of

   • why you believe the items that you wish to search for are at the address that you would like to search

   • why the item(s) constitutes evidence for an offence that has already taken place or will assist an ongoing investigation

   • why the items are important to the investigation

A Sample Search Warrant Application

Let's now look at a sample search warrant, based on the following fictitious scenario. It is alleged that Greg Smith and Lucy Rocci, both of Sudbury, Ontario, are trafficking in various drugs in the city where they live. Based on information gathered from various sources, Detective Dan Hill of the Greater Sudbury Police Service has started an investigation, and he has made the following application for a CDSA search warrant.

Search Warrant—Information to Obtain

APPENDIX A

1. N-methyl-3,4-methylenedioxyamphetamine (N,-dimethyl-1,3-benzodioxole-5-ethanamine) (MDMA)
2. Cocaine
3. Gamma hydroxybutyrate (GHB)
4. Marijuana
5. Crystal methamphetamine
6. Drug paraphernalia, such as scales and packaging
7. Cellular phones, cameras, and their data contents
8. Cash proceeds
9. Documentation regarding the occupancy of 90 Brownstone Street, Sudbury, Ontario

APPENDIX B

1. Gary Smith and Lucy Rocci on or about the 23rd day of August in the year 2014 in the City of Sudbury, Province of Ontario, did unlawfully possess a controlled substance, to wit: cocaine, for the purpose of trafficking, contrary to section 5(2) of the *Controlled Drugs and Substances Act.*

2. And further that Gary Smith and Lucy Rocci on or about the 23rd day of August in the year 2014 in the City of Sudbury, Province of Ontario, did unlawfully possess a controlled substance, to wit: methamphetamine, for the purpose of trafficking, contrary to section 5(2) of the *Controlled Drugs and Substances Act.*

3. And further that Gary Smith and Lucy Rocci on or about the 23rd day of August in the year 2014 in the City of Sudbury, Province of Ontario, did unlawfully possess a controlled substance, to wit: gamma hydroxybutyrate (GHB), for the purpose of trafficking, contrary to section 5(2) of the *Controlled Drugs and Substances Act.*

4. And further that Gary Smith and Lucy Rocci on or about the 23rd day of August in the year 2014 in the City of Sudbury, Province of Ontario, did unlawfully possess a controlled substance, to wit: N-methyl-3,4-methylenedioxyamphetamine (N,-dimethyl-1,3-benzodioxole-5-ethanamine) (MDMA), for the purpose of trafficking, contrary to section 5(2) of the *Controlled Drugs and Substances Act.*

5. And further that Gary Smith and Lucy Rocci on or about the 23rd day of August in the year 2014 in the City of Sudbury, Province of Ontario, did unlawfully possess a controlled substance, to wit: marijuana, for the purpose of trafficking, contrary to section 5(2) of the *Controlled Drugs and Substances Act.*

APPENDIX C

Introduction of the Affiant

I, Dan Hill #44, am a detective with the Greater Sudbury Police Service, assigned to the Sudbury Major Crime Unit. My duties include the enforcement of the *Controlled Drugs and Substances Act.* I am the lead investigator regarding the drug investigation relating to 90 Brownstone Street, in the City of Sudbury.

I have over ten years of experience and training in the investigation of drug related offences. I am a court qualified drug expert for the Greater Sudbury Police Service and I also provide expert opinion evidence on methamphetamine, marijuana, GHB, cocaine, and MDMA.

I have personal knowledge of the facts here and after deposed to, except where same are stated to be on information and belief. During my investigations into this matter, I have read police reports, occurrences, and spoken personally to the police officers, herein named in this application involved in this matter. I have made further inquiries through police computer data banks in relation to the investigation. My investigation and those I oversaw or caused to be done are herein described in this, my information.

I believe that all the information contained in this, my affidavit, is true.

GLOSSARY

The affiant may use the following abbreviations. Their definitions are listed below. These are consistent with their use in the Greater Sudbury Police Service.

a. **CC:** *Criminal Code* (of Canada).

b. **CDSA:** *Controlled Drugs and Substances Act.*

c. **CPIC:** Canadian Police Information Centre—a computer database, which is managed by the Royal Canadian Mounted Police. This database is interfaced with other pertinent data banks, such as the Ministry of Transportation and the Canadian Firearms Program. Information can be added by contributing police agencies. It contains information on a person's criminal record, criminal charges, arrest warrants, probation orders, parole information, weapons prohibitions, firearms registration, motor vehicle registration, and other information that may be of concern to law enforcement officers.

d. **Cocaine:** a controlled substance under Schedule I of the CDSA, usually found in a white powder form snorted through the nose. Can be smoked or injected if altered.

e. **Crystal methamphetamine:** a controlled substance under Schedule I of the CDSA. It is a purified form of methamphetamine that resembles crystals. It can be smoked, snorted, or injected, and is highly addictive.

f. **Det.:** detective—a police supervisor who is also an investigator and performs his or her duties in a plainclothes capacity.

g. **D/C:** detective constable—a police constable who performs his or her duties as an investigator in a plainclothes capacity.

h. **Ecstasy:** a hallucinogenic chemical drug, which is usually sold and ingested in a pill form in various colours and with various symbols stamped on it. Its chemical name is N-methyl-3,4-methylenedioxy-amphetamine (N,-dimethyl-1,3-benzodioxole-5-ethanamine), which is abbreviated as MDMA. It is a controlled drug listed in Schedule III of the CDSA.

i. **Gamma hydroxybutyrate (GHB):** a viscous clear liquid that is orally ingested, and which provides euphoric effects similar to a central nervous system depressant or anaesthetic. It is a controlled substance under Schedule III of the CDSA.

j. **Marijuana:** a controlled substance under Schedule II of the CDSA. It is a leafy green plant material that is usually smoked, but may be eaten.

k. **MDMA:** see "Ecstasy."

l. **PC:** police constable—a police officer who performs his or her duties in a uniform capacity. He or she usually conducts routine patrols in a marked police vehicle, known as a scout car, and responds to radio calls.

m. **GSPS:** Greater Sudbury Police Service.

n. **Sudbury Major Crime Unit:** plainclothes officers of the Greater Sudbury Police Service, whose mandate is to conduct undercover operations and major investigations into offences related to controlled substances

o. **Unified search:** a Greater Sudbury Police Service search engine, which will search the information available to the Greater Sudbury Police Service against the criteria entered. The information database encompasses the following: CPIC, Ministry of Transportation Ontario, field investigative report (a record of police contact with a person), Sudbury Police occurrence reports, photographs of arrested parties obtained by the Greater Sudbury Police Service under the *Identification of Criminals Act.*

SOURCING INFORMATION

a. All police officers named in this affidavit, unless stated otherwise, are members of the GSPS.

b. All locations, unless stated otherwise, are in the City of Sudbury, in the Province of Ontario.

CONFIDENTIAL SOURCE BACKGROUND

See Appendix D.

OVERVIEW

The suspects in this matter are supplying various controlled substances from their home located at 90 Brownstone Street, Sudbury. They supply these drugs to other dealers and friends, as well as supplying drugs to party buses in the downtown Sudbury clubs.

BACKGROUND OF THE INVESTIGATION

1. During the evening of Monday, August 20, 2014, I received a phone call from the Confidential Source, hereinafter called the Source. The Source provided me with the following information regarding the suspects, Gary SMITH and Lucy ROCCI.

   a. A male known as Gary SMITH, but who goes by "Big G," and his girlfriend Lucy ROCCI, are supplying drugs to clubs in downtown Sudbury and the party buses attending the downtown clubs.

   b. SMITH and ROCCI sell powder cocaine, MDMA tablets and powder, GHB, and crystal methamphetamine in large quantities from their house located at 90 Brownstone Street, Sudbury. The drugs are sold to people who deal for them at downtown Sudbury nightclubs and on the "Big Nickel" party buses in the Sudbury harbour.

   c. The Source believes that they have two handguns hidden behind the drywall in their bedroom.

   d. The Source has been buying drugs from SMITH and ROCCI for the past year and goes to their house at 90 Brownstone Street approximately every three days.

   e. The Source has observed other people buy powder cocaine, GHB, MDMA, and crystal methamphetamine on a regular basis. The drugs can always be found in larger quantities in the house, usually in the garage area, which is attached to the house.

   f. The house is described as a single-storey, single-brick and siding house, with a two-car garage, and the front door is back from the garage. The front door is to the left of the garage and there is a kitchen window to the left of the front door. The house has an ABC alarm sign on the front lawn. All the houses on the street are very similar in appearance.

   g. The Source provided me with photos of SMITH and ROCCI via email.

   h. The Source advised that his or her home phone number is 705-555-9087.

2. On the afternoon of Monday, August 20, 2014, the Source contacted me and advised the following:

   a. SMITH and ROCCI were stocking up their house (90 Brownstone Street) for the upcoming Labour Day weekend because they are supplying the "Big Nickel" party buses on Saturday, September 2, 2014 in the downtown area of Sudbury.

   b. SMITH and ROCCI will give the drugs to other dealers to sell on the party buses and at downtown nightclubs.

c. SMITH and ROCCI are in control of the security on the boats, and guns will be present because of the amount of drugs involved.

d. The Source again observed powder cocaine, MDMA, GHB, marijuana, and crystal methamphetamine in the house in large quantities. There is also money in the house, which is the proceeds of drug sales.

e. The Source observed five ounces of powder cocaine, a large quantity of MDMA tablets (ecstasy), numerous Ziploc bags of marijuana, and GHB in a red wooden chest in the corner of the garage.

f. The Source observed powder MDMA in the laundry room in the basement and crystal methamphetamine in paint cans in the basement.

g. The horse equipment in the house leads the Source to believe that ROCCI rides horses.

h. SMITH and ROCCI sell the powder cocaine for $200 for an "eight ball" (3.5 grams), $400 for a 500 mL bottle, $12 per tablet or gel capsule of MDMA, or $3.50 per tablet if you buy in large quantities. (These prices are in line with known drug pricing in Sudbury.)

i. The cash proceeds are in a small safe in a front bedroom on the main floor.

j. The Source is unsure if the handguns are still in the house, but believes they are, considering the amount of drugs at the house.

3. As a result of the information provided to me by the Source, I conducted computer checks on the Internet and with Sudbury Police Unified Search to corroborate the Source's information. I found the following information:

a. Gary SMITH has a date of birth of July 9, 1980. He has been charged with Trafficking a Controlled Substance and Possession of a Controlled Substance for the Purpose of Trafficking. These charges are with the Ontario Provincial Police (OPP), with an offence date of December 13, 2013.

b. Gary SMITH has a criminal record which includes the following convictions:

   • 3 counts of Possession of a Controlled Substance for the Purpose of Trafficking (2007-2010)

   • 1 count of Conspiracy to Traffic a Controlled Substance (2009)

c. Gary SMITH has his Ontario driver's licence registered to 90 Brownstone Street, Sudbury.

d. An OPP booking photo of Gary SMITH shows someone who appears to be the same person who appears in the photo that the Source sent to me.

e. Lucy ROCCI has a date of birth of August 9, 1979. She has no criminal record or outstanding charges. She has an Ontario driver's licence registered to 90 Brownstone Street, Sudbury.

f. Lucy ROCCI has an open Facebook page where she has a profile photograph of herself with a horse. This photo of ROCCI appears to show the same person in the photo that the Source sent me. There are also numerous posts on this Facebook page, posted on July 17, 2014, related to the "Big Nickel" party buses in the downtown core of Sudbury. It appears that she has business dealings with these party buses since she has comments about the company and ticket sales.

g. L. ROCCI is listed under "Admins" on the Big Nickel Party Bus website.

h. On the Canada 411 web-based phone directory, G. SMITH's home phone number is listed as 705-555-9087 and his address is listed as 90 Brownstone Street, Sudbury.

4. On Tuesday August 21, 2014, I advised D/C Brian GREEN #28 and D/C Jerry RED #77 of the Sudbury Major Crime Unit to check 90 Brownstone Street to see what information they could corroborate. At about 2:10 p.m. that day, D/C GREEN advised me of the following:

a. He attended 90 Brownstone Street in Sudbury and observed the house to be a single-storey with a double garage. It is brown brick with green siding. The front door is to the left of the garage and there is a window to the left of the front door. The number "90" is to the left of the garage doors, and there is an "ABC" alarm sign in the front lawn area.

GROUNDS TO BELIEVE THE NAMED OFFENCES WERE COMMITTED

1. The Source has been previously proven reliable (see Appendix D) and the information provided is detailed and compelling. Some of the Source's information regarding the residence and the suspects has been corroborated by the police.

2. The Source has recently attended 90 Brownstone Street, Sudbury, and observed cocaine, MDMA, marijuana, crystal methamphetamine, and GHB. The Source has also bought drugs from the suspects during this time period.

3. The Source is knowledgeable in identifying controlled substances, and has observed illegal drugs being sold from the suspect's home on a regular basis. The drugs appear to be always available for sale in large quantities.

4. Cocaine, MDMA, marijuana, crystal methamphetamine, and GHB are controlled substances under the CDSA and are illegal to possess.

5. Gary SMITH has a criminal history, almost exclusively for selling illegal drugs.

6. Both suspects are linked to 90 Brownstone Street in Sudbury.

GROUNDS TO BELIEVE THAT THE ITEMS SEIZED (AS STATED IN APPENDIX A) WILL AFFORD EVIDENCE OF THE STATED OFFENCES

1. Cocaine, MDMA, GHB, and crystal methamphetamine are controlled substances under the CDSA and cannot be possessed or sold. All of these drugs are incriminating on their face. Marijuana is also a controlled substance under the CDSA and can only be possessed with a Ministry of Health medical marijuana certificate to possess or a marijuana licence to produce.

2. Drug paraphernalia, such as weigh scales and packaging, are used by drug dealers to weigh their product in order to sell them in set weight amounts.

3. A cellular phone is the most common medium of drug sales. It is common to find text messages of drug deals, as well as "trophy" photos of drugs, money, and guns on drug dealers' phones and cameras.

4. Cash proceeds will support a charge of possession for the purpose of trafficking and possession of proceeds of crime. Drug trafficking is generally a cash enterprise.

5. Documentation regarding the occupant(s) of the residence located at 90 Brownstone Street, Sudbury, will show who has knowledge, consent, and control of illegal drugs found in that residence.

GROUNDS TO BELIEVE THAT THE ITEMS ARE AT THE LOCATION TO BE SEARCHED

1. The Source advised that on numerous, as well as recent, occasions, he or she has attended 90 Brownstone Street, Sudbury, where he or she has observed illegal drugs in large quantities on each occasion.

2. The drugs appear always to be in large quantities and available for sale.

3. The Source has been proven to be reliable in the past.

4. Some of the Source's information has been corroborated by police.

5. Gary SMITH has a criminal history, almost exclusively for selling illegal drugs.

6. Both suspects, Gary SMITH and Lucy ROCCI, are linked to 90 Brownstone Street, Sudbury.

Conclusion

As a result of the information provided in my affidavit, I believe the reasonable grounds exist to authorize a search warrant for the dwelling located at 90 Brownstone Street, Sudbury, Ontario. It is respectfully requested that this search warrant application be granted to seize evidence, prevent the repetition of the offence, and to successfully apprehend and prosecute the offenders in this matter.

APPENDIX D

Background of the Confidential Source

The Confidential Source in this matter has one outstanding criminal charge: Theft Under $5,000. The Source has no known criminal convictions.

The Source has provided me with substantial information in relation to drug activities in the Sudbury area. This information has been corroborated by other sources and police investigations. I have specifically used the Source's information on four separate investigations where search warrants were obtained. In all instances, illegal drugs and related trafficking paraphernalia were seized. Several parties were also arrested and charged. To date, none of the search warrants has failed on a court challenge. I continue to rely on the Source's information for other drug investigations.

The Source's motivation to provide information appears to be strictly financial. The Source wishes to get paid for the information provided, but is well aware that payment is not made if the information is found to be not valid or untruthful. The Source is also aware that he or she faces possible criminal charges for misleading the police in these investigations.

The Source has provided information that has been proven to be reliable. It is my opinion that the Source has again provided compelling and reliable information in regards to this investigation.

Request for a Sealing Order

I am respectfully requesting that this search warrant application be sealed for the following reasons:

1. The substance of this search warrant application is based on information provided by a Confidential Source. Information contained in Appendix C and Appendix D will identify the Source to the suspects in this matter. The protection of a Confidential Source's identity is paramount to ensure his or her safety and protect him or her from reprisals and to protect the integrity of the police informant system. The Courts have also consistently recognized that a Confidential Source's identity is protected and privileged information.

2. The sealing of this search warrant in no way prohibits the disclosure of non-privileged information to the accused should the search warrant be unsealed and vetted.

CHECK YOUR UNDERSTANDING

1. Identify six mandatory elements of a search warrant.

2. List at least five details that must be included in a search warrant.

3. Why would a police affiant request that the search warrant application be sealed?

CHAPTER SUMMARY

Individuals in Canada have many rights and freedoms not found in other countries of the world. These rights are entrenched in the Charter. Police officers throughout Canada have many powers that are established in law and granted to them by the various levels of government. However, the police must not overstep these powers and must ensure that the rights of individuals are respected. The law surrounding search and search warrants can be complicated and confusing, and it changes often. Police officers must stay abreast of it and make sure they understand it.

The Charter protects all individuals from arbitrary police power being exercised in illegal searches and intrusions into a person's home, cottage, workplace, or car. If a court determines that the police have illegally obtained their evidence, breaching the Charter, the court will likely exclude the evidence at trial. It is therefore crucial for police officers to follow all the procedures prescribed by statutes, common law, and case law regarding search and seizure. This chapter has focused on the steps and procedures that police must follow when they wish to draft, obtain, and execute a search warrant.

KEY TERMS

affiant, 197

Canadian Police Information
  Centre (CPIC), 215

confidential informants, 206

ex parte motion, 204

information to obtain (ITO), 200

knock and announce rule, 212

nexus of search, 198

night, 213

no-knock entry, 212

police agent, 207

sealing order, 208

telewarrant, 209

Three Fs, 204

REFERENCES

Anderson (Ruling on Voir Dire), Regina v. (2001). 2001 BCSC 674.

Brown, R v. (1999). 74 CRR (2d) 164 (Ont. SC).

Broyles, R v. (1991). [1991] 3 SCR 595.

Canadian Charter of Rights and Freedoms. (1982). Part I of the *Constitution Act, 1982*, RSC 1985, app. II, no. 84.

Collins, R v. (1987). [1987] 1 SCR 265.

Controlled Drugs and Substances Act. (1996). SC 1996, c. 19.

Criminal Code. (1985). RSC 1985, c. C-46.

Garofoli, R v. (1990). [1990] 2 SCR 1421.

Genest, R v. (1989). [1989] 1 SCR 59.

MacIntyre, A.G. (Nova Scotia) v. (1982). [1982] 1 SCR 175.

MacIsaac, R v. (2001). [2001] OJ No. 2966 (Sup. Ct.).

Semeniuk, R v. (2007). 2007 BCCA 399, 224 CCC (3d) 71.

Turcotte, R v. (1987). [1988] 2 WWR 97 (Sask. CA).

FURTHER READING

Anderson (Ruling on Voir Dire), Regina v. (2001). 2001 BCSC 674.

Brown, R v. (1999). 74 CRR (2d) 164 (Ont. SC).

Broyles, R v. (1991). [1991] 3 SCR 595.

Church of Scientology and The Queen (No. 6), Re. (1987). 31 CCC (3d) 449 (Ont. CA).

Collins, R v. (1987). [1987] 1 SCR 265.

Garofoli, R v. (1990). [1990] 2 SCR 1421.

Genest, R v. (1989). [1989] 1 SCR 59.

MacIntyre, A.G. (Nova Scotia) v. (1982). [1982] 1 SCR 175.

MacIsaac, R v. (2001). [2001] OJ No. 2966 (Sup. Ct.).

Pugliese, R v. (1992). 8 OR (3d) 259 (CA).

Semeniuk, R v. (2007). 2007 BCCA 399, 224 CCC (3d) 71.

Turcotte, R v. (1987). [1988] 2 WWR 97 (Sask. CA).

REVIEW QUESTIONS

Multiple Choice

1. A search warrant can be best described as
   a. a written document that represents judicial authorization
   b. a written document that is directed to peace officers
   c. authorization to enter and search a specific place
   d. all of the above

2. Generally speaking, a justice considering a search warrant application needs to be satisfied about five factors. These five factors include which of the following?
   a. the items specified in the ITO exist
   b. the items specified will be found in the place to be searched at the time of the search
   c. the offence alleged has been, or will be, committed
   d. all of the above

3. Which of the following is *not* one of the three things that a search warrant allows investigators to do?
   a. locate evidence
   b. arrest people found inside the premises when the warrant is executed
   c. examine evidence
   d. preserve evidence

4. There are only three circumstances in which the police can search someone while conducting a search warrant. Which of the following circumstances is *not* one of these?
   a. The person at the search location is under arrest.
   b. The police have reasonable grounds to believe that the person is in possession of evidence related to the warrant.
   c. The person whose address is being searched attends to the address while the police are conducting their search.
   d. The police believe that a person at the location of the search is a danger to the officer, to the public, or to himself or herself.

5. If the police wish to search a premises at night they must specifically request a nighttime entry for their search warrant. According to s. 2 of the Code, nighttime refers to the hours of
   a. 6:00 p.m. to 11:00 p.m.
   b. 9:00 p.m. to 6:00 a.m.
   c. 11:00 p.m. to 6:00 a.m.
   d. none of the above

True or False

_____ **1.** An ITO must name the place to be searched and the offence that the evidence being sought will establish.

_____ **2.** A search warrant's authorization ends when the police have searched a premises and then left the same premises. However, the police are permitted to return to that premises and re-search it (without getting a new warrant) if they have reasonable grounds to believe that they may have missed something.

_____ **3.** Exigent circumstances can best be described as circumstances requiring that actions be immediately taken because it is late at night and the courts are not open, which prevents officers from getting a warrant that will permit them to take the actions they would like to take.

_____ **4.** The purpose of a search warrant is to allow investigators to locate, examine, and preserve all the evidence relevant to events that may have given rise to a criminal offence.

_____ **5.** A search warrant can be used to collect evidence supporting a criminal charge, but it cannot be used by the police as a tool to investigate alleged criminal activity. Using it in this way would be a breach of an individual's Charter rights.

_____ **6.** An application for a search warrant consists of two parts: an ITO (Form 1), and the actual warrant to search (Form 5) that the affiant presents to a JP or judge to sign.

_____ **7.** The Charter requires that, for all warrants, police must provide reasonable suspicion, established upon oath, to believe that an offence has been committed and that there is evidence to be found at the place of the search.

_____ **8.** The affiant's reasonable belief does not have to be based on personal knowledge, but the ITO must disclose a substantial basis for the existence of the affiant's belief.

_____ **9.** The ITO should be reliable, balanced, and material. It should also be clear, concise, and legally and factually sufficient, including every detail of the police investigation, no matter how minute.

_____ **10.** The police have to tell a person that they have a search warrant and are at the house to conduct a search. However, they do not have to show the actual warrant, even if the person asks to see it. This removes the risk of the person destroying the search warrant, which is required for evidence.

Short Answer

1. Explain the primary rules of a search warrant.

2. What is the three-pronged test regarding police searches that the SCC set out in _R v. Collins_?

3. The courts have stated that the police must be full, fair, and frank in providing disclosure in the ITO. Explain what this means and the reason that this is a requirement of a search warrant application.

4. What are the objectives of search warrants? Why are searches with warrants deemed preferable to warrantless searches?

5. When do the police use a telewarrant?

It's Your Move, Officer!

You and your partner are on general patrol on a Friday morning. You are driving through a residential area when you get flagged down by a man walking his dog. The man states that he lives down the street and that, while he was setting off this morning with his dog, he saw his neighbour placing what he believes to be marijuana plants into four green garbage bags and then putting the bags out on the boulevard for garbage pickup.

The complainant claims that he knows what marijuana plants look like, and he says that when he walked by the garbage bags he could detect a strong smell of marijuana coming from them. The complainant states that he doesn't know his neighbour other than to say hello, but believes he has lived in the house with his wife for about five years. He tells you that he has nothing against his neighbour, but he simply hates the negative effect that drugs have on people and on neighbourhoods.

The complainant points out the neighbour's house and the four garbage bags sitting out front on the boulevard waiting for garbage pickup. He states that the garbage is usually picked up around noon by the city garbage truck.

It's your move, officer. What are you going to do?

Accountability of Police

10

LEARNING OBJECTIVES

After completing this chapter, you should be able to:

- Explain the importance of police accountability and oversight.

- Explain how an officer's notes contribute to accountability.

- Describe the role of the Charter in police accountability.

- Describe the internal and external mechanisms for enforcing and promoting police accountability.

- Explain the effects that the media and technology have on policing.

ON SCENE

Two police officers are called to a disturbance at a convenience store in a strip mall.

When they arrive, they are met by an anxious store owner. The owner points to a small woman walking hurriedly away from the plaza. He tells them that, a few minutes before, she put her hand in her coat pocket and pointed it at him, demanding the money from his cash register. He complied, afraid she had a knife.

As the officers approach the woman to apprehend her, she bolts. After a short foot chase, one of the officers moves to subdue her. As he wrestles with her on the ground, a passerby stops, pulls out his cellphone, and begins to record the incident. He yells at the police, demanding to know what the woman's crime was. "What right do you have to arrest her?" he yells at the officer. "This is police abuse!"

The officer is out of breath after subduing the woman. But he decides to address the civilian's concerns. He explains that he is performing his duty and that the woman has been accused of a crime for which arrest is mandatory. He also explains that the female has a right to privacy—her Charter rights—and that he intends to respect them. In sum, the officer has taken the time to teach the public about his authority and about his obligations as a police officer.

What do you think of the officer's actions? What would you have done in this situation? How well has the officer balanced the rights and needs of the police, the offender, and the public?

Introduction

Powers over life and death, over freedom and imprisonment—these are among the extraordinary powers given to police. But police must exercise these powers in a way that inspires confidence in an increasingly vigilant public. The search for police officers capable of inspiring such confidence begins during the recruiting process. Police candidates are examined more closely than candidates for almost any other profession. And this close scrutiny does not end with the person's hiring. It continues daily through an officer's entire career.

In our chapter-opening scenario, you see an officer trying to balance the needs and rights of the accused, the police, and a critical, watchful public. You also see that a civilian can record an officer's actions and immediately post this recording to the Internet. More than ever in this information age, police are accountable for—and have to be vigilant about—their behaviour. In this chapter, we will consider what police accountability means, and we will look at the oversight mechanisms that are in place to enforce it.

Police Accountability: An Overview

What does it mean to say that police officers are *accountable*? According to the Merriam-Webster dictionary ("Accountable," n.d.), the word *accountable* means the following: "required to explain actions or decisions to someone"; "required to be responsible for something." To whom are police accountable? Who oversees them and what form does this oversight take?

Oversight is the process of managing police activity. Its instruments range from the duties prescribed by the various police Acts to the various civilian strategies—uploading videos to YouTube, for example—for overseeing police activity. There exist a bewildering variety of mechanisms, official and unofficial, for overseeing police in Canada today.

Oversight begins in the police service itself. All police officers must answer to their superiors: chief, deputy chief, inspector, staff sergeant, and down the line to the sergeant or officer in charge. All are answerable within the chain of command. Police agencies themselves are overseen by the Ministry of Community Safety and Correctional Services. The Ministry conducts audits and ensures that police services meet a certain standard.

Legislation, as mentioned above, is another instrument of police accountability. Police officers in Canada can be charged with wrongful action under the relevant laws of their province. They must be prepared to answer for their actions in court—to be examined by provincial and federal Crown attorneys, by defence counsel, and, of course, by the court justice or judge. They demonstrate their preparedness and accountability through the appropriateness and accuracy of their notes as well as through their testimony on the witness stand.

The Charter provides the fundamental standard by which police actions are judged in criminal and civil courts. Sections 7-14 encompass the basic rights of Canadian citizens with respect to police—including the right to be informed promptly of the reason for their arrest, the right to retain and instruct counsel, the right to be free from arbitrary detention, and the right to be free from unreasonable search and seizure.

Police officers in Canada, then, are accountable to their superiors within the police service, and they are accountable to the prescriptions of police legislation and to the standards of the Charter. In addition to these constitutional and legislative oversight mechanisms, police services in Canada have a strong tradition of *civilian* oversight. In Ontario, these oversight bodies include the Special Investigations Unit (SIU), the Office of the Independent Police Review Director (OIPRD), and the Ontario Civilian Police Commission (OCPC).

Another oversight mechanism, less relevant to day-to-day police work than those listed above, is formal judicial processes such as civil lawsuits against police and inquest recommendations from the Office of the Coroner.

The final player in police oversight and accountability is the media. The traditional public media—newspapers, television, and radio—have always been astute watchdogs of police activity. Nowadays there is a new player: **social media**. This term refers to any online or technologically mediated method of communicating and sharing information. Citizens are now able to upload video recordings of police activity to sites such as YouTube and Facebook. Social media are what make it possible for an officer dealing with a situation in New Liskeard, Ontario to be observed in real time by anyone in the world. Now *that* is accountability on an international, unprecedented scale.

Why do police need accountability and these various forms of oversight? The answer is threefold:

1. Police are given power over the entire citizenry of Canada.

2. Police are entrusted with preserving the safety, security, and property of this same public.

3. Police services cost a lot of money, and this money comes from the pockets of the public. The growing trend toward six-figure salaries for police personnel (once overtime and benefits are factored in) gives the public incentive to watch closely how those salaries are earned. In the eyes of the paying public, the police had better earn that money with honesty, hard work, and integrity.

social media
technologically mediated methods of communication that involves information being uploaded to websites or computer databases and being shared with the public

1. What reasons exist for the extensive accountability of police and the various forms of oversight accorded their activities?
2. How do social media hold police accountable for their actions?
3. What term refers to the management of police activity?

An Officer's Notebook: The First Level of Accountability

Police officers are required to maintain a notebook detailing all of their on-the-job activities. This notebook is a record of the names and details of people with whom the officer has interacted during his or her shift. Each day, an officer begins the notebook record by entering the date, the start-time of the shift, the weather, and the duties he or she has been assigned. Next into the record are notes about ongoing investigations, details that may help other officers. Such information is shared via the various record databases, but the old-fashioned practice of sharing information at a shift briefing is still common.

Importance of Notes

An officer's skill, integrity, and accuracy in keeping notes are essential. Court cases are won or lost on the accuracy of an officer's notes. Lawyers and judges often say, "If it isn't in the notebook, it didn't happen."

Notes are a memory aid and must be trustworthy. They are evidence in themselves, and it is critical that an officer make them independently—that is, based on his or her own perceptions. This ensures that they will withstand the scrutiny of a Crown prosecutor, defence counsel, or justice. It is essential that officers not collaborate with one another in their note-taking. An officer's notes must be made **contemporaneously**—that is, during or as soon as possible after an incident, while his or her recollections are fresh. They are meant to be a precise recording of police activity and of an officer's observations.

contemporaneously
with reference to notebooks, during or as soon as possible after an incident

Lack of consistency in the rules about note-taking has contributed to trial issues and led to wrongful convictions. The Public Prosecution Service of Canada has investigated this matter at length, through the Lamer Commission of Inquiry. The commission, led by former SCC Chief Justice Antonio Lamer, has found that officers sometimes record information in their notebooks inadequately and inaccurately, and sometimes fail to make entries at all. The commission has recommended (Public Prosecution Service of Canada, 2014) that note-keeping practices should be standardized among all police services across Canada. The new and developing practice of using e-notebooks may help achieve this goal.

Basic Rules of Note-Taking

Some basic rules about notebooks do exist. They include the following:

- Entries should be made in black ink (for photocopying ease).
- Notebooks should have pages that are numbered and not easily torn out.
- Officers should not leave blank lines, since these blanks give lawyers room to claim that information was added at a later date. Such claims are not without foundation; officers have been known to backfill notes long after an incident has occurred.

- Officers should not scratch over notes and make them illegible. Doing so opens the way to accusations that an officer is trying to hide information. Instead, they should cross out errors with a single inked line.
- Officers should not add sticky notes to the page.

Notebooks are routinely examined by police supervisors and are kept at the police department when the officer is off duty. Police services prescribe the rules listed above; the courts themselves have no jurisdiction to instruct officers in their note-keeping practices. Courts often mention this fact when they refer to the role of notebooks in trials. For example, at the trial of notorious serial killer Robert Pickton, Justice Williams of the Supreme Court of British Columbia (2007, para. 9) stated the following: "I do not believe it is the role of the court to specifically prescribe or direct officers as to how they are to maintain their notes." The courts rely on police services to teach and maintain good note-taking practices.

Disclosure of Police Notes

Officers' notebooks are subject to the rules of **disclosure**. The case of *R v. Stinchcombe* (1991) confirmed the right of defence counsel to the disclosure of all relevant evidence in a given case. Such evidence includes the investigative information about the case recorded in an officer's notebook. Apart from the disclosure right of the defence counsel, any person with an interest in the case may apply, under freedom-of-information legislation, to have an officer's notes about the case made public. This represents another level of accountability for police.

The Information and Privacy Commissioner of Ontario (IPC), in conjunction with the Durham Regional Police Service, publishes an online guide for police officers, outlining what happens when a citizen requests access to an officer's notebook (IPC, 2001). The public can view this guide online. There are legitimate reasons for refusing a citizen's request for access. These reasons, based on legislation, include such considerations as officer safety or invasion of privacy. However, the public has a right of appeal in this process. In the end, an adjudicator can order the notes to be released.

disclosure
the practice, in criminal cases of the Crown, of providing the defence with all the evidence gathered in an investigation

An Officer's Testimony: From Notebook to Courtroom

An officer's testimony, based on his or her notebook records, has a significant role in the courtroom, where the officer is accountable to the justice presiding over a case. A justice's determination that an officer's testimony is credible can make for a smooth ride in the courtroom for the rest of that officer's career. Conversely, a reputation for unreliability can hurt an officer's career in the courtroom, opening the way to withdrawals of charges, mistrials, stays of proceedings, and acquittals. Whole investigations in which this officer is involved may come to nothing owing to his or her reputation for unreliable testimony.

Let's take a look at the case of *R v. Beaudry* (2007). Early one morning in Quebec, an officer named Alain Beaudry and two of his colleagues responded to a complaint that a car was being driven erratically. The responding officers eventually stopped the vehicle; the driver turned out to be a fellow police officer. During the investigation, Sergeant Beaudry noted that the driver had consumed alcohol, and he was also aware that the driver experienced depression. Beaudry neglected to document certain facts about the incident in his notebook. In addition, he chose not to submit an impaired driving report. His colleagues were ordered to submit one, which they did, although it was an incomplete report. Sergeant Beaudry refused to participate in the submission, claiming he was acting on the advice of his union.

As a result of this incident, Beaudry was charged with obstructing justice under s. 139(2) of the Code. He was convicted in the Criminal Court of Quebec, but he appealed this conviction to the SCC. The conviction was upheld. The conviction was based on the lack of notes and on Beaudry's lack of credibility. The SCC ruling (2007, para. 17) concurs with Judge Beaulieu's finding that the officers were clearly lying, and that their testimony was inconsistent with their reports. In other words, the officers' testimony was measured against their notes. The SCC also confirmed that the officers breached their duty in the way they exercised discretion. Such a breach can lead to charges of misconduct under police act legislation. This case illustrates very well how police are accountable to the criminal justice system, to police oversight legislation, and to the internal authority of a police service.

IT'S YOUR MOVE, OFFICER!

Scenario 10.1

You work for a large police service in a small Ontario municipality. One morning, you receive a call from the principal of the local elementary school. It concerns an incident that took place at the school the day before. She explains that a certain officer was dispatched to the school when his 12-year-old son, a student at the school, was found in possession of a prohibited weapon, a "knuckle knife." The school turned the knife over to the officer, in his capacity as a police officer. The officer assured the principal that his son had been warned not to bring this knife (which he had bought at a yard sale) to school. The principal is now calling because she is concerned about the progress of the investigation.

After speaking with the principal, you look to see if a report was filed. You cannot find one. Your supervisor checks the officer's notebook, which has been left at the station, and does not find any notes about the incident.

1. What would you do in this situation?
2. What *Criminal Code* charges, if any, may apply in this incident?
3. Who is the officer accountable to in this situation?

CHECK YOUR UNDERSTANDING

1. Identify the range of recommended practices that help to ensure that notebook entries are honest.
2. List the people who may see an officer's notebook.
3. Explain the relationship between an officer's notes and his or her credibility in the courtroom.

Accountability and the Charter

In 1991, a young man was accused of brutally raping and murdering a young woman. He showed up at his home after the murder, wet and dirty, explaining that he had been in a fight. Later, after he was arrested, he refused to provide police with samples of his bodily fluids. Upset and crying, he was taken to a washroom where he blew his nose into a tissue. Police seized the discarded tissue for DNA evidence. In their efforts to secure further DNA evidence, police also used threats, forcing the young man to pull out his own pubic hairs. They proceeded to collect other bodily evidence from the accused. Was this type of search and seizure reasonable under the circumstances? Was it simply an extension of the common law right of search incident to arrest? Or was it a violation of the Charter rights of the accused?

The SCC decided in this case, *R v. Stillman* (1997), that the police actions were a violation of s. 8 of the Charter, which guarantees the right to be secure against unreasonable search and seizure. In infringing that right, the police had obtained evidence in a manner that would "bring the administration of justice into disrepute." Therefore, under s. 24(2) of the Charter, the SCC deemed the evidence inadmissible. The court ordered a new trial that would exclude the hair, buccal swabs, and dental impressions that the police had gathered. As this SCC ruling shows, the Charter is the gold standard when it comes to police accountability.

The Charter rights most relevant to police accountability are shown in Figure 10.1. These rights belong to every Canadian. If an individual believes that police have denied or infringed any of them, he or she may, under s. 24(1) of the Charter, apply to a court to "obtain such remedy as the court considers appropriate and just in the circumstances." This remedy can include the reimbursement of legal costs, or even monetary damages by the government. In addition, evidence can be ruled inadmissible, and charges can be stayed or even withdrawn.

The Charter makes the police accountable to Canadians, and it ensures that this accountability permeates the entire criminal prosecution process.

FIGURE 10.1   The Charter: Legal Rights (Sections 7-11)

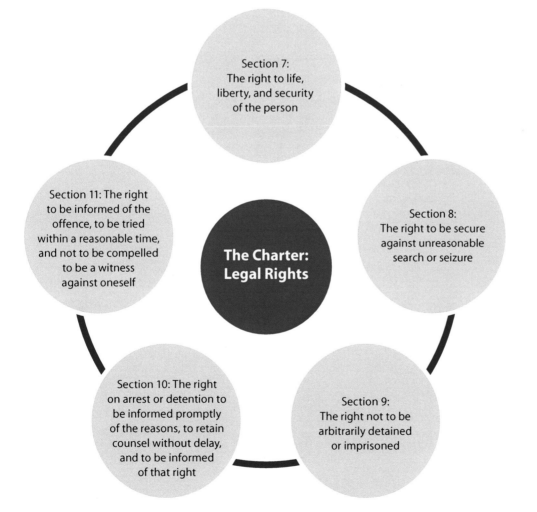

1. Why is the Charter considered the gold standard in police accountability?
2. What is the standard by which an alleged Charter violation is measured, according to s. 24?
3. Identify the remedies available to the court in the event of a Charter violation.

The Police Chain of Command

Police officers are accountable for what they have done and for what they have neglected to do. There are very specific requirements and standards set out in police service legislation across the country. Each province has its own Act—for example, the *Police Services Act* (PSA) of Ontario, the *Police Act* of Alberta, and, federally, the *Royal Canadian Mounted Police Act*. With respect to internal accountability, the chain of command in a police service is shown in Figure 10.2.

Police services in Canada are not uniform in their organizational structure. There are variations on the structure shown in Figure 10.2. That said, there are certain common features. Municipal police services each have a police chief, along with a deputy chief. The OPP and the RCMP have similar positions, but they are called *commissioner* and *deputy commissioner*. The other positions are shown in the bottom level of boxes in Figure 10.2, in order of authority as you move from left to right. Details of organizational structure

FIGURE 10.2 The Police Chain of Command

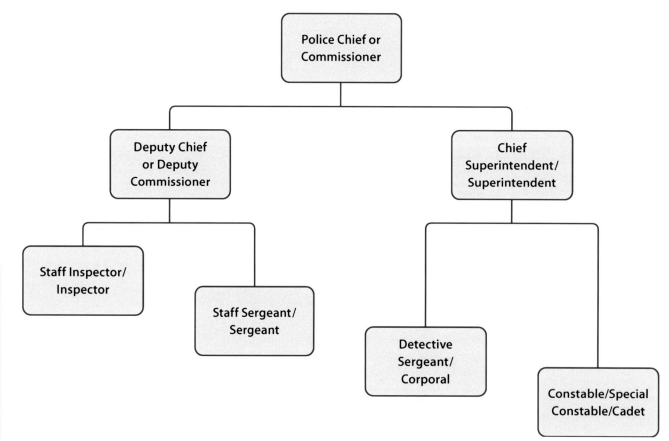

specific to each police service—whether provincial, municipal, or federal—can be found at each service's website. The names and particular areas of responsibility in each organization are available for public perusal.

A primary function of the organizational structure is to order and clarify accountability within the police service. In a general way, all officers are accountable to each other. Practically speaking, however, lower ranked officers are supervised and managed by senior staff, who try to ensure that their juniors adhere to their sworn duties in their day-to-day activities, and uphold the applicable code of conduct. A police service will conduct its own investigation into an officer's misconduct, ultimately deciding whether an officer should face disciplinary charges under the applicable legislation—Ontario's PSA, for example. Charges can range from discreditable conduct, neglect of duty, breach of confidence, and deceit, to corrupt practice, unlawful exercise of authority, and improper use of firearms.

Part V of the PSA permits a police chief to lodge an internal complaint against a member of his or her police service. If the officer is convicted at a subsequent PSA hearing, a variety of penalties may be imposed, including suspension, demotion, or dismissal. A common penalty is forfeiture of pay or of days off. An officer may be required to work additional time without pay.

If an officer in Ontario is dissatisfied with the results of an internal PSA hearing, he or she can file a disciplinary appeal with the Ontario Civilian Police Commission (OCPC). This commission has been developed and is regulated through the PSA. If the officer is then dissatisfied with the OCPC's decision, and the issue relates to an incident that occurred prior to October 19, 2009, the decision may be appealed to the Divisional Court for Ontario, as per s. 71 of the PSA. If the incident being examined occurred on or after October 19, 2009, then the decision of the commission is final (OCPC, n.d.). Civilians can also appeal the results of an officer's disciplinary hearing—if, for example, the civilian thinks an officer has been treated too leniently or too harshly. The OCPC hears these civilian appeals, which amount to civilian oversight of the police discipline process.

CHECK YOUR UNDERSTANDING

1. What are some examples of penalties a police chief in Ontario can impose if he or she finds against an officer under the PSA?

2. How does the hierarchy of a police organization contribute to accountability?

3. Identify three examples of legislation that governs police organizations provincially or federally.

External Oversight of Policing

In a small town in Canada, a police chief opted for a unique approach to a domestic complaint. A woman had complained to the chief that she was fearful of her ex-husband and asked the chief, "How am I to protect myself?" As told by *The Toronto Star* (Rush, 2012), the chief decided to give the woman a can of pepper spray to protect herself.

An officer in the service advised the chief that he had made an error. The pepper spray was retrieved, but not without triggering a complaint to the OCPC. Pepper spray is a prohibited weapon in Canada, its possession limited to police and armed forces. A subsequent hearing found the chief guilty of discreditable conduct under the PSA.

Is this the kind of decision-making we want to see in our police services? What if you or a member of your family is a casualty of such police error? How can we ensure that police know we are watching them?

Canadian society has decided that police should be accountable to and overseen by agencies, such as the OCPC, that are made up of the very civilians that police are responsible for protecting. A tradition of civilian oversight has developed in Canada over the past several decades. Ontario has the OIPRD, the OCPC, and the SIU. In other provinces, there are similar organizations to which the public can take a complaint. Half the provinces have an organization similar to the Ontario SIU—for example, the Alberta Serious Incident Response Team (ASIRT), the Nova Scotia Serious Incident Response Team (SiRT), and the Independent Investigations Office (IIO) of British Columbia. The RCMP is not subject to the provincial oversight bodies. On occasion, however, when an incident involving the RCMP is serious enough to demand examination, an external review body is set up.

Let's consider the Ontario model.

Role of the OIPRD

The OIPRD is the "go-to" organization for public complaints against the conduct of an officer in Ontario. It is an arm's-length agency of the Ontario Ministry of the Attorney General staffed entirely by civilians (OIPRD, 2013).

Complaints may concern the policies or the services of a police department, or they may involve the actions of an individual officer. A complainant need not be directly involved in an incident; he or she may simply be a witness to it. Complaints are investigated either by the OIPRD or by the police service in question. Or the complaint may be referred to another police service.

If an incident is minor, the OIPRD encourages the public to go through a "local resolution" complaint process rather than bring the complaint to the OIPRD. In other words, a person is encouraged to complain to the management of the unsatisfactory police service. In that event, the police service must document the process with the OIPRD. If the civilian prefers not to go this route, he or she may complain directly to the OIPRD. Details of the complaint process, along with all required forms, are available online at the OIPRD website. They are also available at every police agency in the province, conspicuously placed, in most cases, in a brochure holder at the station's main entry. A complaint may be made online, by regular mail or fax, or in person at the organization's office.

Generally speaking, a complaint must be filed within six months of the incident in question. There are exceptions to this requirement. If the complainant is a minor, is disabled, or is charged in relation to the event, or if the complaint in some way serves the greater public interest, the director may proceed with the investigation after the six-month period has expired.

Resolution of a complaint can take various forms: an informal resolution (that is, a warning); disciplinary hearings or actions against a police officer; changes to police service practice and policy; or, in some cases, a determination that no action need be taken. Informal resolution is common; often, a complainant simply wants to be heard, and it is good public relations for a police service to address a complaint directly and to the satisfaction of all parties. In one Ontario police service, police administrators will go so far as to visit complainants at their homes or meet them outside of regular office hours, in a genuine effort to reach out to the community. If no action is taken, it is usually the result of a lack of evidence, of witnesses being unwilling to speak out, or of an officer against whom the complaint was made having left the police service.

Investigations of a police service usually stem from a public complaint about a single incident. However, the OIPRD, which prides itself on its objectivity, will sometimes undertake a systemic investigation. In 2014, for example, the OIPRD made a commitment to examine the Toronto Police Service's use of force. This was a response to a series of high-profile incidents involving this service's use of lethal force on people with mental health problems or emotional disturbance (OIPRD, 2014).

IT'S YOUR MOVE, OFFICER!

Scenario 10.2

You are patrolling in a marked police cruiser one night when a dishevelled woman waves you over. She appears upset. She is well known to police in the community. Neighbours often call in complaints about her rowdy behaviour. She has recently returned to the neighbourhood from a brief stay in the psychiatric wing of a local hospital. She has a room in a boarding house.

You stop and get out of the car to speak with her. As she begins to explain why she accosted you, a male officer pulls up. Ignoring him, the woman tells you that she called police earlier to complain that she'd been robbed—that someone had taken cash from her purse when she set it down on a bench. She is still upset about the money, but is even angrier that the officer who responded to her earlier call treated her dismissively. The officer who just pulled up is the one that responded to her earlier call. She tells you that he said to her, "What money? How do you even know you had any money in your purse? You're too out of it to know anything! This is a waste of my time." She claims he then spoke abusively to her, swearing and telling her to get off the street and clean herself up.

The other officer listens to what she says to you, laughs, walks away, and leaves in his cruiser.

1. What advice could you give the woman?
2. Which process do you think would be most beneficial for the woman, and why?

Role of the OCPC

The OCPC is an independent oversight organization that ensures that police are accountable to the public. Its mission statement (OCPC, 2014) explains that it is "an independent oversight agency committed to serving the public by ensuring that adequate and effective policing services are provided to the community in a fair and accountable manner." The commission's primary functions are to oversee how police serve the citizens of Ontario and to ensure that these services are fair and equitable. Since the OCPC represents the interests of civilians, its full- and part-time members are community members and include such individuals as health professionals, lawyers, politicians, and teachers.

The OCPC does not hear initial complaints; it is responsible for hearing appeals, both from officers and civilians. Under the PSA, police officers may appeal the outcome of a disciplinary hearing before a tribunal. Civilians have two possible reasons for filing an appeal with the OCPC:

1. to appeal the finding of a police disciplinary hearing, if the incident that instigated the hearing involved the civilian;
2. to appeal the penalty outcome of a hearing for an incident in which the civilian was involved.

OCPC appeal hearings, in keeping with the notion of public accountability and transparency, are open to the public. Information about hearings is available on the OCPC website.

Many of the appeals heard by the OCPC concern not only police constables and sergeants, but senior administrators, including chiefs and deputy chiefs. The OCPC may even scrutinize police services boards and police organizations.

Ontario's Special Investigations Unit and Oversight Bodies in Other Provinces

At one time, police services investigated themselves or each other. The public came to view this arrangement skeptically. How can police be seen as objective investigators of themselves when they have their own reputation to protect? *Why is the mouse guarding the cheese?* In Ontario, this concern on the public's part led, in 1990, to the amendment of the PSA, with s. 113 introduced to provide a framework for the Special Investigations Unit (SIU). The SIU is a civilian organization, independent of any connection to a police service.

The SIU investigates incidents in which a police interaction with the public has led to death, serious injury, or even allegations of sexual assault. It is responsible for overseeing all municipal, regional, and provincial police officers in Ontario. Other organizations oversee the RCMP, military police, and First Nations police. In Alberta, British Columbia, Nova Scotia, and Manitoba, there are organizations equivalent to the SIU. The scope of their responsibilities is slightly larger than the SIU's in Ontario; they oversee the RCMP as well as all of the police officers working within their provinces. These various civilian oversight bodies, new on the police scene, reflect the general trend in Canada toward more accountability and oversight for police.

Criteria for hiring investigators to work on these oversight bodies vary from province to province. The SIU investigators are peace officers, with backgrounds in law, health and safety, immigration, and national security (SIU, 2014a). Some are former police officers, in which case they are prohibited from investigating members of the police services they once worked at. The director of the SIU cannot be a former police officer. The director of the SIU has the power to commence criminal investigations and cause criminal charges to be laid against police officers. However, he or she is not able to recommend charges under the *Police Act* or under any other provincial laws.

Nova Scotia's SiRT has an equal number of civilian investigators and police investigators. The police officers are seconded or "on loan" from the RCMP and Halifax Regional Police service (SiRT, 2014). In the case of the Independent Investigations Office of British Columbia, no investigator is permitted to have worked as a police officer for the previous five years (IIO, 2014). These rules reflect a common effort to satisfy the public's desire for distance between the watchdog organization and the police.

Ontario's SIU, in keeping with its ideal of transparency, maintains a comprehensive website providing up-to-date statistics, news releases, and publications, as well as a description of the organization's structure and what it does. The organizations in the other provinces reach out to the public in similar ways, providing information through their websites. There are some interesting differences between the organizations in this respect. Some provide a detailed summary of investigations and their outcomes. Others indicate the types of investigations they carry out, but they don't provide a detailed summary of them. The various organizations learn from one another's successes and failures.

As mentioned above, the SIU deals with serious incidents, as do its counterparts in other provinces. There are slight differences in this respect, too. The SIU limits itself to on-duty police incidents, whereas Nova Scotia's SiRT investigates off-duty incidents as well. Each investigative body has its own rules. Figure 10.3 shows the kinds of complaints investigated by the SIU from its inception in 1990 up to 2011. During this period, a total of 102 cases led to charges being laid against 116 officers.

Nova Scotia's SiRT has been in existence since 2012. In that time, it has investigated a total of 22 incidents, some involving off-duty allegations. Thirty-four officers were investigated, and six were charged. Figure 10.4 identifies the types of complaints against police that SiRT has investigated.

FIGURE 10.3   SIU Distribution of Complaints by Category, 1990-2011

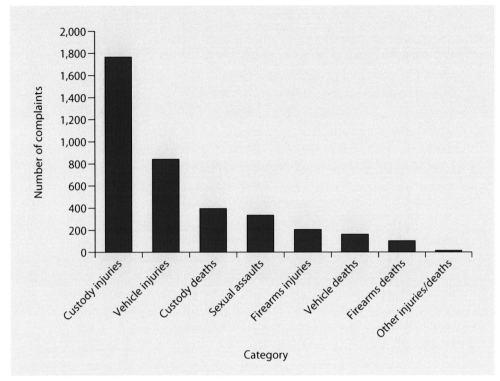

SOURCE: Special Investigations Unit (2014b).

FIGURE 10.4   SiRT Investigations by Category

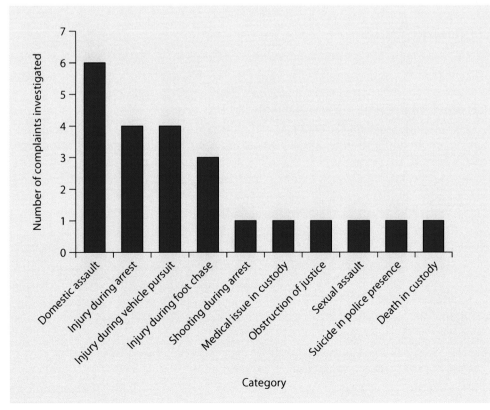

SOURCE: SiRT (2013, p. 8).

The Investigation Process

Following are the general steps in an oversight body's investigation process:

1. *Reporting the incident.* The police chief or other officer in charge must immediately report to an investigations unit any incident that falls within the mandated categories. In the case of the SIU, any civilian, not just a police chief, can report an incident to the investigations unit.

2. *Assessing the complaint, to decide on an appropriate response.* Once the SIU has been notified, it assesses the complaint and decides on a response. The complaint may be referred to one of the other complaint processes mentioned in this chapter, or the SIU may move forward with an investigation of its own.

3. *Conducting the investigation.* The ensuing investigation will look like any other police investigation; it will involve locating and interviewing witnesses, including police officers. The incident scene will be examined and evidence seized for forensic purposes. If there has been injury, as is often the case with these incidents, the unit will need to stay on top of the victim's medical condition and to notify next of kin. If there has been a death, the investigations unit will work with the coroner. The director will receive updates on the progress of the investigation, and reports and public statements will be issued. Publicizing details of the incident will be kept to a minimum, however, so as not to compromise the outcome of the case.

4. *Submitting a report at the end of the investigation.* Once the investigation is complete, a report is submitted to the director, who then decides what actions to pursue.

5. *Resolving the investigation.* The director determines whether or not criminal charges should be laid against the officer(s) involved. Personal visits to the next of kin are often undertaken as part of the investigation's resolution, to help them understand the process (SIU, 2010).

Contentious Issues

Most police officers take an unfavourable view of civilian oversight bodies and do not welcome their investigations. No officer likes to have his or her work examined—to have split-second decisions, often made under enormous pressure, scrutinized by critical outsiders. Such investigations are stressful for police.

Police officers face some difficult issues when the SIU is engaged to investigate an incident. To whom does the officer speak after an incident? Does he or she have the right to retain a lawyer? The answer to the second question depends on the function the lawyer is retained to serve. Until a recent Ontario Court of Appeal decision, police officers being investigated by the SIU were able to enlist a lawyer's aid in preparing their notes. In *Schaeffer v. Wood* (2011), however, the Ontario Court of Appeal decided that enlisting a lawyer's aid violated the principle that an officer's notes are an independent action, prepared by the officer alone. At the same time, the court accepted that officers who are under investigation by the SIU may receive ordinary legal advice regarding their rights and obligations.

Ian Scott, the director of the SIU, cross-appealed the Ontario court's decision. He took the position that police–SIU transparency is compromised by police consulting with lawyers during an investigation. When this case went to the SCC, the justices decided (*Wood v. Schaeffer*, 2013) that officers' notes should be made immediately after an incident, not after the officer has consulted with—and had the notes vetted by—a lawyer.

What the SCC ruling means, from a practical point of view, is that an officer's own notebook entries are *now more important than ever*; there's no longer any prospect of their being vetted by a lawyer if the officer has to account for his actions. They are required to be more independent and contemporaneous than ever before. The *Wood v. Schaeffer* case has a more general significance, too, apart from the particulars of the case. By weighing in on a case having to do with civilian oversight of police, the SCC is acknowledging the social importance of this legal area.

CHECK YOUR UNDERSTANDING

1. What has led to the development of independent investigation organizations?
2. Describe an officer's right to counsel in an SIU investigation.
3. What are the five basic steps in a complaint investigation?

Other Oversight Mechanisms

Tribunals

Provincial tribunals in Ontario are hearings conducted in response to complaints against individuals and, in some cases, against police officers and police services. Examples of tribunals include the Ontario Human Rights Commission (OHRC), the Landlord and Tenant Board, the Child and Family Services Review Board, and the Ontario Labour Relations Board. The complaints submitted to the OHRC regarding police are numerous enough that there is a special category on the OHRC website dedicated to this subject. According to the commission, there are more complaints against police than against any other group. This is not an encouraging pattern, and it appears to be a consistent one. While some of these complaints have concerned employment issues, the majority (almost two-thirds) have been based on prohibited grounds of discrimination—race, colour, ethnic origin, ancestry or place of origin, disability, or sexual orientation.

The complaints brought to the OHRC have almost always concerned how a police service treats the public. Most complaints have been about police discrimination based on race and disability, but a significant number have been about police discrimination based on sexual orientation.

The values and attitudes of individual police officers are what lead them into violations of the Ontario *Human Rights Code* (HRC). Biased officers, as they rise to senior positions in the force, are often disseminating their attitudes through the police service they serve, and the service has no systemic means of safeguarding against them. Police services focus on training in law enforcement, not on awareness of social justice issues. Stereotypes are not challenged sufficiently in the normal course of police training. Currently, police recruits receive no mandatory human rights training outside of being taught basic Charter issues.

The OHRC (2011) has noted that common human rights complaints against police concern the following:

- racial slurs being used by police when they are conducting vehicle stops, making arrests, and responding to 911 calls;
- degrading treatment of suspects—for example, strip-searching a suspect on a street;
- racial profiling, or treating a person differently because of his or her race—for example, flocking in excessive numbers to a low-risk call owing to the suspect's race; and
- releasing police-record information (for example, information that a person was once apprehended for suicidal behaviour) on request to private and public organizations such as volunteer organizations, schools, and employers, which has resulted in discrimination against the individual within his or her community or workplace.

Many police services in Canada have responded in a proactive and positive manner to such complaints. They have acted on the recommendations from human rights commissions that they implement human rights training and institute organizational change. A human rights complaint against an officer or service can now result in a finding of responsibility that brings with it a fine or a requirement that the officer undertake further human rights training.

Such measures amount to punishment, but human rights commissions are ultimately more focused on initiating organizational change than on pursuing punitive measures. The mechanism they offer for hearing human rights complaints provides a further mechanism for overseeing police powers—and another way of ensuring police accountability.

Civil Lawsuits

Beyond the external and civilian oversight organizations discussed above, there is another formal mechanism for enforcing police accountability, and it is a measure available to everyone. A member of the public can simply sue a police officer or a police service. Lawsuits against police are part of many law firms' regular caseloads. These lawsuits concern various allegations against police, including unlawful detention, wrongful arrest, injury, negligence, assault and battery, malicious prosecution, and property damage. Police do lose these lawsuits; judges find for the **plaintiffs** sometimes. In one example, *Joel Elliot v. Waterloo Region Police Services* (2011), a judge criticized the police service for its officers' excessive actions in executing a search warrant and arresting the homeowner. The judge found the police actions unreasonable and ordered police to return all seized property to the plaintiff, who also received $32,000 in damages. The civil law system can be used to attain justice when the police exceed their authority.

In *Penner v. Niagara* (2013), the SCC ruled that a lawsuit against a police officer can go forward even if he or she has been charged, investigated, and exonerated through a PSA hearing. In this case, the complainant was seeking compensation for injuries sustained from what he alleged was unnecessary use of force and wrongful arrest. In the PSA hearing, the arrest in question was determined to be lawful and the misconduct complaint dismissed. The Ontario Court of Appeal supported the police finding and ruled that the legal principle of **res judicata** prevented the civilian's lawsuit from proceeding beyond the hearing. The SCC disagreed, asserting that it was unfair for a PSA hearing, headed by a police chief, to judge whether lawsuits made against police should go forward. The court ruled that if the Ontario Court of Appeal's decision had been permitted to stand, it would have undermined public confidence in the complaints process against the police. This is another instance of the SCC bringing its attention to bear on the question of who should oversee police.

plaintiff
a person bringing a civil action or lawsuit

res judicata
Latin for "already decided"; a special plea with which the accused argues that the charges against him or her have already been dealt with in a court of law

Criminal Charges

As we have seen, there are many different mechanisms for ensuring police accountability—internal and external mechanisms, including civil suits. No discussion of this topic would be complete without some mention of the *Criminal Code*. It too has a role in making police accountable for their actions.

Police officers derive their authority from the Code, but they are also accountable to it for their actions. The laws of Canada apply to police as to other citizens. An investigation by one of the oversight bodies may reveal evidence of criminal wrongdoing by police. (The inverse is also possible: what begins as a criminal investigation against an officer may end up being referred to one of the other oversight processes.)

The criminal charges that may be levelled against an officer relate to offences mentioned throughout this textbook. If convicted, an officer can receive a criminal sanction ranging from an absolute discharge to imprisonment. A common criminal charge levelled against police officers is assault under ss. 265 and 266 of the Code. This charge tends to result from excessive use of force by police. Such cases appear regularly in the news.

An egregious case occurred in Barrie, Ontario in 2010 (McLaughlin, 2014). A man committed the offence of mischief when he broke a Christmas ornament on a tree in the local mall. The responding officer took the man to the rear of the mall, handcuffed him, and violently beat him. The officer then lied to investigators and the court about the event. The mall's surveillance footage captured the entire assault and exposed the officer's lie. The officer was subsequently convicted of assault causing bodily harm and given a jail sentence. He also resigned as a police officer. His violation of the Code cost him his career, his freedom, and his reputation.

CHECK YOUR UNDERSTANDING

1. What is the primary goal of the Ontario Human Rights Commission (OHRC)?

2. Identify an action that could typically lead to a civil lawsuit against police.

3. Explain the legal principle of *res judicata*.

In the Camera's Eye: Media and Police Accountability

IT'S YOUR MOVE, OFFICER!

Scenario 10.3

You are running a multidirectional radar in a marked police cruiser on Highway 401, looking for speeders on a stretch of highway notorious for fatalities. A car whizzes past at 143 km/h; the speed limit on the highway is 100 km/h. You activate your lights and siren and set off after the speeding driver. No one gets by you. You are a seasoned traffic enforcer.

Today, you are tired and cranky, having worked late attending a fatal collision the night before. You only got about five hours of sleep. You are not in the mood to listen to excuses from this driver.

As you approach the car, the driver exits the vehicle. This puts you on alert. The driver asks why he has been stopped. You point out that the licence plate is registered to a suspended driver. You also inform the driver he was speeding, and you ask him for his driver's licence, ownership, and insurance. As you are doing this, a woman gets out from the passenger side and starts accusing you of racial profiling; she says you checked the plate only after noticing that the driver was Aboriginal. Then she begins recording the interaction with her cellphone.

How would you handle this situation? Would you ask her what she is doing, and why? What action should you take, if any?

Cameras are everywhere. They are mounted on dashboards, pinned to police officers' hats or shirts, attached to buildings, and placed at street intersections. Most pervasive of all, however, is the use of cellphones for video recording. In 2013, Canadians possessed more than 26 million cellphones, most of them equipped to record video or audio data (mobiThinking, 2014).

Cameras as a Useful Investigative and Oversight Tool

Cameras have long been a useful tool for police investigations. Police have used videos as evidence, and they have used them to catch criminals. In the past, video technology's usefulness was limited by the storage capacity of the systems then available. Data not needed for ongoing investigations had to be deleted after a certain period of time. Today, many cameras have the ability to upload automatically into Cloud storage systems. This is a great benefit to police services; they can keep unlimited video evidence in the Cloud.

Some security personnel and police, and even some civilians, use pin cameras to record events. In a panel discussion published in the RCMP magazine *Gazette*, officers gave their views on body-worn cameras (RCMP, 2014). One officer pointed out that 77 percent of officers who wore them as part of an evaluation stated that these cameras improved their own professional behaviour. The evaluation also showed a significant decrease in complaints against police. Officers spoke approvingly, as well, of the cameras' "de-escalating" effect on potentially violent individuals, once these individuals became aware that an officer was wearing a camera. Technology can be used to expose police misbehaviour, but it can also work in favour of police, protecting them from false allegations of abuse.

Is It a Crime to Record Police?

Video cameras can also be used to monitor police activities and behaviour—as shown by the Barrie assault case described above. Civilians have often used cellphones to record police. The images thus captured can be uploaded immediately to the Internet, and they cannot be destroyed once they are there. A quick search of sites such as YouTube reveals dozens of channels devoted to monitoring and recording police behaviour. Social websites often intersect with traditional media. In 2013, after the shooting death of Sammy Yatim by Toronto police, several videos were uploaded to YouTube without any police intervention. What these videos revealed was reported in daily newspapers and TV news.

Is the recording and posting of police actions legal? Donald Fraser, a privacy lawyer who hosts the Canadian Privacy Law Blog website, has stated that people "can photograph or video police in public in Canada" (Fraser, 2014). *There is no law prohibiting recording police activity in Canada.* The courts have been consistent in this regard. In *R v. Zarafonitis* (2013), the court stated that, outside of safety considerations, police do not have lawful authority to advise the public not to record or photograph their activities. Controlling the public is not an officer's job, unless doing so is required for law enforcement or safety. The court has ruled that police officers' awareness of a citizen's right to record and photograph their activities should help prevent them from abusing their authority. Cameras, in other words, have been judged an informal but valuable method of overseeing police.

The notorious death of Robert Dziekanski at the hands of police in 2007 is another case where civilian videotape played a major role in overseeing police and contributing to justice. A civilian witness, Paul Pritchard, videotaped the incident. Dziekanski had arrived at Vancouver airport from Poland. The immigration process that he had to undergo was delayed. After about ten hours, he became distressed and agitated. He spoke no English and was unable to communicate his needs. Security contacted the RCMP, who tasered Dziekanski. He died within minutes. RCMP officers stated that he had approached them screaming and that they were fearful. The video evidence contradicted this statement and other

Source: Reuters/Paul Pritchard/HO/Landov.

Police officers approach Robert Dziekanski at the Vancouver airport in this image from Paul Pritchard's video.

claims in their testimony. This case was a turning point for police and the public; it showed the enormous role that video evidence could have in the pursuit of justice. Without Pritchard's video, the RCMP claims might have gone unchallenged.

While an officer can *ask* an uninvolved witness for a copy of his or her recording, the witness can *choose* whether to comply (Andreatta, 2013). Also, police cannot demand that witnesses hand over their phones or cameras. In the Dziekanski case, witness Paul Pritchard offered the camera to police. When he asked for the return of his camera, he was told that it would be at least a year and a half before it would be returned. Pritchard engaged a lawyer and his case went to court. In the end, the British Columbia Supreme Court ordered the camera returned, smoothing the way for future on-the-spot recordings of police activity by civilians ("Man Who Recorded," 2010).

The Code makes both police and civilians accountable for their actions. While recording police actions is not unlawful, a person doing so could be obstructing justice. Most people recording police are not obstructing the officer, but a person who physically steps between an officer and a person the officer is lawfully arresting or searching would be obstructing justice. Officers warn people of the potentially "obstructing" nature of their behaviour as a matter of practice. Section 129 of the Code states that someone who "wilfully obstructs" police as they exercise their lawful duty is guilty of this offence. It is also the case, however, that if police seize a cellphone in the belief that it is evidence of obstructing justice but it is later determined that this was not the case, the victim can lay a charge of mischief against police. Section 430(1.1) of the Code defines the offence of mischief in relation to data as follows:

(1.1) Every one commits mischief who wilfully
    (a) destroys or alters data;
    (b) renders data meaningless, useless or ineffective;
    (c) obstructs, interrupts or interferes with the lawful use of data; or
    (d) obstructs, interrupts or interferes with any person in the lawful use of
data or denies access to data to any person who is entitled to access thereto.

Any action by police that includes any of the elements set out in s. 430(1.1)—for example, erasing or destroying data—could result in charges.

CHECK YOUR UNDERSTANDING

1. What would an officer need to prove to demonstrate obstruction of justice by a witness?

2. Explain the rationale behind the rule that police cannot advise a bystander not to record an incident.

3. Go back to Scenario 10.3. Has your answer changed?

CHAPTER SUMMARY

In this chapter, we have looked at various aspects of police accountability and at various mechanisms for overseeing police. We have considered the importance of an officer's notebook as an instrument of police accountability. We have explored how the Charter limits police powers and holds police accountable for their actions while protecting the rights of individuals. We have discussed police oversight and accountability as they are imposed through the police chain of command and through provincial oversight bodies such as the OCPC, the OIPRD, and the SIU. The courts themselves, including the SCC, have proven to be an oversight mechanism, as various judicial decisions demonstrate. People harmed by police action can sue police in civil court.

Finally, we have considered how the media oversight of police has evolved owing to technological changes. Media outlets—online, television, radio, or print—have been powerfully affected by the accessibility of cellphone videos. These recordings increase the possibility for objective interpretation of interactions between the police and the public. The courts have made it clear that the public has a right to videotape police activity in public areas, and that police must respect that right. These video recordings are increasingly used within the criminal and civil justice systems to ensure police accountability. As the methods for ensuring the accountability of police continue to develop, so must police awareness of these methods, and their willingness to accept them.

KEY TERMS

contemporaneously, 230
disclosure, 231
plaintiff, 242
res judicata, 242
social media, 229

REFERENCES

Accountable. (n.d.). In *Merriam-Webster Online*. Retrieved from http://www.merriam-webster.com/dictionary/accountable.

Andreatta, D. (2013, August 2). Witnesses to crimes have no obligation to hand cameras to police. *The Globe and Mail*. Retrieved from http://www.theglobeandmail.com/news/toronto/witnesses-to-crimes-have-no-obligation-to-hand-cameras-to-police/article13571607.

Beaudry, R v. (2007). 2007 SCC 5, [2007] 1 SCR 190.

Canadian Charter of Rights and Freedoms. (1982). Part I of the *Constitution Act, 1982*, RSC 1985, app. II, no. 44.

Criminal Code. (1985). RSC 1985, c. C-46.

Human Rights Code. (1990). RSO 1990, c. H.19.

Fraser, D.T.S. (2014, May 1). We seriously need transparency about law enforcement demands. Canadian Privacy Law Blog. Retrieved from http://blog.privacylawyer.ca/2014/05/we-seriously-need-transparency-about.html#uds-search-results.

Independent Investigations Office of BC (IIO). (2014). Agency. Retrieved from http://iiobc.ca/agency.

Information and Privacy Commissioner of Ontario (IPC) & Durham Regional Police Service. (2001). *Police officers' notebooks and the Municipal Freedom of Information and Protection of Privacy Act: A guide for police officers*. Information and Privacy Unit, Durham Regional Police Service. Retrieved from http://www.freedominion.com.pa/images/police_notebooks.pdf.

Joel Elliot v. Waterloo Region Police Services. (2011). 2011 ONSC 6889.

Man who recorded Dziekanski tasering chronicles G20 confrontations. (2010, July 6). *The Globe and Mail*. Retrieved from http://www.theglobeandmail.com/news/british-columbia/man-who-recorded-dziekanski-tasering-chronicles-g20-confrontations/article1390340/.

McLaughlin, T. (2014, May 14). Former Barrie cop convicted in brutal beating. *The Barrie Examiner*. Retrieved from http://www.thebarrieexaminer.com/2014/05/13/former-barrie-cop-convicted-in-brutal-beating.

mobiThinking. (2014). Global mobile statistics 2014—Part A: Mobile subscribers; handset market share; mobile operators. *mobiForge*. Retrieved from http://mobiforge.com/research-analysis/global-mobile-statistics-2014-part-a-mobile-subscribers-handset-market-share-mobile-operators.

Office of the Independent Police Review Director (OIPRD). (n.d.). Talk to us: Step-by-step how to make a complaint against the police. Retrieved from http://www.oiprd.on.ca/EN/PDFs/Talk-to-Us-Step-by-Step_E.pdf.

Office of the Independent Police Review Director (OIPRD). (2013). About the OIPRD. Retrieved from http://www.oiprd.on.ca/EN/AboutUs/Pages/AboutUs.aspx.

Office of the Independent Police Review Director (OIPRD). (2014, February 24). OIPRD to review Toronto Police Service's use of force. *News*. Retrieved from http://www.oiprd.on.ca/EN/Education/Pages/News.aspx.

Ontario Civilian Police Commission (OCPC). (n.d.). *Public complainant's guide to disciplinary appeals*. Retrieved from http://www.ocpc.ca/stellent/groups/public/@abcs/@www/@ocpc/documents/abstract/ec081083.pdf.

Ontario Civilian Police Commission (OCPC). (1996). Maintaining public trust: An introduction to the Ontario Civilian Police Commission. Retrieved from http://www.ocpc.ca/stellent/groups/public/@abcs/@www/@ocpc/documents/webasset/ec079255.pdf.

Ontario Civilian Police Commission (OCPC). (2014). Mission statement. Retrieved from http://www.ocpc.ca/english/index.asp.

Ontario Human Rights Commission (OHRC). (2011). Complaints and allegations against police. *Human rights and policing: Creating and sustaining organizational change*. Retrieved from http://www.ohrc.on.ca/en/human-rights-and-policing-creating-and-sustaining-organizational-change/5-complaints-and-allegations-against-police.

Penner v. Niagara (Regional Police Services Board). (2013). 2013 SCC 19, [2013] 2 SCR 125.

Pickton, R v. (2007). 2007 BCSC 2029.

Public Prosecution Service of Canada. (2014). Chapter 11—other issues. *The path to justice: Preventing wrongful convictions*. Retrieved from http://www.ppsc-sppc.gc.ca/eng/pub/ptj-spj/ch11.html.

RCMP. (2014). Panel discussion. *Gazette, 76*(1). Retrieved from http://www.rcmp-grc.gc.ca/gazette/vol76no1/discussion-debat-eng.htm.

Rush, C. (2012, August 24). Stirling-Rawdon police chief disciplined for giving pepper spray to woman to protect herself. *The Toronto Star*. Retrieved from http://www.thestar.com/news/crime/2012/08/24/stirlingrawdon_police_chief_disciplined_for_giving_pepper_spray_to_woman_to_protect_herself.html.

Schaeffer v. Wood. (2011). 2011 ONCA 716, 107 OR (3d) 721 (CA).

SiRT. (2013). *The first year in review: 2012-2013 annual report*. Retrieved from http://sirt.novascotia.ca/sites/default/files/reports/First_Annual_Report_20130814.pdf.

SiRT. (2014). About SiRT. Retrieved from http://sirt.novascotia.ca/about.

Special Investigations Unit (SIU). (2010). Investigative process. Retrieved from http://www.siu.on.ca/en/process.php.

Special Investigations Unit (SIU). (2014a). Organizational chart. Retrieved from http://www.siu.on.ca/en/org_chart.php.

Special Investigations Unit (SIU). (2014b). SIU occurrences since inception. Retrieved from http://www.siu.on.ca/pdfs/siu_occurrences_since_inception.pdf.

Stillman, R v. (1997). [1997] 1 SCR 607.

Stinchcombe, R v. (1991). [1991] 3 SCR 326.

Wood v. Schaeffer. (2013). 2013 SCC 71, [2013] 3 SCR 1053.

Zarafonitis, R v. (2013). 2013 ONCJ 570.

FURTHER READING

Braidwood Commission on the Death of Robert Dziekanski. (2010, May 20). *Why? The Robert Dziekanski tragedy.* Braidwood, QC, Commissions of Inquiry. Retrieved from http://www.braidwoodinquiry.ca/report/P2Report.php.

Enhancing Royal Canadian Mounted Police Accountability Act. (2013). SC 2013, c. 18. Retrieved from http://laws-lois.justice.gc.ca/eng/annualstatutes/2013_18/page-1.html.

RCMP. (2014). Does body worn video help or hinder de-escalation? *Gazette, 76*(1). Retrieved from http://www.rcmp-grc.gc.ca/gazette/vol76no1/discussion-debat-eng.htm.

REVIEW QUESTIONS

Multiple Choice

1. There are a variety of ways to manage police activity. The term used to describe this is

    a. accountability

    b. oversight

    c. *Police Act* charges

    d. exclusion

2. Officers are accountable through

    a. the OIPRD

    b. the SIU

    c. the OCPC

    d. all of the above

3. Police need oversight

    a. because of the power they hold

    b. because of the cost of police services

    c. because they are given the public trust

    d. all of the above

4. An officer's notes must be made

    a. before the officer leaves shift

    b. contemporaneously

    c. independently

    d. b and c

5. Who is entitled to the disclosure of an officer's notes?

    a. the defence

    b. the media

    c. the jury

    d. the witnesses

True or False

_____ **1.** Officers can usually take home their notebooks to catch up on the day's notes.

_____ **2.** In *R v. Stinchcombe*, disclosure was defined as including the relevant pages of an officer's notes.

_____ **3.** Section 8 of the Charter is the right to be free from unreasonable search and seizure. This right is not relevant to the application of police powers.

_____ **4.** The gold standard when it comes to police accountability is the Charter.

_____ **5.** Ontario and Nova Scotia are the only two provinces with civilian-led oversight bodies for investigating police.

_____ **6.** An officer can appeal a disciplinary decision by the OCPC.

_____ **7.** Civilian complaints against police can only be made in person to the police service in question.

_____ **8.** Police officers are exempt from being sued if another complaint process is under way at the time.

_____ **9.** Police officers have the right to ask a member of the public for a copy of any recording he or she may have made of a police incident.

_____ **10.** It is unlawful in any circumstance to record police activity.

Short Answer

1. In the case of *R v. Pickton*, why do you think the justice was compelled to comment on the role of the courts in note-taking practices?

2. What is the effect of the OCPC's having the "final word" on an officer's appeal of a disciplinary hearing disposition?

3. Compare Figure 10.3 and Figure 10.4. Why do you think that the two graphs have different complaint categories?

4. Which of the various mechanisms for overseeing police in Ontario do you think are most effective in today's society? Why?

5. Video recording of police activity has become commonplace. What restrictions, if any, do you think should be placed on this activity?

It's Your Move, Officer!

A. One evening, at about 6:00 p.m., you receive a call from your supervisor saying that she needs to speak with you. She is a staff sergeant and has been a difficult supervisor. She always sends you to calls that are time-consuming and uninteresting, and she has often made you work overtime, thus forcing you to miss time with your family.

She tells you to pick up a pizza at the local pizza shop, known for providing pizza to officers at no charge. When you ask for money to pay for the pizza, she sneers, "They won't make you pay."

On your way to the pizza shop, you have mixed feelings. You feel you must get the pizza or risk your supervisor's ire (and more bad treatment from her). But you are uncomfortable being given free food. At the pizza shop, you knock on the back door, which opens into the kitchen. It is the usual entry for police picking up free food. When the cook hands you a pizza, you take out $20 and offer it to him. The cook waves you away. "It's on the house," he says. The cook then opens up a cupboard and jots down your badge number along with the time and date. While he is doing this, another officer, a newer recruit, walks into the kitchen. The recruit observes you and the cook. Just as you are trying to decide what to say and do, the radio crackles, "PC Antonelli, have you picked up that item yet?" It is the staff sergeant.

1. What would you do next? What would be the oversight mechanism for this scenario? How might a member of the public view this incident?

B. While on foot patrol on a busy city street one Saturday evening, you and your partner notice a crowd gathered in a circle at an alley entrance. Based on what you can hear and see, they are watching a street fight between two men. The crowd yells at the combatants, "Finish him! Put him down! Hurt him!" Several members of the crowd are recording the fight with their smartphones.

As you approach, intending to break up the fight, the crowd begins to disperse. Some people remain to continue filming. Backup officers arrive at the scene. The combatants stop, but some crowd members continue to yell at the combatants, telling them to keep fighting.

You and your partner arrest the combatants for causing a disturbance. That is when you realize that there are smartphone cameras recording the incident.

1. What would you do? Would you interview witnesses and ask for their phones? Would you seize the phones as evidence or ask for voluntary sharing of the recording?

2. Would your actions be different if the offence were different? What if one of the combatants possessed a weapon or seriously injured the other?

Glossary

A

accountable required to explain actions or decisions to someone

actus reus Latin for "a guilty act"; an *actus reus* is the physical component of committing a criminal act

affiant the police officer who writes the warrant application

amalgamate combine two or more existing organizations to form one; in policing, two or more municipal police forces may be combined to form one police force serving multiple municipalities

amendments changes made to enacted legislation to modify and improve it

appearance notice a notice in Form 9, issued by a peace officer (street level), that compels an accused person to appear in court at a specific date, time, and location

arrest warrant a court's written order, directed at all police officers within the jurisdiction where the order is valid, to find and arrest an identified person and return that person to the court that issued the order

B

bail any form of interim release authorized by law

behavioural factors attributes of the responding officer(s) that affect how he or she manages an incident

behavioural profile one measure of the risk posed by a subject, categorized as either cooperative, passive or active resistant, assaultive, or threatening grievous bodily harm or death

bench warrant an arrest warrant for a person, previously arrested and released, who fails to appear in court to answer to his or her charge(s); a written order from the police notifying all other peace officers to arrest the person named on the warrant

bill a proposed new or amended law in the provincial/territorial or federal legislative process

British North America Act Canada's original constitution, which united the separate colonies of Quebec, Ontario, Nova Scotia, and New Brunswick to form Canada

bylaws regulations and rules adopted by local or municipal governments

C

Canadian Charter of Rights and Freedoms a constitutional document that sets out the rights and freedoms of all people in Canada

Canadian Police Information Centre (CPIC) the central police database used by all Canadian police services to access information on a number of matters, including the current charges individuals may be facing and any criminal record they may have

Charter remedies remedies that the courts provide to ensure that any information or evidence gathered by police was obtained in accordance with the accused's Charter rights; may include the exclusion of items from evidence at trial

codified written down

collective bargaining rights the rights of employees, such as safety, wage, and working hours, negotiated through a process called collective bargaining; the PSA allows police officers to be members of an association for the purpose of negotiating these rights with their employer

colour of right an honestly held belief in entitlement to property; a defence to a charge of theft

common law the body of judge-made law not found in statute

community-based policing police policy and philosophy that includes the people of the local community in the operations and activities of a police service

compelling document a document that compels an individual to attend court to answer a criminal charge (for example, a summons, an appearance notice, a promise to appear, a recognizance to officer in charge or justice, or an undertaking entered into before a justice)

concurrence agreement that negates the intrusive potential of a search-and-seizure activity; principle whereby a search consented to by the person being searched requires no authorizing document from police

confidential informants informers who provide valuable information to the police and whose identity cannot be revealed by the Crown or the police unless the informant agrees to it

constitution the fundamental law of a nation or state, written or unwritten, that establishes the character and conception of the nation's government

constitutional supremacy a doctrine that places final decision-making power in legal matters in the hands of the judiciary

contemporaneously with reference to notebooks, during or as soon as possible after an incident

continuity break the transfer of any property or evidence from one location to another, or from one person to another

core police services a collection of services required to be performed by every police service in Ontario; failure to provide these services may lead to a dismantling of a police service and the installation of another police service

criminal offence any act or activity that violates an Act of Parliament; any offence found within the *Criminal Code* or any other federal statute that lists criminal offences

Crown attorney a lawyer responsible for prosecuting criminal offences in the province of Ontario

D

delegated legislation legislation such as regulations and bylaws created by subordinate governmental bodies such as branches and agencies rather than the legislature

direct discrimination discrimination directed toward characteristics such as age, gender, culture, and sexual orientation

disclosure the practice, in criminal cases of the Crown, of providing the defence with all the evidence gathered in an investigation

discretion the freedom or authority to make judgments and to act as one sees fit

discretionary release release of the accused by a peace officer or the officer in charge that is not mandatory, but is done on the basis of the officer's own judgment

discrimination treating people differently as a result of prejudice

division of powers refers to the specific powers granted to the federal and provincial levels of government, respectively, by ss. 91 and 92 of the *Constitution Act, 1867*

doctrine of precedent or rule of precedent a doctrine that requires a judge, in resolving a particular case, to follow the decision in a previous case where the facts in the two cases are similar

dual procedure (hybrid) offences offences that can be dealt with as either summary or indictable; always treated as indictable by arresting officers

E

entrenched firmly established

evidential chain the chain of evidence establishing the events that, seen in sequence, account for the actions of the suspect, the victim, and even the witnesses in an incident; can also account for different forms of evidence found within the time frame in which the crime may have occurred

***ex parte* hearing** a court proceeding held in the absence of the accused person

***ex parte* motion** a legal term referring to a proceeding or application where one of the parties has not received notice and, therefore, is neither present nor represented

excessive force force whose use in the given situation does not accord with ordinary common sense

exigent circumstances an emergency that permits police to make a warrantless entry or arrest

expressed consent direct and specific permission

F

facts-in-issue the components that must be established by police to make an arrest—day, date, time, and place; identity; *actus reus*; and *mens rea*

federation a group of independent states, provinces, or territories that have agreed to unite under a central or federal government

Feeney warrant a warrant that gives police authority to enter a residence to effect an arrest where there is no consent or permission to enter

force psychological or physical contact with another person, used by officers in the course of performing their duties

found committing a situation in which a person actually witnesses a crime taking place

freedom of expression a right guaranteed under s. 2(b) of the Charter that ensures everyone the right to manifest thoughts, opinions, and beliefs, including all expressions of the heart and mind regardless of how unpopular or distasteful they may be

fundamental justice rights that belong to us all and originate either in the express terms of the Constitution or, by implication, in common law

G

governor general the monarch's representative in the federal legislature

H

hot pursuit an exigent circumstance in which police can continue the pursuit of a suspect into a building, including a dwelling-house, to make an arrest without a warrant

I

implied consent a person's actions that are inferred by a police officer to be permission

indictable offences the most serious types of offences, with a maximum penalty of life in prison

indirect discrimination discrimination, generally unintentional, that results from a policy or practice that on the face of it seems reasonable, such as a height requirement for police

informant the person laying an information under oath before a justice

information a document that begins all criminal proceedings and that contains the charge (counts) against the accused

information to obtain (ITO) a statement of facts concerning the investigation, the place to be searched, the items being sought, and the reason for their being sought

informed consent voluntary consent, revocable at any time, from a person who is fully aware of the intent of the police and the consequences he or she may face if consent is given

integrity soundness of moral character

interim release releasing an accused person from custody with a document compelling his or her appearance in court

investigative detention a situation where reasonable grounds to arrest a person are absent, but police detain the person to determine whether he or she is involved in the crime

J

jurisdiction a body's sphere of authority to do a particular act—for example, the authority of a court to hear and determine a judicial proceeding

K

knock and announce rule a rule that requires police to announce their presence outside of the dwelling and to announce that they have a search warrant

L

legislate to make or enact laws

legislative process process by which the elected representatives of government make laws

lethal force force that is intended or is likely to cause death or grievous bodily harm

lieutenant governor in council the monarch's representative in the provincial legislature; official name for the provincial Cabinet

M

mandatory release compulsory release of the accused from custody by the peace officer or officer in charge

mens rea Latin term meaning "a guilty mind"; an element of criminal responsibility; a guilty or wrongful purpose; a criminal intent

misconduct improper behaviour; behaviour that contravenes certain standards or laws; an Ontario police officer is guilty of misconduct if he or she commits an offence described in s. 80 of the PSA or O. Reg. 268/10

N

nexus of search a direct relationship, or nexus, between the offence that has been committed, the evidence that the police need to secure in their investigation, and the location where the police believe the evidence will be located

night defined, in s. 2 of the *Criminal Code*, as the hours between 9:00 p.m. and 6:00 a.m. of the following day

no-knock entry police entry into a location undertaken with a warrant but without any announcement of their presence outside the premises; used where the affiant believes that announcing the police presence could endanger police or jeopardize vital evidence

O

objective standard a standard based on how an ordinary person would have behaved in the same circumstances; used in determining whether an officer had *reasonable grounds* for his or her actions

offensive weapon an object designed to be used or intended to be used to cause injury, death, threat, or intimidation

oversight the management of police activity, both internally and externally

P

parliamentary supremacy a doctrine that places final law-making power in the hands of the legislature

patriation the process of changing the Canadian Constitution so that control of legislation was moved from the British Parliament to the Canadian Parliament

plain-view doctrine a doctrine according to which a police officer who is lawfully in a place can seize items that are in plain view and that are, on their face, illegal; requires that the initial intrusion by police be lawful and that the evidence be discovered inadvertently

plaintiff a person bringing a civil action or lawsuit

police agent a person who, acting under the direction of the police, goes out into the field to gather, obtain, and convey to the police the information he or she receives

PRICE acronym for the criteria applied by police when deciding whether an arrested person should be released; the same as RICE except that it also includes "public interest" (Public interest, Repetition, Identity, Court, Evidence)

prima facie Latin for "at first look"; evident from the facts; evidence that, if not contradicted, will be sufficient to prove a particular proposition or fact

promise to appear a promise in Form 10, issued by an officer in charge (station level), requiring the accused person to attend court at a specific date, time, and location

R

racial profiling practice that targets for police investigation people of a particular race, based on stereotypes

reasonable force the force that any person with ordinary common sense would exercise if placed in the officer's position

reasonable grounds a set of facts or circumstances that would cause an ordinary and cautious (in other words, prudent) person to form a belief

recognizance a document, issued by the officer in charge or by a justice, that requires an accused person to agree to meet certain obligations in exchange for being released from custody, and that also requires the accused person to appear in court at a specific date, time, and location

regulations a type of subordinate legislation that carries out the intent of the statute under which it is made; generally concerned with the detail and technical aspects of the law

report to justice a legal document, commonly referred to as a "5.2," that police use when asking a justice of the peace or judge for lawful permission to hold seized property for further investigation or until the completion of the trial

res judicata Latin for "already decided"; a special plea with which the accused argues that the charges against him or her have already been dealt with in a court of law

return radius an area, specified in an arrest warrant, within which a found suspect must be returned to the police that requested the warrant

RICE acronym (Repetition, Identity, Court, Evidence) for the criteria applied by police when deciding whether an arrested person should be released

royal assent approval of the British monarch through his or her representative

S

sealing order an order that the details of a warrant and an ITO not be disclosed to the public after the warrant has been executed

situational factors environmental factors in a situation that are beyond the officer's control; can include time, place, and the suspect's characteristics

social media a technologically mediated method of communication that involves information being uploaded to websites or computer databases and being shared with the public

solicitor general of Ontario the elected official and Cabinet member of the political party in power in Ontario; charged with duties pertaining to law enforcement and correctional services in Ontario; this position is held by the minister of community safety and correctional services

stare decisis a common law doctrine stating that the decision of a higher court in a particular jurisdiction acts as a binding authority on a lower court in the same jurisdiction

statutes codified legal provisions developed and adopted through the parliamentary and legal process

subjective elements elements composing the officer's personal interpretation of the situation, used in determining whether he or she had *reasonable grounds* for his or her actions

summary conviction offences the least serious of the offences set out in the *Criminal Code*, most with a maximum penalty of $5,000 and/or six months in jail

summons a summons in Form 6, issued by a justice or judge, requiring an accused person to appear in court at a specific date, time, and location (the document is later served on the accused person personally)

sureties the deposit of something of value with the police or court to ensure that the accused person will attend court

systemic discrimination discrimination in which certain attitudes or values become the accepted standard in an organization or even a community

T

tactical factors skills and resources available to an officer in helping him or her manage an incident

telewarrant a warrant requested by telephone or other telecommunication means, most often a fax machine; used in circumstances where it is impracticable for the affiant to apply for the search warrant in person

third-party consent search consent given by someone other than the accused

Three Fs describes the criteria for search warrant applications—full, fair, and frank

U

undertaking an undertaking in Form 11.1 or 12, used in conjunction with a promise to appear or with a recognizance (if issued by the officer in charge), that requires an accused person to meet certain obligations in exchange for being released from custody and that may also require (if issued by a justice) the accused person to attend court at a specific date, time, and place

unsatisfactory work performance work performance that does not meet the standards established by the policies of chiefs of police

Use-of-Force Continuum model a model, used by police, that aligns the suspect's behavioural responses and profiles with suggested police responses

V

voluntary accompaniment a situation where a person who is neither under arrest nor being held for investigative detention chooses to accompany or remain with police for investigative purposes

W

warrant in the first instance an arrest warrant issued in circumstances where the police are unable to locate the suspect, or where the suspect, knowing that he or she is wanted, is evading police or other authorities

warrantless search a search conducted without a warrant; presumed to be unreasonable unless the Crown demonstrates, on a balance of probabilities, that it is reasonable

Index